AN ANTARCTIC AFFAIR

AN ANTARCTIC AFFAIR

*A story of love and survival by the great-granddaughter
of Douglas and Paquita Mawson*

EMMA MCEWIN

East Street Publications

www.eaststreet.com.au

Published by East Street Publications
11 Gibson Street, Bowden, SA 5007, Australia
www.eaststreet.com.au

First published 2008

The National Library of Australia
Cataloguing-in-Publication

    McEwin, Emma (Emma Louise), 1969–

    An Antarctic Affair / author, Emma McEwin.

    ISBN 9781921037306 (pbk.) :

    Includes index.
    Bibliography.

    Subjects: Mawson, Douglas, Sir, 1882–1958.
                Mawson, Paquita, 1891–1974.
                Explorers—Australia—Biography.
                Geologists—South Australia—Biography.
                Women civic leaders—South Australia—Biography.
                Women authors, Australian—South Australia—Biography.
                Long-distance relationships—Australia.
                Long-distance relationships—Antarctica.
                Marriage.
                Antarctica—Discovery and exploration—Australian.

    919.89040922

Front cover photographs of Douglas Mawson and Paquita Delprat kindly supplied by the
    Gareth Thomas Collection.
    Ninnis driving a team of dogs. Photograph by Mertz. Courtesy Mawson Collection, South
    Australian Museum. Back cover photograph by Frank Hurley of a turreted iceberg. Courtesy
    Mawson Collection, South Australian Museum.
Cover design by Ellie Exarchos, Scooter Design
Map by DEMAP
Sketches by Emma McEwin
Design and typeset by David Bradbury
Typeset in 12/15 Adobe Garamond
Printed and bound by Griffin Press, South Australia

To the memory of Oma

Have you ever seen the midnight sun? Have you ever flirted with the penguins and beguiled them into parting with their eggs when you were hungry? Have you ever seen the snow, nothing but snow, miles upon miles, and then more miles, all around and underneath? If you ever had experienced these, and a few more attractions the Antarctic has to offer, you would not ask me why I am going back.

Douglas Mawson in an address to the Canadian Club in Montreal,
Montreal Herald Daily Telegraph, 23 January 1915

Contents

1   An Explorer in the House   1

2   Adventure Bound   9

3   Finding Antarctica   15

4   How Douglas Mawson Ended up in Antarctica   21

5   Paquita   26

6   The Making of the AAE   34

7   South Bound   44

8   Winter Pursuits   56

9   Sledging into the Interior   63

10 The Race Back   75

11 The Loss of Mertz   83

12 Surviving Alone   93

13 Defying Death   100

14 A Will to Live   108

15 Love and Responsibility   114

16 A Miraculous Return   123

17 Providence   132

18 *A Shadow of Himself* 143

19 *The Aborted Rescue* 150

20 *Telegram from Antarctica* 154

21 *Lost Letters of Love* 162

22 *Descent into Darkness* 166

23 *Madness and Misunderstanding* 176

24 *Anxiety about the Future* 181

25 *Thoughts of Reunion* 187

26 *Coming Out of the Cold* 193

27 *A Knight to Remember* 201

Appendix

Abbreviations 218

Metric Conversions 218

Timeline of Arctic and Antarctic expeditions mentioned 219

Members of the AAE (1911–1914) 222

Endnotes 224

Reference List 244

Index 250

List of maps and illustrations

Maps

1   Map of Antarctica 1912   XIV
2   Route map of Far-Eastern Sledging Journey   5

Photographs

1   *Aurora* alongside the Mertz Glacier Tongue   13
2   Paquita, Douglas and Henrietta Delprat   29
3   Loading stores, Queen's Wharf, Hobart 1911   38
4   *Aurora* after a blizzard   49
5   The Wireless Station, Macquarie Island   51
6   Mid-Winter's Day in the Hut, 12 June 1912   58
7   The air tractor sledge   65
8   Crevasse   67
9   Douglas Mawson and sledge   68
10 Blizzard the pup   81
11 Shovel   88
12 Douglas Mawson's half-sledge   138
13 Douglas Mawson, 1913   147
14 Commonwealth Bay and Hut   172
15 The Mawson's house at Brighton   190
16 Paquita holding a husky called Admiral D'Urville   195
17 Douglas Mawson, Jessica and Pat, at home 1930   204

18   Paquita and Douglas with baby Pat   207
19   Douglas Mawson knighted, June 1914   210
20   Paquita and Douglas, Adelaide circa 1915   212
21   Some Mawson family members   215

Black and white plates

1   Life in the Hut
2   AAE men on the *Aurora* 1914
3   Members of the AAE
     Douglas Mawson, John King Davis, Frank Hurley
     John Close, Robert Bage, John Hunter
     Eric Webb, Xavier Mertz, George Ainsworth
     Percy Correll, Charles Laseron, Alfred Hodgeman
     Walter Hannam, Herbert Murphy, Belgrave Ninnis
     Frank Stillwell, Leslie Whetter, Archie McLean
     Cecil Madigan, Frank Bickerton, Frank Wild
4   Paquita in Broken Hill, circa 1900
5   Paquita aged 11 at Robe
6   Paquita in Holland, 1912
7   Mawson wedding party

Acknowledgements

I would like to thank Mark Pharaoh for giving me so much of his time, and for sharing his extensive knowledge of Douglas Mawson with me, for his editorial guidance, for providing and helping select photographs from the Mawson Collection at the South Australian Museum, and for his friendship. I would also like to thank Nancy Robinson Flannery for giving me access to all the material she has collated on the Mawsons, in particular on Paquita and the Delprats, for compiling the index, and for her continued generosity and support despite her own frail health. I am very grateful to Gareth Thomas for putting his private collection of family papers and photographs at my disposal, and for helping me on many occasions, often at short notice, and, to Alun Thomas for providing me with material from his own collection. The other people I would like to thank are my family, in particular my parents, and my godmothers, Doody Taylor and Deb Lavis, for supporting me in so many ways, Barbara Wall for her valued comments on an early draft of this book, my publishers, Michaela Andreyev and Jane Macduff, and all my friends, especially Shane Le Plastrier, who have supported and encouraged me throughout the writing of this book.

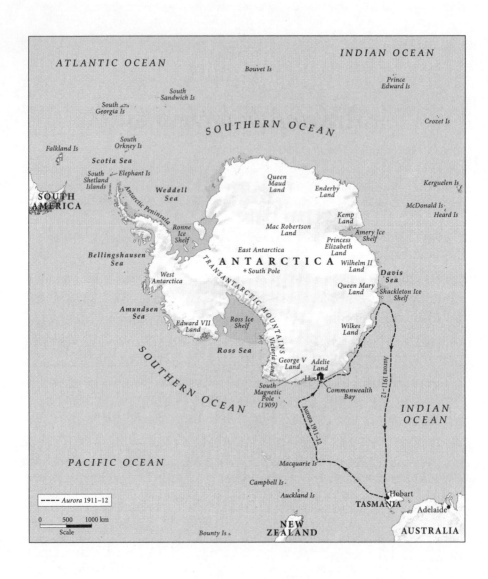

I

An Explorer in the House

Unfortunately, I never met my paternal great-grandfather, Sir Douglas Mawson. A geologist and an Antarctic explorer, he died in 1958 when my father was twelve.

As a child I slept in his reindeer skin sleeping-bag and ran around our garden in his yellow snow goggles. I lay under our quince tree to escape the heat, my heart pounding in my head, and tried to imagine the cold of Antarctica and Douglas walking for miles and miles in a great expanse of sparkling white snow. In our house we had pictures of elephant seals, penguins, ships and blue-white icebergs. For a while, his younger daughter, Jessica (my grandmother, Oma), had a rickety old table in her kitchen that had come from Aladdin's Cave, a shelter for explorers that Douglas and his men had dug out of the Antarctic ice in 1912 on a wind-swept plateau where tents do not survive. Oma hulled strawberries on it while my brothers and my sister and I tore in and out of the house, unaware then of the full story of our great-grandfather or of the value or significance of this table and other things that belonged to him. We knew only the gory details that appealed to our young minds; that he ate his dogs to survive; that his beard fell out in clumps in the snow; that the soles of his feet came away.

In fact, he went to Antarctica on three expeditions. It was the second, the Australasian Antarctic Expedition (AAE) 1911–14, which he led and on which he narrowly escaped death that earned him his knighthood and a place in the annals of polar history. Among the books in Oma's house and in ours, were *The Home of the Blizzard*, his account of this expedition, as well as his biography, *Mawson of the Antarctic*, by his wife and my great-grandmother, Paquita, who died six days after my fifth birthday.

Five is very young but a few vivid memories of her remain. She was a tall woman with wide hips and she parted her hair down the middle, which accentuated her Roman nose. When I think of her she is always dressed in black. I recall her walking towards Oma's house in the country and stepping onto the front veranda that was covered in the pink leaves of a glory vine, while I watched her from the edge of a small forest near the house. I remember her as a frail woman being wheeled into a dining room and placed at the head of a table to face a dark porch where I was playing. In a family movie, made in the thirties, she climbs gingerly over fallen tree trunks in long boots and jodhpurs; laughs (silently) as she pours water from a watering can over the ferns in her glasshouse; hugs a young Oma in plaits. In the portrait of her that has always hung above the fireplace in every sitting room in every house my parents have ever owned, she is a serious young woman in a green dress against a raspberry background.

I visited her in hospital in the final weeks of her life. I was with my mother and my sister. We didn't stay long because Paquita was tired. She was wearing a thin nightdress and her trademark art deco glasses with the black rims. Her chihuahua, Trinnie, was perched on her left shoulder. A spoilt, yapping dog, Trinnie cocked his leg wherever he pleased and left yellow stains in the corners of rooms. It was because of Trinnie and to differentiate between my grandmother and my great-grandmother that I called Paquita 'Other-one-Oma-with-the-dog' but in the following pages, I shall call her Paquita.

I first read *Mawson of the Antarctic* in London when I was in my early twenties. I borrowed it from the Kensington Library and later discovered that Paquita had written most of it in a bedsit not far from this library, on a board balanced across the arms of a chair. This was in 1959, a few months after Douglas's death. (It was her second book, her first being, *A Vision of Steel*, a biography of her father.) She and Douglas had talked about writing his life together and later he had said he thought she should do it and gave her many details. She went to England for research purposes because that was where Douglas was born and it was also where he had received a lot of support for his expeditions.

British explorer, Sir Ranulph Fiennes, who made the first unsupported crossing of Antarctica in the early 1990s, argues that Douglas Mawson 'missed out on lasting fame, even in his native Australia, partly because he went on to die naturally in old age'.[1] Certainly, while working on *Mawson of the Antarctic*, Paquita was frustrated that no one in England knew who Mawson was. When she was introduced to people as 'Lady-Mawson-whose-husband-went-to-the-Antarctic', she was always asked, 'Did he go with Shackleton or with Scott?' These two men were his contemporaries and they were both in Antarctica at around the same time that Douglas was there from 1911–14 and their stories are partly responsible for obscuring his name. The tragic death of one and the heroics of the other, together with the outbreak of war in 1914, largely eclipsed Douglas Mawson's achievements. That he did not die young or in a spectacular fashion perhaps further explains, as Fiennes suggests, why he is so little known on an international or even on a national scale.

Yet, now we are seeing a revival of interest in him, as predicted by Archibald Grenfell Price who wrote the story of Douglas's third and final expedition to the Antarctic, the British Australian New Zealand Antarctic Research Expedition (BANZARE) 1929–1931. Grenfell Price wrote: 'Although future generations may continue to afford a high place to the gallant men of several nations who reached the South Pole, or who died in the attempt or achievement, they will, I think, pay increasing honour to the man who, of all southern explorers, gave the world the greatest contributions in south polar science and his own people the greatest territorial possessions in the Antarctic'.[2]

The 1930 popular edition of *The Home of the Blizzard* was republished in 1996 and became a bestseller. A new biography, *Mawson: A Life* by Philip Ayres, came out in 1999. The name, Mawson, lives on when it would otherwise have been forgotten since Douglas had no sons and Bob, the only son of his brother, William, died unmarried and childless in an aeroplane accident in 1939. Many things have been named in his honour, including buildings, fossils and geographical features. Yalumba, the winery that provided wine for BANZARE 1929–1931, has produced two 'Mawson' wines. The name 'mawsoni' applies to over sixty biological species of groups of invertebrates, algae, lichen and fish. There is 'Mount Mawson' in Tasmania, complete with 'Mawson's Hut' at its peak and there is even a 'Mawson cherry' that is particularly resistant to cold and frost. The Winter Quarters he established in Antarctica in 1912 have been restored some thirty years after Paquita, concerned it would fall into disrepair, appealed, unsuccessfully, to the then prime minister of Australia, Sir Robert Menzies, for it to be dismantled and reassembled in South Australia. It continues to be maintained. Mawson Station, the oldest continuously operating scientific research station south of the Antarctic Circle*, and one of three permanent Australian stations, was established in 1954.

Douglas's achievements as a pioneering scientist in the south polar regions are celebrated in South Australia, where he lived and set off on all three polar expeditions.** There is a bust of him outside the University of Adelaide where, just over a hundred years ago, he began his appointment as a lecturer in mineralogy and petrology in the department of geology in 1905. There is a large rock specimen on either side of him, one from Antarctica and the other from the Flinders Ranges, two regions of particular geological interest to him. In 1921, he was appointed Professor of Geology and Mineralogy, a position he held until the end of his working life. During his career he was offered the Chairs of Geology at Manchester, Liverpool and Harvard, as well as the vice-chancellorship at the University of Sydney but he remained committed to developing and expanding teaching and research in the Department of Geology at the University of Adelaide. Having raised the funds, he helped design a new building to house the department, later named the Mawson Laboratories. It was completed in the early 1950s and he occupied a room there for the last year of his professorship in 1952. When Douglas died he was accorded a Commonwealth state funeral. The bells of his local church, St Jude's at Brighton, tolled seventy-six times to mark the years of his life.

His image has appeared on several Australian postage stamps and his unshaven face, framed by a balaclava, appeared on the first Australian one hundred-dollar bill. This same image, enlarged, hangs in the main

---

* The Antarctic Circle is an imaginary line on the surface of the earth at 66°30S which marks the southernmost point at which the sun can be seen during the summer solstice, and the northernmost point at which the midnight sun can be seen in south polar regions.

** The British Antarctic Expedition (BAE) 1907–1909; the Australasian Antarctic Expedition (AAE) 1911–1914; the British Australian and New Zealand Antarctic Research Expedition (BANZARE) 1929–1931.

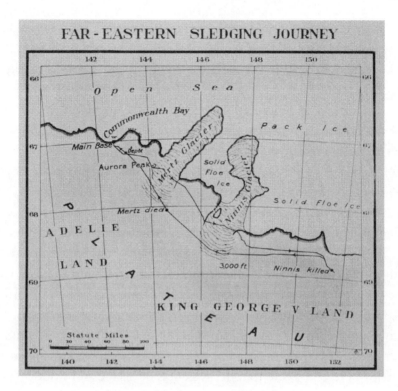

Route map of the Far-Eastern Sledging Journey
(*Mawson Collection, South Australian Museum*)

foyer of the South Australian Museum. From behind glass, he faces out onto the street he walked along almost every day of his working life (the university is two buildings away). If one looks down to the museum from the footpath, and stands on the plaque placed there in his memory, it is possible to see his image through the window. His features are sharp and delicate, almost fox-like. His strong, distinctive nose, the wrinkles around his eyes and the stubble around his mouth give him a rugged, weathered appearance and there is something about the balaclava that makes him look like a medieval knight.

Upstairs, in the museum, there is now a permanent exhibition drawing on his personal collection. Much of this polar heritage was once part of the Mawson Institute for Antarctic Research, established within the University of Adelaide in 1959. It comprised of Douglas's library of polar literature, a large collection of his papers and letters, records and artefacts related to his work in the Antarctic, some of which were on display, as well as his Antarctic diaries, slowly transcribed over a period of years and finally published in 1988 by the Director of the Institute, Dr Fred Jacka and his wife, Eleanor. However, there were many other objects of interest and importance, belonging to the collection of some 100 000 items, that were deteriorating in the basement of the geology department. This concerned Paquita who had always wanted Douglas's collection to be exhibited and properly maintained.

At the age of seventy-eight she was asked how Douglas's achievements in Antarctica might best be commemorated. She said, 'I see a hall located possibly somewhere in the northern parklands with relics of Antarctic explorations around the walls. The main exhibit should be a large relief map of Antarctica showing landmarks and features, and lit up from underneath so that it looks like a miniature Antarctica reduced to scale'.[3] The Mawson exhibition, 'In the footsteps of Sir Douglas Mawson', appropriately housed in the museum where he was Honorary Curator of Minerals for more than fifty years and Chairman of the Board from 1940 until his death in 1958, is even more comprehensive than she had imagined and has helped create a greater public awareness of his life and work.

As part of the exhibition, extracts from the films of his expeditions run continuously to the eerie sound of a moaning wind, recorded almost a hundred years ago. In a fur hat and in a slightly nasal voice and in an educated, faintly English accent, he proclaims Antarctic territory for the British Crown in the name of King George V and Queen Mary. He mapped 2500 kilometres of coastline on BANZARE 1929–1931, one section of which was named the Mawson Coast in 1961[*]. Stuffed huskies, snow petrels, albatrosses and plump penguins stare out from behind glass cabinets. Strange sea creatures float in jars. There are snow boots, sledges that look surprisingly flimsy, faded and worn down by the incessant polar winds, sepia photographs, books and food cans and even a doll that the dancer, Anna Pavlova, gave to Douglas in 1910, when she christened his ship in London with a bottle of champagne.

---

[*] Currently, no one owns Antarctica. The Antarctic Treaty, signed in 1961, has suspended all territorial claims but Australia is nevertheless recognised as having the largest territorial claim of 42% of the continent, officially established in 1936, much of which was first explored and annexed by Douglas Mawson on The Australasian Antarctic Expedition 1911–1914 and also on his British Australian New Zealand Antarctic Research Expedition 1929–1931.

In December 2006, English polar explorer, Tim Jarvis, who has attained the North Pole and made the fastest unsupported journey to the South Pole with fellow explorer, Peter Treseder, retraced the sledging journey that almost claimed Douglas's life. Although Tim was not permitted to visit the exact area that Douglas Mawson explored, he faced similar terrain. Had Tim got into serious trouble, which fortunately he didn't, he could have called for help on the satellite telephone and arranged for a helicopter to airlift him to safety. Yet he embarked on the journey knowing there were no guarantees he would make it out of there alive. The territory is still relatively unknown and he was afraid of losing the cameraman down a crevasse or of falling down one himself. Wearing clothes similar to those worn by Douglas in 1912, he ate equivalent food rations of equivalent protein. Before he left for the Antarctic, I asked him why he chose Douglas Mawson's trek and he replied, 'Because it's the hardest one I could find and one of the greatest stories of lone survival'.

Indeed, it is an amazing and inspiring story, and what makes it so extraordinary and distinct from other instances of survival in polar regions is that in the last month of the journey, Douglas was completely alone. Part of the appeal of exploration for Tim Jarvis is that for him it is a spiritual experience, and I imagine never more so than when he found himself alone, chasing the ghost of Douglas Mawson.

The story I understood as a child was much simpler than the one I have since discovered through my reading and research, which has prompted me to wonder beyond the straightforward explanations I had been given as to how Mertz and Ninnis died and to consider why Douglas survived. There are many reasons why he did survive and these reasons illuminate his character and explain his greatness. To survive he had to draw on many things; his motivation for being there, his past knowledge and experience, his mental and physical strength, his aspirations for the future.

At the time of this expedition Douglas was engaged to Paquita whose love was one of the major driving forces in his struggle to reach safety. It seems, at least in this case, that there is some truth in the saying, 'Behind every great man there is a woman'. Research has proved that the survival rate of single or unmarried people is lower than that of married couples. Of all the explorers I refer to in this book, many failed to maintain successful relationships or to provide their families with the stability they needed, many fell victim to their adventurous spirits and died young and in tragic circumstances.

Yet, while Douglas and Paquita enjoyed a long and happy marriage, they had a difficult beginning. Due to what transpired on the sledging journey in 1912–13 they did not see each other for more than two years. The letters that Paquita wrote to Douglas, which shed light on the hardships they both faced, were discovered amongst his papers at the University of Adelaide in 1991. Six years later, in 1997, Douglas's letters to her at this time were found in a box in Pat's house (the Mawson's elder daughter and my great-aunt), after which the collection was published in its entirety.*

Although she eventually came to see the value in publishing the letters, Oma revealed to me that she initially felt uncomfortable about releasing them into the public domain. The letters are very personal and she found it hard to read them. It was less difficult for me, three generations removed. Their words moved me. They are at once full of anguish and of hope and I soon realised that they are crucial to an understanding of the whole story. Reading them gave me an insight into their marriage in so far as I could see how the expedition and the separation it enforced, shaped their partnership and that neither was left unscathed.

The most extraordinary thing about these letters is that most of them remained undelivered at the time as there was no such thing as a mail boat steaming back and forth from Antarctica. The 'everlasting silence', as Paquita described it, put an enormous strain on their relationship and, for her, in particular, this became almost 'unbearable'.

This is the story of their love, their legacy, their survival.

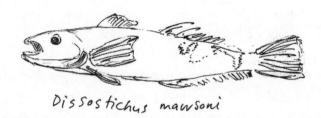

Dissostichus mawsoni

---

* Nancy Robinson Flannery, ed., *This Everlasting Silence: the Love Letters of Paquita Delprat & Douglas Mawson 1911–1914*, Melbourne University Press, 2000.

2

Adventure Bound

Survive *verb* **1** *trans., intrans.* to remain alive or relatively
unharmed in spite of (a dangerous experience); to come
through. **2** to live on after the death of. **3** *intrans.* to remain
alive or in existence. {from Latin *super,* beyond + *vivere,* to live}

survivor *noun* **1** one who survives **2** one who survives another.[*]

On 21 June 1884, the surviving members of an American expedition led
by US Army officer, Adolphus Greely, were rescued from the Canadian
Arctic by the *Aurora,* the ship that Douglas Mawson would one day buy
and take to the bottom of the world. Only seven of the original twenty-
five men, including Greely, were found alive at remote Cape Sabine. Their
relief ship had failed to arrive the previous year, and they had survived
for eight months in a crude hut made of stones and an upturned boat,
existing on lichen, shrimps, birds and Arctic foxes. Their situation was so
desperate, that on the one occasion they caught a bear, they even salvaged
the sections of snow into which its blood had run. Their food supply
almost completely diminished a few days before they were saved and,
as a last resort, they had begun to roast and eat the hair of their sealskin
sleeping-bag covers.

---

[*] *Oxford Paperback Dictionary,* Oxford University Press, 2000.

The survivors were found lying motionless and glassy-eyed, just hours from death. One man, who later died on the return journey to New York, had lost both hands and feet to frostbite. A spoon was attached to the stump of his right wrist. Someone knelt down beside Greely, who was almost unrecognisable under his long beard, and told him his wife and daughters were well and waiting for him. He had not seen them for three years. The half-buried bodies of the eighteen dead, one of whom had been shot for stealing food, lay strewn around the camp. Cold, hunger and isolation had led to cannibalism, madness and death.

Douglas Mawson was two years old at the time that this rescue was being carried out. Twenty-seven years into the future the *Aurora* would take him on an expedition and away from his fiancée, Paquita, for almost two and a half years. This same ship would rescue him as it had rescued Greely, but from a place much colder and crueller than the Arctic. The events of his life would lead him to Antarctica, the highest, driest, coldest, stormiest, remotest, most barren and most inaccessible continent on earth, where the only permanent inhabitant is a tiny, wingless fly*.

In June 1884, two-year old Douglas was sailing south on the clipper ship, the *Ellora* with his parents, Margaret and Robert Mawson and his elder brother, Will. They were bound for Sydney Australia. Two years before, in the year that Douglas was born in Shipley, Yorkshire, his long-widowed paternal grandmother had died and upon her death, Harewood, the family property, was sold, the proceeds of which were divided between Robert and his sister, Sarah. This left Douglas's father free to start a new life elsewhere. Having dabbled in various business ventures, none of which were very successful, (he had already lost half of his inheritance in a cloth-making business that had gone bankrupt), Robert was only too pleased to start afresh in a new country. He was a bit of a dreamer, more interested in reading the classics than in making money. A frustrated adventurer, had he been a single man, he might have gone to the South Pacific Islands or to the Far East, areas about which he had read widely, but with a family to consider, Australia was a safer option.

In her prologue to *Mawson of the Antarctic*, Paquita described the

---

* While the male Emperor penguin remains on the continent throughout the year in some parts of Antarctica, there are no permanent land inhabitants in the region that Douglas Mawson explored between 1911–1914.

young Douglas escaping from his cot and crawling out onto the deck of the *Ellora* to climb the rigging. 'Up went little Douglas Mawson' she wrote, 'never looking back, always on and up, so engrossed that he did not hear the sharp order from the bridge nor notice the movement that shook the ropes until strong hands plucked him bodily from the rigging. Kicking and protesting loudly he was brought down by the grinning sailor'.[1] Douglas caused his parents 'anxiety' Paquita claimed for 'one could never know what he wanted to do next'.[2]

Years later, in 1913, while Douglas was in Antarctica, Paquita met her future mother-in-law, Margaret Mawson, for the first and only time in New South Wales. What drove Douglas to explore might well have been something the two women discussed and it is likely that in the course of it, Margaret told this story of how her son's adventurous nature was evident from as early as two years old. Such a story could belong to any number of mischievous, spirited young boys, except that Douglas Mawson continued, throughout his life, to achieve things that set him apart from his peers.

As a boy he was enchanted by tales of adventure such as *Robinson Crusoe*, *The Swiss Family Robinson*, Rudyard Kipling's *Kim* and the novels of Joseph Conrad. In Sydney, his mother took in boarders. One lodger was the son of the last whaling captain to sail around New Guinea and the north of Australia. He delighted Douglas with stories of attacks by 'natives'. Douglas shared, with his brother, Will, a love of the outdoors and of the natural sciences. Yet, like his contemporaries, Ernest Shackleton and Robert Falcon Scott, he didn't grow up wanting to be a polar explorer. It is unlikely the idea ever occurred to him. Rather, how he ended up in Antarctica resulted from a combination of character, chance and circumstance.

His early childhood in Australia was spent on a farm at Rooty Hill, west of Sydney, where his father bred pigs, made wine and then jam and started the first fruit cannery in New South Wales. However, again, without much success, largely as a result of the land boom smash in the early 1900s. Robert had borrowed hundreds of pounds from friends and it would take him years to pay this money back. Douglas's mother, Margaret, comes out as the dominant parent, particularly after Robert gave up his position in Sydney at around the time that Douglas was starting university, and 'went north' to follow up an investment in cedar forests, which incidentally also failed. Margaret Mawson was from the Isle of Man and grew up in its capital, Douglas, after which Douglas was presumably named. Given that her father, Thomas Moore, was the owner of a large metal works on the Isle and chairman of the most important lead mines in the United Kingdom, it is fair to assume that Margaret had led a fairly comfortable childhood. Robert's failed investments caused her much anxiety, and, according to Douglas, 'permanently reduced her vitality'. And yet, she was enterprising in the face of financial ruin, and bore the social humiliation of taking in boarders to supplement her husband's modest income. She taught Douglas and William at home before they went to school and she was ambitious for her sons, encouraging them to gain a profession, something Robert did not have.

It was not until a wealthy timber merchant employed Robert, putting him in charge of his lumberyards in Sydney, that the Mawson family's prospects began to improve. After a number of moves they settled at Glebe Point, partly to be near Fort Street Public School, a secondary school with a good reputation. It was at this school that Douglas's leadership skills were recognised and commented upon. Incredibly, his headmaster, a Mr Turner, accurately predicted his future when he said, at the end of Douglas's final year, 'If there be a corner of this planet of ours still unexplored, Douglas Mawson will be the organiser and leader of an expedition to unveil its secrets'.[3] Another teacher at the school reminded Douglas of this comment upon his return from the Antarctic in 1914 and Douglas confessed that he had never forgotten it.

Dr Walter Henderson, a man who worked closely with Douglas on the promotion of BANZARE 1929–1931, said of him: 'His personality was cast in the heroic mould. He had a comprehensive mind which would have taken him to a foremost place in any profession he might have chosen'.[4] Douglas even said of himself, in a letter, years later to Paquita, that, had he not lived in the twentieth century, he might have been a crusader or a buccaneer. Had he lived in the twenty-first century he might have been an astronaut. David Parer and Elizabeth Parer-Cook, authors of the book and film, *Douglas Mawson: The Survivor*, have also produced a film comparing Douglas's 1912 sledging journey in Antarctica with modern-day voyages to outer space in which they argue that he possessed the

Aurora alongside the Mertz Glacier Tongue
(*Mawson Collection, South Australian Museum*)

temperament and the survival skills to qualify as an astronaut. However, Douglas's life spanned the late nineteenth century to the middle of the twentieth century. The period in which he was born goes a long way to explaining his career path. When he was a young man, Antarctica was the last great geographical goal and the last great scientific mystery and the modern subject of geology was an ideal combination of laboratory science and field work.

In his lifetime the world was mysterious in a way that it isn't now. At the time of his birth in 1882, the motor car hadn't been invented, the telephone was only a few years old. When he was five, a young engineering student invented the first calculator that could automatically multiply. When he was six, Jack the Ripper began murdering women in London and getting away with it. (At the time, forensic science was in its infancy. The idea of taking fingerprints had not been invented and it was not yet possible to distinguish human blood from animal blood.) When Douglas was thirteen, the first motion picture theatre opened in Paris. It was not until 1911, the year that he sailed to Antarctica as the leader of the AAE that the last horse-drawn bus in the London General Omnibus Company was taken out of service to make way for the motor car.

In terms of exploration, most blank spots on the map of the world had more or less been filled in. Advancement in ships and nautical skills had led to more thorough exploration. Australia had been mapped by Matthew Flinders and Nicholas Baudin, and John McDouall Stuart had solved the mystery of its interior. Contrary to popular belief, there was no inland sea or oasis. McDouall Stuart was several million years too late. Scraps of opalised shell around Coober Pedy and other relics provide evidence that there was once an inland sea running through the middle of Australia, but what Stuart found was just one vast, unrelenting desert. The medical missionary, Dr David Livingstone, had opened up much of Africa in his quest to find the source of the Nile, reputedly having traversed more than 30 000 miles and mapped even more. The Northwest Passage, a navigable seaway believed to exist between the Pacific and North Atlantic Oceans linking Europe with China, continued to elude explorers. No one had reached the North Geographical Pole, though men had suffered, and many had died, in their obsession with solving the riddle of the Arctic. At the southern end of the globe, Antarctica lay almost completely unexplored. It was not even known if it was a continent. There was the possibility that it was even two continents or just a group of ice-capped islands.

a Royal Penguin

3

Finding Antarctica

*They are ill discoverers that think there is no land, when they can
see nothing but sea.*

Francis Bacon (1561–1626)

The last of the world's seven continents to be discovered, Antarctica
was not sighted until 1820 by a Russian navigator, Fabian von Bellingshausen, who preceded a British explorer, Edward Bransfield, by three
days. Trade and adventure lured men to the far-south on and off for
the next eighty years or so, although there were years in between during
which no one went at all. The real unveiling of the continent only began
in earnest at the very end of the nineteenth century and the beginning
of the twentieth century with the advent of ships equipped with reliable
steam engines and improved knowledge of magnetism and navigation.
Before that explorers were hindered by the thick pack-ice and poor light,
which only afforded them glimpses of land. It was not until as late as
1945 that Antarctica began to be thoroughly photographed from the air
and then, later still, by satellite.

The belief in the existence of Antarctica goes back as far as the Ancient
Greeks. They believed there was a southern continent to counterbalance
the northern one at the other end of a spherical earth. This made sense
to them geographically. They imagined it was a rich, fertile land, and

assuming it was populated, voyagers even packed gifts for 'the natives'. This belief was upheld for several hundred years. Throughout the seventeenth century, the discovery of lands in the southern seas, such as the New Hebrides (present-day Vanuatu), the Solomon Islands, the Carolines and Marianas, and later, Tahiti, were considered confirmation of the existence of a flourishing southern continent.

The notion that it was a habitable, temperate land was largely dispelled when Captain James Cook circumnavigated Antarctica in 1773. He did not sight the continent but saw enough to put him off for life. He surmised that there was very probably a great southern landmass lying beyond the ice, though to his mind impenetrable, inhospitable and of little benefit to mankind. Forced to retreat due to the heavy pack-ice, he was not in the least sorry to leave the discovery of what promised to be an unfruitful land, to some other unfortunate explorer.

However, while Cook's bleak impressions did little to encourage further geographical investigation, he discovered and named the South Sandwich Islands and South Georgia, on which he reported having sighted numerous seal colonies. This created a reason to go south and, by the 1820s, seals were being slaughtered indiscriminately, fur seals for their brown, velvety pelts, primarily used for making slippers, and elephant seals for their oil. At this time there were more than two hundred ships in operation. Fur seals were the most sought after. When breeding, in September, they congregate in large numbers, making them easy targets. Sealers would systematically work their way along a beach and slaughter every seal, including mothers and their fluffy, black pups. It didn't take long to wipe out an entire colony as a good sealer could kill and remove the pelt of a seal in sixty seconds. This forced sealers to search for new fishing grounds, which inevitably led to the unofficial discovery of many of the Antarctic and sub-Antarctic islands. In fact, the little that was known about the area was almost entirely learnt from sealers and later, whalers, but new finds were kept secret, for as long as possible to ward off competition, and thus few charts were published. With such rich pickings on the fringes of Antarctica, there was no need to push further south towards the continent, bearing in mind that this was in the days before steam ships. The frozen sea was an added deterrent for ships that were totally at the mercy of the wind, as Cook's ship was decades before. That he had got as far as he did without mishap is truly remarkable.

It was not until 1823, fifty years after Cook's voyage, that his latitude 71°10'S was bettered by a British sealer, James Weddell, who happened to encounter an exceptionally good season in the normally ice-infested sea that was subsequently named after him. Weddell's furthest south, 74°15'S, was surpassed by another Englishman, naval officer James Clark Ross, some twenty or so years later during a flurry of activity in Antarctica, precipitated by a wave of scientific enthusiasm. Ross, a naval officer and experienced Arctic explorer, led one of three national expeditions sent south, the others being an American one under Lieutenant Charles Wilkes and a French one under Captain Jules Dumont D'Urville. These three men sailed around an area of the continent directly south of Australia, which was to become the region that Douglas Mawson would explore seventy years later.

For a period of fifty years after Ross, no one, apart from a solitary American sealer, went down to Antarctica as all interest was diverted to the Arctic when Sir John Franklin, a British naval officer, vanished with 128 men in 1847. He was then on his third expedition to the Arctic and on a quest to find the Northwest Passage. Franklin was the nephew of Matthew Flinders and had accompanied his uncle on the first circumnavigation of Australia in the early 1800s, and served as Lieutenant Governor General of Tasmania from 1834–1845. His disappearance precipitated, over a twelve-year period, no fewer than twenty-six search expeditions. This inadvertently led to the unveiling of the Canadian Arctic[*].

While searches for the missing Franklin party became largely responsible for the advancement of geographical knowledge in the north polar regions, exploration of Antarctica began quite differently. It was instigated by a conscious decision to investigate a part of the world that had, until then, inspired only spasmodic interest and had otherwise been largely ignored. At the Sixth International Geographical Congress of 1895, Sir Hugh Robert Mill, librarian at the Royal Geographical Society in London, drew attention to this fact. By then no one, apart from that lone

---

[*] Expeditions to establish the cause of the deaths of Franklin and the 128 who vanished with him were still being carried out as recently as 1992.

American sealer, had visited Antarctica since Ross in 1839. Mill urged Britain and other countries to organise expeditions before the close of the century. And so began the 'Heroic Era of Antarctic Exploration' to which Douglas Mawson belongs.

The phrase, 'Heroic Era of Antarctic Exploration', was first coined by Antarctic historian, John Gordon Hayes. It was characterised by the fact that it involved penetrating the interior of the continent on foot or with the assistance of dogs, ponies and primitive mechanised equipment, such as motor cars, motorised sledges, and even balloons, as opposed to surveying the continent from ships as earlier explorers had done. Most expeditions of the period had a scientific bent and the idea was to map the coastline, or rather, correct the coastline, as well as map the mountains and glaciers. There was not much scope for the study of vegetation, which is limited to lichen and mosses, but the rich sea life more than compensated. Geologically, there was much to learn. The continent is separated into east and west by the Transantarctic Mountains and inside this range are several dry valleys, where rain has not fallen for several million years. The cold conditions have ensured the preservation of animal and plant fossils in the rock layers.

According to Hayes, the era began with Scott's first expedition, the British National Antarctic Expedition 1901–04, and ended with Shackleton's Imperial Trans-Antarctic Expedition 1914–17, on which he tried, unsuccessfully, to cross the entire continent from sea to sea via the Pole, or, more specifically, with his death in 1922. Although the era involved more than twenty expeditions, four men stand out and they are Roald Amundsen, Douglas Mawson, Ernest Shackleton and Robert Scott.

During this period of exploration, several European countries launched expeditions to Antarctica and an enormous amount of knowledge, previously unknown, was accumulated in a relatively short space of time. The first claimed landing on the continent had only taken place as recently as 1893 by an expedition party led by Henryk Johan Bull, a Norwegian businessman and Australian immigrant. Virtually nothing was known of the interior and only small sections of coastline had been chartered, and some incorrectly, by the turn of the twentieth century.

Most of the Antarctic coastline is lined with high, ice cliffs and few rock exposures and the polar light is such that it gives the impression of land where there is none. Thus it was very difficult for Cook and other early explorers, who sailed south sixty years after him, to distinguish land from icebergs because their ships were enshrouded by one big blur of white. This resulted in phantom sightings or the locating of coastline sometimes hundreds of miles from its actual position. Wilkes claimed to have discovered eight new lands, six of which were later found to be non-existent by his contemporary, Ross, and by subsequent explorers, such as Scott and Douglas Mawson who sailed into open sea where he had purportedly seen land and mountains.

Ross enjoyed greater success than Wilkes, who, although later acquitted, returned to a court martial for, among other things, fabricating sighting land. Ross, who had successfully located the North Magnetic Pole in 1831, had been sent by the Admiralty to find the South Magnetic Pole on the British Antarctic Expedition of 1839–43. He did not find it but is credited with discovering the Ross Sea, the Ross Ice Shelf, which he named the 'Great Ice Barrier', occupying an area the size of France, and Victoria Land, a large region in West Antarctica which became the launching pad for both Shackleton's and Scott's assaults on the South Pole. Ross sighted and named Victoria Land from a considerable distance in his ship but it was Scott and Shackleton who later explored it. They ventured hundreds of miles beyond Ross's furthest point and examined a long section of coastline that their predecessor had merely glimpsed.

Scott was a lieutenant in the Royal Navy with no prior experience of exploration when he was appointed to lead the British National Antarctic Expedition 1901–04 but he saw it as a quick route to promotion in the navy during peacetime. The main purpose of this expedition was to reach the South Geographic Pole. Lieutenant Shackleton, a charismatic Irishman with ten years' experience in the merchant navy, joined the expedition and was chosen, along with Dr Edward Wilson, the expedition's artist and scientist, to march with Scott to the Pole. They did not reach the Pole and the return journey was particularly arduous. They were all suffering from scurvy when they eventually reached the ship, with only two of the nineteen dogs they had set out with. Shackleton was the worst affected and Scott invalided him home on a relief ship, together with the rest of the merchant navy men, while he remained, with all the other Royal Navy men, his ship *Discovery* remaining trapped for a second season.

Once back in England, Shackleton started making plans for an expedition of his own, which became the British Antarctic Expedition (BAE) of 1907–09, with the aim of attaining the South Pole by the same route. However, he, too, failed to reach it, although he achieved a new farthest south, coming within a mere ninety-seven nautical miles of it. Douglas Mawson became a member of this expedition. His involvement incited him to organise the Australasian Antarctic Expedition (AAE) 1911–14, to explore an untouched part of the continent he had glimpsed while sledging on the BAE. It was a domino effect. Scott introduced Shackleton to Antarctica and Shackleton introduced Douglas Mawson. They all fell under the spell of the continent. They all returned more than once and all became famous, for very different reasons, for later visits.

a killer whale

4

How Douglas Mawson Ended up in Antarctica

Do not go where the path may lead, go instead where there is no path and leave a trail

Ralph Waldo Emerson (1803–1882), American essayist and poet

Scott was fourteen years older than Douglas and while he was heading for the South Pole at the beginning of last century, Douglas was a lean teenager in Australia coming to the end of what would be only his first degree. He had entered the University of Sydney at the age of sixteen at the same time that his elder brother, Will, began his medical degree. In 1902 Douglas became one of the youngest students to ever graduate from the university, when he qualified for the degree of Bachelor of Engineering. Soon afterwards, at just nineteen years old, he was appointed as a junior demonstrator in the Department of Chemistry. He held this paid position for three years, throughout studying for his second degree, which helped as his parents were never in a strong financial position. He was recommended by the Professor of Geology, TW Edgeworth David, whose teachings inspired Douglas's interest in geology and who was to become responsible, also, for securing him a place on Shackleton's BAE

1907–09. In his letter of recommendation, David described Douglas as 'a very good student, of above average ability', with 'a good capacity for original research', 'an enthusiastic worker, of sound physique and good address'.[1] Such qualities hint at the scientific explorer and leader he was destined to become.

Three years later Douglas gained a Bachelor of Science, majoring in geology, again from the University of Sydney. His first experience of scientific exploration and of unknown lands came in between degrees when he took six months leave from his studies in 1903 and went on an expedition to the New Hebrides, present day Vanuatu. This was once again at the instigation of Professor David and, at the invitation of the then commissioner of the New Hebrides, Captain EG Rason. At the risk of contracting malaria and, in the knowledge that the natives were canni-bals, Douglas made the first thorough geological survey of the islands. Although he later talked of going back, and even to New Guinea, the tropics were never to hold his interest as Antarctica did.

However, this trip was significant, not least of all because it was his first real test of endurance; he almost lost a leg. While trying to obtain a specimen from a rock face with a geological hammer, a piece of rock flew out and lodged itself under his kneecap. It seemed nothing at first, but then the pain set in and serious swelling ensued. Far from anywhere, he and two other men rowed for some thirty-six hours to a naval ship for medical help. By the time they reached the ship, Douglas was almost unconscious and his leg was black to the groin. It looked doomed for amputation, which would have abruptly ended any chance of a life of exploration. Fortunately, the leg was saved, it was opened up and large amounts of dark fluid drained from it, but, according to Paquita, he was dangerously ill in the ship's hospital for weeks afterwards. In relating this incident in *Mawson of the Antarctic*, Paquita made mention of his stoic attitude to pain and his strong constitution, both of which were to prove important factors in his greatest survival test of all, less than ten years later.

As unlikely as it sounds, Douglas's interest in Antarctica was inspired by his interest in the geology of South Australia. Before qualifying for his Bachelor of Science, he successfully applied for the position of Lecturer in Mineralogy and Petrology at the University of Adelaide, which commenced in March 1905. Then only twenty-three years old, he worked alongside a man called Walter Howchin, who had gained international recognition for finding evidence of glaciation in South Australia of Pre-Cambrian age, the earliest known geological age dating back more than 500 million years. Douglas already had an interest in glaciation as this was Professor David's area of expertise.

In between lecturing at the university, Douglas went on geological excursions, mostly to the country around Broken Hill, which in those days, was a desert almost as hostile and remote as the frozen wastes of Antarctica. On these trips he travelled by horse and gig and later, by motorcycle, and encountered daytime temperatures that soared well over 100° F in the shade, contrasted by very cold nights. It was rocky, dusty, lonely terrain and obtaining water was always a challenge. In September 1907, while he was on one such excursion, he wrote to Professor David from Broken Hill, upon hearing that his old lecturer and mentor had been invited to go on the BAE as far as Edward VII Land.* David was then a world expert on glaciology and later used his considerable influence in political circles to help Shackleton to obtain a grant of £5000 from the Australian government and a further £1000 from the government of New Zealand.

Upon his return from Broken Hill, Douglas met Shackleton in Adelaide and asked him, not for a place on his expedition, but if he, too, could sail with him on the *Nimrod* to Edward VII Land and work on the ship to earn his passage. For both men it was an opportunity to see glaciation first-hand. There were many theories about how Antarctica had evolved. Of Douglas's opinion, Shackleton wrote in an article for the *The London Magazine*: 'Dr Mawson, for instance, regards as almost conclusive the evidence that, in a geologically recent past, there existed a habitable Antarctic continent, stretching out to what are now South America, New Zealand and South Africa; that volcanic activity brought about a separation; and that an Ice Age of fearful severity afterwards extinguished the life of the present Polar area'.[2] This was a relatively new theory. The idea that continents were not fixed but constantly shifting, was most famously

---

* Edward VII Land in north-west Antarctica, lies east of the Ross Ice Shelf and was discovered by Scott on 30 January 1902.

proposed in 1912, by German geologist, Alfred Wegener. While not the first to put this idea forward, Wegener was the first to support the theory with evidence in his book *The Origin of Continents and Oceans*, published in 1915. However, he could not sufficiently explain how the continents had moved and continental drift was not fully embraced until after the rise of the theory of plate tectonics in the 1960s that put forward a mechanism.

The existence of metamorphic rocks all over Antarctica, rocks that are formed as a result of intense heat or pressure, and the discovery, on previous expeditions, of coal in the Transantarctic Mountains, tended to support this theory. The discovery of animal fossils and tree and plant fossils that could only have existed and thrived in temperate or even tropical conditions, as well as traces of fossilised wood, all of which suggested a once fertile land that had been overwhelmed by ice, only strengthened this argument.

Just days following their meeting, Douglas received a telegram from Shackleton in Sydney inviting him to join the expedition as physicist. He was a little surprised by the offer, as physics was not his chosen area of study, but when Professor David intimated that there would be opportunities for geological work as well, he finally accepted and gained a year's leave of absence from his lecturing post at the University of Adelaide, which was later extended to two years. At some later stage, it was decided that Professor David, despite being fifty years old, would also remain for the duration of the expedition to offer advice and assistance to the scientific staff. This occured once both were on board *Nimrod*, in the Antarctic, having set sail from New Zealand on New Year's Day, 1908.

With the Professor, Douglas became one of six to make the first ascent of Mount Erebus, the only active volcano in Antarctica, and, was among the first three to reach the South Magnetic Pole on what became the longest unsupported* journey across Antarctica. It is significant that he was chosen by Shackleton for these two important journeys, particularly given that he was a late addition to the expedition. Furthermore, in

---

* Unsupported in this context denotes travelling on foot without the assistance of animals or machinery.

the event of the non-return of Shackleton's South Pole party,* he was appointed to lead the search party to look for them. His sixteen months of apprenticeship on this BAE, on which he also served as unofficial photographer, sewed the seeds for his own expedition and thus began his long association with Antarctica.

A weka

---

* While Professor David, Dr Mackay and Douglas Mawson went in pursuit of the South Magnetic Pole, Shackleton led a party in the direction of the South Geographical Pole, the attainment of which was the main objective of the British Antarctic Expedition 1907–09.

5

Paquita

*Believe me Paquita, I have never at any time loved anybody as I
love you. Never had it entered my head before I met you to wed
anybody. This is perhaps one reason why I love you so much.*

Douglas Mawson to Paquita Delprat, written aboard the *Aurora*,
Antarctic [sic] Ocean, 26 December 1913

It was at this stage in his life, at twenty-seven years of age and soon after
his return from Antarctica, that Douglas met Paquita Delprat. By March
1909, he had resumed his job at the University of Adelaide. In August of
that year he went to Broken Hill to research for his Doctor of Science,
which he gained in December 1909, and to give a talk on his experiences on Shackleton's expedition. One evening, during his stay, he was
invited to dine with the Boyd family, who lived in the centre of town,
in the first house that Paquita and her family had occupied upon their
arrival in Australia from Europe in 1898. Paquita's father, Guillaume
Daniel Delprat, known by all as GDD, was the General Manager of
Broken Hill Proprietary Limited (BHP), then the largest silver mine in
the world. GDD later played a leading role in the company's move into
steelmaking in 1915, hence the title of Paquita's biography of him, *A
Vision of Steel*. Mr Boyd, the dinner host, was the Underground Manager
at the 'Big Mine', the silver and lead mine.

GDD was Dutch by birth and educated in Amsterdam. He was a mining engineer and had worked in Spain for some twenty years for an English mining company overseeing the running of a number of mines in Andalusia where, near Cordoba, he had successfully unearthed an ancient Roman silver mine that had been in disuse for two thousand years and which contained many valuable artefacts. He had subsequently unearthed other mines in southern Spain with equal success. His reputation had spread throughout the mining world, eventually reaching Australia where he was offered the position of Assistant General Manager of BHP and soon afterwards, General Manager.

Paquita was the sixth of his seven children and his youngest daughter. When her family emigrated to Australia, she was just seven years old. Douglas was nine years older. When he entered university, she was still a child running barefoot around the palm trees in the garden of her Broken Hill home. On arrival in Australia, she spoke only Spanish and Dutch and, even after learning English, she retained a foreign accent for the rest of her life. At primary school in Broken Hill she was labelled a foreigner and a heretic, perhaps partly on account of her dark Basque looks, which she had inherited from her father, whose ancestors were Basque Huguenots. For years I understood that her name, Paquita, a diminutive of her real name, Francisca, meant 'little one'. In a way it does. She was born premature in London on 19 August 1891, the only one of her siblings to be born outside Spain. She weighed just four and a half pounds and for a long time I was under the impression that, due to her small size, she had been shipped out to Australia in a shoebox.*

In fact, Paquita grew into a very tall woman, inheriting her height from her mother, Henrietta. In 1909 she was seventeen and taller than her father, at almost six feet tall. The previous year she had passed her senior exams at a progressive private girls' school, Tormore House, in North Adelaide, which offered the subjects of chemistry, biology and even geology. At the time of this dinner engagement at the Boyds,

---

* In the biography of her father, *A Vision of Steel*, Paquita quoted a Spanish nurse as saying to her mother, Henrietta, at the birth of one of the Delprat children, born premature: 'Don't worry…there will be no expense. You can bury it in a shoebox'. This is possibly where my idea came from. It was disappointing to learn that Paquita had emigrated to Australia at the age of seven, as this destroyed my long-held image of a crying baby in a lone shoebox on a wide, open deck.

Paquita had just completed a year of piano and singing lessons at the Elder Conservatorium of Music in Adelaide and was enjoying a summer holiday in Broken Hill with her father and her sister, Leintie.

Paquita was aware of who Douglas Mawson was. In fact, she had secretly admired him for a year. In *Mawson of the Antarctic* she described how she was first struck by his smile, which she had witnessed from a distance on a foggy winter's day in the university grounds. She had also attended his lectures to the public on polar exploration and, years later, affectionately recalled him arriving in the complete polar outfit and peeling off layers as the lecture proceeded until he stripped down to a dinner suit. More recently she had seen his picture in the paper. Upon his return from the BAE in March 1909, he had received a hero's welcome in Adelaide. Some of his students had kidnapped him, and carried him in a hand-held cart all the way along North Terrace from the Adelaide Railway Station to the university, chased by a policeman intent on retrieving the porters' cart.

Despite her youth and inexperience, Paquita had a strong sense of self-worth and this undoubtedly attracted Douglas. A photograph of her sitting on a rock at the beach at Robe, when she was eleven years old, gives some indication of her allure. She was tall, even then, and her mature, self-assured gaze makes her look much older and wiser than her years. She appears strong and independent, qualities that were to stand her in good stead as the fiancée and later, wife, of an often absent explorer.

After this initial meeting in Broken Hill, Douglas invited Paquita to a musical comedy and she was so excited that she failed to remember a single word of the performance. He was subsequently invited to dinner at the Delprats' home in Tynte Street, North Adelaide, where he and Paquita pored over the photographs he had taken in Antarctica and in the New Hebrides. It is likely that he was persuaded to play billiards with his future father-in-law, who was a keen player. Apparently GDD had bought the house without a full inspection of all the rooms, having looked no further than the billiard room.

It seems Douglas was at ease in female company, perhaps on account of his good relationship with his mother. It would not be long before he was writing letters to his future sisters-in-law and addressing each as 'sister', and his future mother-in-law as 'mother'. The Delprat women

Paquita, Henrietta and Douglas, Adelaide, circa 1910
(*Gareth Thomas Collection*)

were no ordinary women. All were highly educated. Paquita's mother, Henrietta, was an accomplished pianist and spoke several languages; two of Paquita's sisters, Lica, then 27, and Mary, 23, were studying medicine at the University of Adelaide; 20-year-old Leintie was a pianist and another sister, Carmen, at just 25, was a concert violinist of international renown. Paquita's elder brother, Theo, who was 28, a year older than Douglas and the eldest of the Delprat siblings, was then working for BHP having studied mining engineering at his father's encouragement. Theo later took up medicine as did Paquita's younger brother, Willy, who was fifteen years old in 1909.

All of Paquita's siblings were very much in awe of Douglas. Theo was flattered when Douglas apparently announced that he wanted to see more of him, but he soon realised he was just 'a milepost' on the explorer's way to his youngest sister's heart. Sometimes Douglas joined the Delprats for weekends at El Rincon, their holiday house at Brighton, where he eventually proposed to Paquita on the veranda one night. She instantly accepted and forever afterwards associated the sound of waves in the dark with the moment she knew her feelings for him were reciprocated.

Douglas then wrote a seven-page letter to GDD that would appeal to even the hardest-hearted person, asking for his permission to marry Paquita. In it he claimed that he had never loved any women before nor spoken to any 'in terms of wedlock' and that if a lifelong union with Paquita was not realised, his life would be 'forever blighted'. He admitted that he had 'but poor means' to support Paquita, which is interesting in that, years later, when Peter McEwin wanted to marry his daughter Jessica (i.e. Oma), Douglas was fiercely opposed to it on the grounds that Peter had no money behind him. However, in 1910 Douglas was young and confident. He detailed to GDD his family background and education. His father was well-educated but had not had much luck in business and this had put his mother under enormous strain. He recalled as well, his plans to lead an expedition to the Antarctic spanning fifteen months and commencing early in 1911.[1]

Needless to say, GDD was not very happy to learn that Douglas wanted to marry his daughter, only to dash off into the unknown. Douglas was going to a hostile, almost entirely unexplored continent, and there was a very real chance that he wouldn't come back at all. He could vanish as John Franklin had vanished into the Arctic; as the Prussian explorer, Ludwig Leichhardt, had disappeared into the Australian desert sixty years before, in his attempt to cross the country from east to west. Antarctica in 1910 was as mysterious as Australia had been in the mid-1800s.

Although the list of casualties was short in comparison to that of the Arctic, several men had died on previous expeditions to Antarctica, since the turn of the century. While not all of the deaths were caused by the harsh conditions, the risk to life was always there. Also, there was the possibility that Douglas might return badly injured or even return an invalid. Permanent damage to his health could affect his ability to work or his ability to have children and where, wondered GDD, would this leave Paquita?

On a hot fly-ridden day in Port Pirie, with the smoke from the works billowing around the house, GDD replied to Douglas's letter. He wrote that, while he did not know of a better man to whom he would trust the future happiness of his daughter, he questioned whether it was fair of Douglas to put a woman through such a separation and expose her to months, perhaps years, of anxiety. With reference to Antarctica, he wrote: 'You have made a great name for yourself there already—what good can a second trip do you?…it would be a terrible strain on Paquita which would not do her any good. Have you thought this well over?… Every man must fight his battle in his own way, but as your success is my girl's happiness—and if anything happened to you her life would be blighted…I fully understand that to give up such an expedition, must mean a tremendous lot to you. Do you think you can do it? You want a great deal—is it worth the sacrifice? I am sure it is.'[2]

However, GDD stressed in his letter, that he did not wish to place any conditions on the marriage, perhaps because he understood the desire for adventure. After all, he too, was a pioneer. In his foreword to *A Vision of Steel*, Paquita's biography of her father, the then prime minister Sir Robert Menzies described GDD as 'an explorer', likening him to his 'celebrated son-in-law'.[3] Like Douglas, GDD's adventurous spirit had driven him to take risks. He had been so confident of finding silver in the Roman mine in Spain that, despite having a young and large family to support, he had offered to put in every penny he had. Furthermore, he had taken his wife, Henrietta, to Spain, which was not as remote, nor as perilous as Antarctica, but then, in the late 1800s, it was a far-off country. He had left Henrietta alone in remote countryside for long periods of time, while he rode off to inspect mines. She had given birth to six of their children in primitive conditions. Apparently, on one occasion it had been necessary to lock the local doctor up for two weeks to ensure he would be sober for the event. The days were hot and dusty and swarming with mosquitoes and at night wolves howled around the house. Relatives had asked 'Was it wise?' 'Why not remain in your own

country where there is plenty to do for a clever energetic young man?'.
Now it was twenty years later and GDD was posing a similar question
to his future son-in-law: 'Would you not be able to find as wide a field
for your energy in the inhabited world?' he asked.[4]

GDD's pleas fell on deaf ears. It was too late. Antarctica had, by
his time, got well and truly under Douglas's skin. He was adamant
that he would not give up the expedition. Douglas had begun to seriously formulate his plans for what would become the AAE 1911–14 in
February 1910. His letter to GDD was written in December 1910, by
which time plans were already underway. In his letter of reply, GDD
asked Douglas to 'think it over again' and suggested he talked to Henrietta in the meantime. GDD was not due to return to Adelaide from Port
Pirie until the following week upon which, he explained, he would have
'a final discussion'[5] with Douglas. However, this discussion probably
never took place for the engagement between Douglas and Paquita was
announced in the papers just two days after GDD sent his letter.

Paquita admitted to her daughters, years later, that her father had
expressed his objections to the expedition by walking out of the room
whenever he saw Douglas and her sitting together and holding hands,
but that he eventually came to accept the inevitable. Certainly, Douglas
was about to embark on a dangerous mission, but it was not a reckless
one and perhaps GDD realised this. He wasn't just tearing off on a whim
to the ends of the earth and he was not the sort of man to do anything
without serious research and consideration. He was then in his late
twenties and more than capable of leading an expedition. He had some
prior experience of the continent and this was surely some comfort, and
would later prove an enormous advantage on what became known as the
Far-Eastern Sledging Journey.

Initially, Paquita had not wanted Douglas to go but once she realised
there was no chance of changing his mind, she claimed 'he had no keener
supporter'.[6] It was perhaps a good thing that she was largely ignorant of
the dangers he would face. Neither she nor Douglas ever imagined he
would nearly lose his life. They were young, full of hope and courage.
Paquita might never have let him go had she seen the advertisement
for willing recruits for the BAE a few years before, which Douglas had
joined. It read: 'Men wanted for hazardous journey. Low wages, bitter

cold, long hours of complete darkness. Safe return doubtful, honour and recognition in the event of success'.[7]

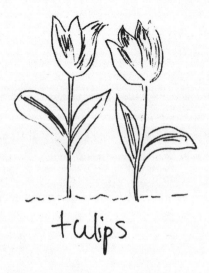

tulips

6

The Making of the AAE

Tell me not sweet, I am unkind,
That from the nunnery
Of they chaste breast and quiet mind,
*To Antarctica I fly.**

From Douglas to Paquita, 10 December 1911

In considering his own expedition, Douglas's main objective was to investigate a largely unknown section of coastline directly south of Australia, stretching in an east-west direction for some 2000 miles. The significance of this was that by applying the polar precedence from the Arctic, Douglas could rightfully make claims for Australia of land directly to the south. The territory he had in mind lay between Cape Adare in the east and Gaussberg in the west, discovered in 1902 by the German Antarctic Expedition under geologist, Erich von Drygalski. Of this coast, as Douglas later explained when describing how his expedition plan came about, 'only the barest evidence had been furnished'. This area which

---

* This is the first stanza of a poem, 'To Lucasta, going to the Wars' by English poet, Richard Lovelace (1618–1658). Douglas changed the last line of this stanza from 'To war and arms I fly' to 'To Antarctica I fly'.

Douglas called his 'Land of Hope and Glory'[1] had not been visited since
Dumont D'Urville* had navigated these waters some seventy years before.
Dumont D'Urville had sighted the area near where Douglas would land
in 1911 and named it Adélie Land after his wife. Many explorers, such as
Scott and Shackleton, focused on the better-known Ross Sea region as a
base for the attainment of the South Geographical Pole. Douglas believed
it would be more beneficial, particularly from a scientific perspective, to
concentrate on the large expanses of the continent adjacent to Australia
that remained unknown.

Given Antarctica's proximity to Australia, he felt that Australians
should have a special interest in investigating this territory. He advocated
that geographically it belonged to Australia and ventured to refer to it
as 'the Australian quadrant'. Hinting at the potential economic value of
Antarctica to Australia, he wanted to investigate the whale oil and seal
skin industries, (incidentally the whaling industry was flourishing**) and
thoroughly explore the region for mineral deposits. In announcing his
plans for the expedition, he argued that Australians were, 'just as well
fitted constitutionally to stand the rigorous conditions of life in high
latitudes as are people originating from colder climates'.[2] His own experiences in the deserts of Australia had involved enduring extreme conditions, albeit at the opposite end of the temperature scale. This had proved
good preparation for the BAE, on which two Australians, namely he and
Professor David, had made the greatest achievements, and now Scott,
who was also in the midst of planning an expedition to the Antarctic, had
recruited two Australian scientists, Griffith Taylor and Frank Debenham.
An Australian-led expedition, Douglas advised, would raise the profile of
the country and show that Australia was not only as capable as any other

---

* Dumont D'Urville had circumnavigated the world twice, (1822–25 and 1826–29) when he successfully
applied to the French government in 1837 to undertake a third circumnavigation. King Louis-Philippe
personally instructed D'Urville to better James Weddell's farthest south of 74°15'S, which he succeeded in
doing in January 1838. While on this expedition, D'Urville discovered and named Adélie Land.

** The Antarctic whaling industry was founded by a Norwegian explorer, Carl Anton Larsen. He established
the first whaling station in the Antarctic on South Georgia in 1904, which resulted in the relocation of
most of the Norwegian whaling industry to southern waters. Interest was initially sparked by James Clark
Ross (1839–43) who claimed to have seen right whales in the Ross and Weddell Seas. The industry was
concentrated on Deception Island and South Georgia, the latter being where Shackleton arrived in 1916 after
his epic 800-mile voyage across the South Atlantic from remote Elephant Island following the sinking of his
ship, *Endurance*.

nation in the realm of scientific exploration, but that it had as much right, if not more right, as Antarctica's closest neighbour, to claim territory for the British Crown. If Australia did not act swiftly, other nations would, with less right as Douglas saw it, secure this part of the continent for themselves.

It was a huge undertaking to organise an expedition, not least of all because it was so costly. Finding money was the hardest part of the preparation. Many explorers had faced the problem of insufficient funds. Scotsman, William Speirs Bruce, had proposed a trans-continental expedition to Antarctica to begin in 1911, but it never materialised due to a lack of financial support. At around the same time, Dr Mackay, who had trekked to the South Magnetic Pole with Douglas in 1908 on the BAE, put forward a plan to study the Antarctic coastline as opposed to the interior but he, too, failed to attract the necessary support. To escape his creditors, whom he realised he was unable to pay, and reluctant to abandon his expedition to the Arctic in 1903, the Norwegian, Roald Amundsen, had resorted to sailing out of Oslo (then Christiana) in the middle of the night. For his South Pole expedition he had mortgaged his house. When organising the BAE, Shackleton had run out of money by the time he reached Australia. Without Professor David's influence, it is unlikely the expedition would have got underway. Associating oneself with high profile people was a sure way of gathering support and Douglas immediately thought of Scott, who was busy organising another expedition to the Pole. On 9 December 1909, Douglas set sail for England and cabled Scott from Perth to arrange a meeting.

When Douglas met Scott in London, he quickly realised Scott had misinterpreted the reason for his visit. Scott, who had been advised in a cable by Professor David, to take Douglas with him to Antarctica, asked him to join his expedition, though not as chief scientist. Scott's good friend, Edward Wilson, had been offered this position. Douglas could not be persuaded to join the expedition, even when Scott, who had barely met him, promised to include him in the march to the Pole and to pay him £800 for two years, which was a lot. He had other ideas. Seeing little value in a dash for the Pole, it had occurred to him that he could join Scott's expedition in another capacity. It would save him the trouble of organising his own. He proposed that the Englishman land him and a party of three at Cape Adare, adjacent to the unknown coast to the west, where they could carry out scientific research as an independent unit. Scott thought this over and, although he eventually decided it was not feasible, he continued to hold out hope that Douglas would join him in his own venture, keeping him on his staff list until the last possible moment. Scott even enlisted his wife, Kathleen, in pursuit of this. However, on this Douglas would not change his mind and he began preparing to mount his own expedition to accommodate his ambitious plans.

The final idea was to land three parties of men on the Antarctic continent and one on Macquarie Island, a sub-Antarctic island which lies between New Zealand and the Antarctic mainland (although this was later reduced to two parties on the continent itself). There were, at the time, a number of wireless stations in the Northern Hemisphere that had supplied meteorological records for some years from near or within the Arctic Circle. 'The bearing of Antarctic meteorology on Australian weather is apparent to all', Douglas was quoted as saying by the *Daily Telegraph*. Of his plans to establish a wireless relay station on Macquarie Island and another station on the continent itself, he argued, 'It is only along this particular coast to be investigated by this expedition that a suitable Far South station can be erected. The meteorological conditions come from the Cape, sweeping along the coast of Adélie Land, reaching Australia'.[3] Thus, sending daily weather forecasts and storm warnings would benefit mariners and Australian farmers in so far as it could assist in the prevention of shipwrecks and the destruction of crops and, on a wider scale, possibly reveal something of the bearing of Antarctic meteorology on world climate. Douglas planned to also erect a wireless station on the continent, something that had never been done before. This was an ambitious undertaking given that the Italian physicist, Guglielmo Marconi, had succeeded in sending wireless messages over a long distance, across the Atlantic, only a decade before.

Douglas set out his plans in writing to Shackleton, who had recently been knighted for his achievements on the BAE, in the hope that he would offer support. Shackleton subsequently more or less poached his idea. One day he entered the small office from which Douglas was operating in Regent Street, and suggested the same plan, only with himself as leader and Douglas as Chief Scientist. Added to this, some

Loading stores, Queen's Wharf, Hobart, 1911 (*Mawson Collection, South Australian Museum*)

money donated to the expedition, via Shackleton, seemed to have all but disappeared. Douglas felt he had been cheated but he had the sense to see that Shackleton, a man of great charisma and influence, and, who was now well-known in polar circles, would be far more successful at procuring further funds. Shackleton was restless and constantly changed his plans. He proved unreliable and eventually relinquished command of the expedition to Douglas, although he agreed to continue to support it and, without Shackleton, and the help of other explorers, including Jean Charcot and Adrien de Gerlache, it may never have happened.

Yet, even with the assistance of people of influence, there was an enormous amount of work to do. Douglas later wrote, 'The date of departure south was fixed for 4 p.m. of Saturday, December 2, and a truly appalling amount of work had to be done before then'.[4] And this was after the exhausting and, as Douglas described it, 'soul destroying' task of raising the thousands of pounds needed to cover all their costs. It was hard work trying to gather support for a journey to a land no one knew much about and with no guarantee of success. (In *The Home of the Blizzard* Douglas referred to Antarctica as 'the supposed continent'.) He wrote regularly to Paquita in Adelaide and kept her up to date with all the arrangements, although, more often than not, she read of his movements in the newspapers long before his letters arrived. Her love was a tremendous support and inspiration, spurring him on to success and she occupied his thoughts on long train journeys. 'I could never have been so happy had I not found you out',[5] he confessed.

In the months leading up to his departure south, set for 2 December 1911, in between lectures at the university and field trips into the outback, Douglas travelled interstate to raise funds. It took courage to leave out the glamour of the Pole in his programme. It was harder to argue the benefit of intellectual gain. He attracted interest from political and scientific bodies and from the general public by stressing that this was the first expedition to be undertaken by Australians outside Australia. He had the backing of Professor David and professor of chemistry at the University of Melbourne, Orme-Masson. They were leading figures on the committee of eighteen scientists established by the Australian Association for the Advancement of Science to promote and support the expedition, the estimated cost of which was £40 000. Support came from the British government, the Australian government, the governments of four states of Australia, the government of New Zealand, as well as private donors.

On evenings when he wasn't giving a lecture on polar exploration or meeting a sponsor, Douglas would visit Paquita and they would check lists together. She was astonished at the quantity of food required, some sixteen tonnes for twelve men to be supplemented by penguin eggs and seal meat. In January 1911, shortly after he became engaged to Paquita, he again went to England, because many rich Australians were in London for the coronation of George V. It was also where he purchased many of the provisions and where he bought the *Aurora*, a thirty-eight year old steam-powered whaler made of oak and fir. She had been used, primarily, to ship tonnes of seal oil to Dundee, but was better known for her part in the rescue of Greely from the Arctic in the late 1880s.

It was largely due to Shackleton's intervention and the cooperation of the *Daily Mail* that money started rolling in. Shackleton wrote a letter, published in the *Daily Mail*, in which he appealed to the British public for donations to cover the cost of £12 000 for a ship for Douglas Mawson. He argued that Australians had supported British south polar ventures, financially and otherwise, not least of all his own expedition of 1907–09. Within two days the money had been raised by donations from both England and Australia and British firms had offered, at no cost, to supply nearly all the food needed. The man Douglas had chosen to sail the ship was Captain John King Davis and it was through his efforts that the *Aurora* was finally purchased for £6000, less than half its original price of £13 000.

Captain Davis was also to act as Douglas's second-in-command. An Irishman with short red hair and a red beard, he was pencil thin and looked older than his twenty-eight years. Nicknamed 'Gloomy' because of his pessimistic disposition, he had run away to sea at the age of sixteen. Douglas had met him on the BAE 1907–09 on which Davis had been appointed first mate of the *Nimrod* at the age of just twenty-five. For both men it was their first voyage to Antarctica. They had become friends on the outward voyage when Davis found a severely seasick Douglas lying in a lifeboat and fed him tinned pears. A master at avoiding icebergs, Davis arguably became the greatest captain of his time to navigate in Antarctic waters. He was at his best when pushed to the limit. His whole countenance changed in rough seas. His booming voice could be heard over the loudest hurricane and, exhilarated by the danger, he was rarely off the deck where he was known to break out into song. The voyage of the *Aurora* in 1911 was the second of seven voyages Davis undertook to the Antarctic, and he later described it as his 'main life's work'.[6] His last polar voyage was as captain of the first of two summer cruises led by Douglas in 1929 on BANZARE.

The South Pole had been the last place on Davis's list of desirable places to visit when he was appointed first mate and later, Captain of the *Nimrod*. Like Douglas, Davis more or less happened upon the BAE by chance. On the spur of the moment, he had accompanied a friend to London's Lower Regent Street to an exhibition of polar equipment Shackleton was intending to take with him to the South Pole. After hearing that some difficulty was being experienced in finding a suitable first mate, he was taken to meet Shackleton, after which he passed a map of Antarctica in the hall. It was barely filled in. Its proposed coastline, indicated by dotted lines, looked to Davis like, 'some gigantic, empty spider's web'.[7] However, even as he studied this almost featureless map, he began to feel excited and, like so many polar adventurers, after his first visit to the Antarctic, he wanted to go back.

The other key member of Douglas's expedition was Frank Wild. An Antarctic veteran, he had first gone to Antarctica with Scott in 1901 and then again in 1907 with Shackleton on the BAE on which he had been a member of the Pole Party. It was also where he met Douglas. After the AAE, Wild went on Shackleton's second expedition in 1914, as well as his third and final expedition from 1921–22,* thus he was periodically a part of the 'heroic age' from beginning to end. Born in Yorkshire and reputed to be a direct descendent of Captain Cook,** Wild had served in the merchant navy for twelve years after which he had joined the Royal Navy. Sporting a tattoo on each forearm, he was relatively short, standing at not quite five feet five inches tall but was a strong man with huge stamina. Douglas held him in high esteem, which was important given that Wild was appointed to lead one of the land bases, what became the Western Base, from which Douglas would be too far away to supervise.

With regard to the rest of the staff, the majority of the thirty-one men chosen for the expedition were from Australia or New Zealand as this was promoted as an Australasian expedition.*** However, there were a handful of non-Australians, apart from Wild, including the two men who are especially important to this story, Belgrave Ninnis from south London and Dr Xavier Mertz from Basel, Switzerland. Ninnis was a skilled surveyor and a lieutenant in the Royal Fusiliers. His father had been surgeon on an Arctic expedition in 1875 led by British naval officer, George Nares. A few years before this, Nares had sailed south in command of *Challenger*, the first steam-driven ship to enter Antarctic waters. It was the founding voyage of oceanography, then a relatively new science, and the rocks dredged up from the sea floor provided further proof that Antarctica was a continent rather than a collection of islands.

---

* Shackleton died of a heart attack in the Antarctic on board his ship, the *Quest* in January 1922, and on his death, Wild took over as leader of the expedition.

** That he was a descendant of Cook was claimed by Wild himself, but this is disputed by his biographer, Leif Mills.

*** Unfortunately there is no record of how many men applied for a position on the AAE although it was probably somewhere in the thousands. Twelve scientists were chosen to join the BANZARE 1929–31 from 1200 applicants, twenty-five of whom were women.

Mertz, a qualified lawyer, had a background in engineering and, as a teenager, had worked as a carpenter, plumber and blacksmith. An expert skier, and the champion Swiss ski jumper of 1908, he was also a mountaineer. He had worked as an alpine guide and climbed all the major peaks of Switzerland, including Mount Blanc. Both Ninnis and Mertz joined the expedition from England, sailing with the dogs in *Aurora* from London to Hobart.

The equipment and stores for the expedition weighed about fifty tonnes and had to provide for four Antarctic bases for at least a year. The food, mostly tinned or dry, was heavily represented by cans of fruit and vegetables to reduce the risk of scurvy. Tonnes of fresh potatoes were also taken, chocolate, biscuits, cocoa, flour, wines and whisky, sauces and pickles, ham and bacon, canned meats, cereal meals, custard powder, malted milk and 'fancy biscuits'.

The mountaineering equipment was obtained from Switzerland, the dogs from Greenland and the sledges, made of hickory and ash with a decking of bamboo, came from Norway and Australia, based on the Norwegian explorer, Fridtjof Nansen's design.* Much of the equipment and clothing was based on designs learnt from previous explorers who had lived with the Eskimos (Inuit) and taken them on their Arctic journeys, such as Robert Peary who claimed to have reached the North Pole in 1909 with the help of twenty Eskimo families. He had employed the women to work as seamstresses. The best boots were made from the fur on a reindeer's leg as this is the toughest and resistant to snow. They were lined with sennegras, a type of Scandinavian grass that keeps the feet warm, particularly when wet.

Some polar explorers of the age, such as Peary, favoured Eskimo clothing which is extremely warm and was perfect for his purposes. He travelled by dog sledge which involved sitting in one place for hours at a time. On his assault on the North Pole in 1909 his clothes included, for example, a sheepskin coat, bearskin trousers, hareskin stockings and deerskin boots. Amundsen dressed similarly. Although Antarctica is colder than the Arctic, for explorers like Scott, Shackleton and Mawson, who

---

* Fridjof Nansen (1861–1930), Norwegian scientist and Arctic explorer, was the first to cross Greenland (1888–89) during which he all but pioneered skiing as a means of polar travel. Finding his sledges too heavy he adapted them, based on those used by Norwegian farmers, with wide runners.

travelled mainly on foot, animal skins were too heavy and bulky. They required clothes that allowed for greater flexibility, that were warm but also light and easy to remove, hence their preference for wearing many layers. Only their gloves and their footwear were made of animal skins. They wore finnesko, boots made of reindeer skin fur, and wolfskin mitts. Their undergarments were made of wool, all-in-one Jaegar fleece suits made by tailors in Hobart over which they wore light, waterproof Burberry jackets and trousers, designed by Thomas Burberry of Hampshire, who had discovered that a close weave was the key to keeping out the rain. The disadvantage of such clothing was that the men grew cold very quickly once they stopped moving, partly because their sweat, absorbed by the fibres, froze on their bodies, unlike synthetics worn by modern-day explorers which are more effective at rejecting sweat and also dry very rapidly. The clothes for the men going to Macquarie Island, where it was warmer and wetter, varied slightly and included rubber boots and oilskins.

As Charles Laseron, taxidermist and biological collecter on the AAE later wrote in his book, *South With Mawson*, 'Whether we needed a sewing machine or a toothpick, every want seemed to have been anticipated'.[8] It was just as well, as Douglas noted, 'the most careful supervision was necessary to prevent mistakes, especially as the omission of a single article might fundamentally affect the work of a whole party'.[9] In a shed on Queen's Wharf at Hobart they stored all the equipment and the food, all of which was divided up into 5200 packages that needed to be sorted and checked. By the time they'd transported it all on to the ship, there was barely a space on the deck that wasn't filled, nor a man who wasn't utterly exhausted.

a leopard seal chasing an Adelie Penguin

7

South Bound

And now there came both mist and snow,
And it grew wondrous cold:
And ice, mast-high, came floating by,
As green as emerald.

From *The Rime of the Ancient Mariner*, Samuel Taylor Coleridge (1772–1834)

When Douglas set sail from Hobart on 2 December 1911, Antarctica was a remarkably busy place*. Between the years 1910–14 there were five expeditions in operation. Professor David's daughter, Mary, recalled that her father referred to this period as 'the overcrowding of the South Pole'.[1] A German expedition led by Wilhelm Filchner was bound for the Weddell Sea with the aim of carrying out hydrographical and scientific work and a Japanese expedition under Lieutenant Nobu Shirase, who had originally wanted to organise an expedition to the North Pole. Upon learning, in 1909, of both Frederick Cook and Robert Peary's claims to have reached the North Pole, Shirase had turned his attention to attaining the South Pole. He had launched an expedition to Antarctica in 1910 with this aim, but ice and strong winds had prevented him from landing at his chosen sight near Edward VII Land. He had been forced to leave as he was not

---

* Today a few thousand people live in Antarctica during the summer, but the population reduces to the hundreds in the winter months.

equipped for the winter and could not afford to be frozen in. After a year berthed in Sydney, during which time he replenished supplies and hired new men, Shirase set off for Antarctica a few weeks before Douglas. By then he had abandoned his ambition to reach the South Pole, choosing instead to explore Edward VII Land.

Roald Amundsen, a professional Norwegian explorer, who had successfully navigated the Northwest Passage in a small herring boat in 1905, had, like Shirase, abandoned his life-long plan to sledge to the North Geographic Pole after hearing that Peary had purportedly beaten him to it. Quite uninterested in going where someone else had been or in tracing the same trail in a different way, Amundsen had made an impulsive decision to sail to Antarctica on 9 August 1910 with his sights set on reaching the South Geographic Pole instead. His arrival came as a surprise to Scott, who was already down there making his own Pole preparations. He had not anticipated any competition. Scott had openly planned his second expedition for two years and his proposed route to the Pole was well-known. By contrast, for Amundsen it was a snap decision he kept secret until he reached South America, confiding only in his brother. Suddenly Scott and Amundsen became engaged in what the public labelled a race for the Pole. It was the British versus the Norwegians and everyone was eager to learn the outcome.

Both Amundsen and Scott were still making their way to the Pole when Douglas sailed out of Hobart to the sound of a band and guns firing on the afternoon of 2 December to cheers from the crowd that had gathered to farewell him from Queen's Wharf. The Premier, Sir Elliot Lewis and the Governor of Tasmania, Sir Harry Barron and his wife, Lady Barron, had stepped aboard to say goodbye in the final moments before departure. Paquita was not there. A letter Douglas wrote to her in September 1911 indicates that she was originally going. 'I am looking forward with great joy to that trip to Hobart. What a jolly time it will be',[2] wrote Douglas. However, it was later decided by both Paquita's mother and Douglas that Paquita would be too emotional on the day. Not being there to see him off was something she later came to regret when she realised the enormity of the occasion and in light of the fact that he so very nearly didn't come back. (She would make up for this years later when she joined the crowds cheering and fluttering their handkerchiefs to wave him goodbye from Hobart on 22 November 1931 as he sailed to Antarctica for the last time.) By December 1911 she had not seen Douglas for a month and very little of him in the preceding months. She would not see him again for more than two years. In a parting letter to her, Douglas wrote, 'You may be sure that I am going away this time far happier than last when there was no gem of priceless worth awaiting my return'.[3]

The ship was heavily overloaded and every space was utilised to the extent where, Douglas observed, 'the deck was so encumbered that only at rare intervals was it visible'.[4] It consisted of wireless masts, the building materials for three huts, cases of dog biscuits, thousands of gallons of benzine, as well as an aeroplane. In 1901 Scott had made the first flight over Antarctica in a hot air balloon, but Douglas was the first to take a plane. However, the plane that cluttered the deck of the *Aurora* was without wings. It had crashed in a demonstration flight in Adelaide a few weeks before. Douglas made the decision to take it anyway, minus the pilot who was sent home to England, with the idea of using it to transport supplies across the ice. Such was the excitement surrounding the exploits of Scott and Amundsen that, despite his plane's wingless state, there were suspicions that Douglas was harbouring a secret plan to fly to the Pole.* Nothing could have been further from his mind.

The aeroplane aside, the *Aurora* was loaded up with 500 tonnes of coal for sixty-two days of steaming and thirty-six dogs that were collected from quarantine on the way out of the harbour. Transported in a ketch, some swam ashore on the way out to *Aurora* and had to be recaptured. Eventually all were secured and tethered on top of the deck cargo. Thirty-six is the number Douglas gives in *The Home of the Blizzard*, although he quoted thirty-nine in his lectures following the expedition. Due to the constant breeding and the fact that some died on the voyage, the number of dogs originally taken differs in every account of the AAE. Forty-nine sailed from Cardiff but many died on the voyage to Hobart, either as a

---

* Another South Australian scientist and explorer, Sir Hubert Wilkins, made the first Antarctic flight in Western Antarctica in a monoplane in November 1928. In 1929 Douglas helped pioneer flying in Eastern Antarctica in a Gypsy Moth piloted by Lieutenant Stuart Campbell. They made aerial surveys and discovered a new coastline Douglas named MacRobertson Land. In the same year American admiral and explorer, Richard Byrd, who was first to fly to the North Pole in 1926, became the first to fly over the South Geographical Pole, although now it is thought that he did not.

result of being washed overboard or from distemper, a contagious disease affecting dogs, which attacks the central nervous system causing fever and coughing. Most pups born on the voyage from England did not survive because they were either killed or eaten by the adult dogs. A second ship, the *Toroa*, had been engaged to follow them as far as Macquarie Island with some of the men and extra supplies, including ninety tonnes of coal for *Aurora*, forty-five live sheep, some of which were deposited on the island, as well as a number of cats.

It was a perilous voyage. Even today ships travelling to and from Antarctica have to pass through very rough seas and through what are called 'the roaring forties', the 'furious fifties' and 'the shrieking sixties', areas of strong westerly winds that sweep right round the earth.* The first hurdle for all explorers was getting there. Many previous expeditions had met with disaster on the voyage to the continent. The Belgian Antarctic Expedition 1897–99 under Adrien de Gerlache crossed the Antarctic Circle in February, 1898. A young seaman was washed overboard in a heavy sea and soon afterwards the ship became stuck in the ice and de Gerlache and his men became the first party to experience an Antarctic winter. University geology lecturer, Otto Nordenskjöld led a Swedish expedition to Antarctica in 1901 and was forced to remain a second winter when his ship, *Antarctic*, met the same fate. The pressure of the ice damaged the keel to the extent that it sank when it eventually sailed into open water, though fortunately no lives were lost.** A few years later, in January 1905, while in search of territory not previously explored by Gerlache and Nordenskjöld, the Frenchman, Jean-Baptiste Charcot, hit a submerged rock near Alexander Island in his ship, *Francais*, which, incidentally, Douglas had considered buying for the AAE. For the remainder of Charcot's expedition the crew only managed to keep the vessel afloat by pumping water by hand forty-five minutes of every hour. Erich von Drygalski's German expedition had become trapped in the pack in the *Gauss* in 1902. In March 1904, the *Scotia* of the Scottish National Antarctic Expedition led by William Speirs Bruce was lucky to

---

* As of 2006 there are flights from Australia to Antarctica whereas it has been possible to fly to the continent from the US and New Zealand for many years.

** After surviving a winter on the ice, the expedition members and crew were rescued by an Argentinian relief ship in 1903.

escape being crushed in the Weddell Sea when it was caught in a blizzard and lifted out of the water by the ice rather than wedged in. A few days later the wind changed direction and the temperature rose enough to cause the ice to break up and the ship was set free. More recently, Scott had landed at Cape Evans on 4 December 1910, only after finding it impossible to land at Cape Crozier, his first choice for a wintering base. He had lost two ponies on the voyage down and one dog. In a fierce gale he had been forced to throw some supplies and ten tonnes of coal overboard as violent seas threatened to capsize his heavily overloaded vessel. Wilhelm Filchner had left for Antarctica from South Georgia only a few days before Douglas left Hobart and by 15 March 1912, Filchner's ship, *Deutschland*, would be frozen into the pack for eight months.

In December 1911 the *Aurora* was lucky and Davis was an exceptionally good captain but it was far from a comfortable voyage. Seas flooded all parts of the ship. The thirty-six huskies tied up on the cluttered deck, howled in misery as the waves swept over them again and again. Douglas was frequently awoken when thrown from his 'couch', while on night watch, into several inches of cold seawater that flowed back and forth across the floor. The starboard bridge was completely washed away (fortunately the officer on watch was on the other side at the time), and much of the drinking water became contaminated with seawater when the deck plug of one of the freshwater tanks was washed away. The galley was repeatedly deluged, leaving the cook in a sea of floating food and utensils. If, in the chaos, he succeeded in making a meal, there was no guarantee a sudden lurch wouldn't send it to the floor on its way to the table. To make matters worse, Davis noted in his diary that, even apart from the challenges of preparing meals in a rough sea, the food was 'very bad' as they had unfortunately employed, 'a poor sort of cook'.[5]

They arrived off Macquarie Island, approximately 850 miles from Hobart, dirty and dishevelled, a little over a week after they had left Tasmania. After anchoring one and a half miles off shore, supplies were disembarked in boats. Twenty miles long and five miles at its widest point, this hilly, foggy island was discovered in 1810 by Frederick Hasselborough, a Norwegian sealer who had emigrated to Australia. He had named it Macquarie after the then governor of New South Wales. Frequent visits by sealers in the 1820s had wiped out the fur seal population (none

Shovelling ice from the deck of the *Aurora* after a blizzard
(*Mawson Collection, South Australian Museum*)

were sighted in the two years that Douglas's men spent on the island).
In fact, Douglas was so disgusted by the continuing destruction that he
later played a leading role in campaigning for it to be made a wildlife
sanctuary, which it was in 1933.

In 1911, the island, which had not been investigated in any detail or
from a scientific perspective before, was teeming with wildlife. Mother
Cary's chickens (Wilson's Petrel, *Oceanites oceanus*), King penguins
(*Aptenodytes patagonica*), Royal penguins (*Eudyptes schlegeli*) with golden
feathers on their heads and above their eyes which give the appearance
of eyebrows, giant petrels (*Macronectes giganteus*) and brightly coloured
Maori hens, also called wekas (*Ocydromus scotti*), crowded its shores.
Leopard seals (*Hydrurga leptonyx*) appeared here and there and huge,
clumsy elephant seals (*Mirounga leonina*), or sea-elephants, as the AAE
men called them, lazed on the beach in their thousands, and wallowed in

the muddy patches between the tussocks that dotted the island, the males covered in scars from fighting.

Five men under the command of thirty-three year old meteorologist, George Ainsworth, were to make a complete survey of the island. The party, all in their twenties, apart from Ainsworth, included two wireless operators, Arthur Sawyer and Charles Sandell, a biologist, Harold Hamilton, and surveyor and geologist, Leslie Blake, who would produce the first accurate map of the island. Part of the programme included making a special study of elephant seals. The party was also to establish and operate a wireless station to relay messages between Australia, where they were to send daily weather reports to the Meteorological Board in Melbourne, and Douglas's base on the Antarctic continent.

Upon arrival the men on the *Aurora* were met by a crew of shipwrecked sealers who were living with a party of men under the lessee of the island, a Mr Hatch, who had permission to collect oil from the resident elephant seals. After the blubber was boiled down in digesters, the oil was shipped in casks to Australia. The *Clyde* was the third ship Hatch had lost and the most recent wreck of the several that littered the shores of the island. It had been preparing to take a shipment of oil to New Zealand when it was wrecked. It was arranged for the *Toroa*, which left the island on 16 December 1911, three days after it arrived, to take the sealers and their oil back to Tasmania, which, incidentally, covered the expense of originally hiring it. One of the sealers, however, replaced the incompetent cook and was engaged to sail south with the *Aurora*.

At home in Adelaide, Paquita learnt of the wreck of the *Clyde* in the papers and also of how the *Aurora* had hit a submerged rock and narrowly escaped disaster. Davis, who had been sleeping at the time of the accident, was furious with the second mate who had failed to notice the ship was dragging. Although, fortunately no damage was done, Davis observed that, 'it might easily have been a total loss'.[6]

Paquita, who kept track of Douglas's movements from Adelaide and later, from Europe, where she spent more than a year, while Douglas was away in the Antarctic, pasted into her scrapbook articles regarding both incidents. Her scrapbook contains news clippings about the AAE and other polar expeditions that were happening at the time. It includes, from the *Sydney Daily Telegraph*, a previously unpublished picture of the *Nimrod*

The Wireless Station in winter, Macquarie Island (*Mawson Collection, South Australian Museum*)

of Shackleton's 1907–09 expedition almost completely submerged under a huge wave. Only the stern and masts are visible. Given that Douglas had been aboard the *Nimrod* in 1907 and was at the time sailing across the same tempestuous seas in only a marginally larger vessel, such a picture would hardly have put her mind at ease. News of the sinking of the *Titanic*, a much bigger ship than the *Aurora*, its hull punctured by an iceberg in the comparatively calmer North Atlantic Ocean a few months later, would only have compounded her fears for Douglas's safety.

The men were lucky that during the days they were unloading stores by whaleboat and motor launch, onto the notoriously windy island, the weather remained relatively calm, and that they did not meet with any serious accident. A headland they named Wireless Hill, 300 feet above sea level, was chosen as the site for the wireless station and all crew and expedition members helped to erect it, transporting the materials by a flying fox given to them by the sealers. They worked sixteen-hour days. Sometimes there were as many as twenty men on the hauling-line, singing as they worked, partly to scare away the skua gulls that regularly swooped upon them. Davis described it as, 'altogether one of the most exciting and strenuous weeks I have ever spent', noting that, 'Mawson throughout worked like a Trojan'.[7] A week later, *Aurora* was loaded up again, with the dogs, and the sheep that had been disembarked to graze. The ship's crew and AAE members, who were going south with Douglas, totalling fifty men, farewelled Ainsworth's island party at dusk on the beach on 23 December.

The appearance of an Antarctic petrel, three days later, heralded the beginning of the pack-ice. They were held spellbound by the scene before them. Mertz marvelled at the icebergs, sometimes up to forty miles long, sculptured into huge marble-like columns and arches resembling the ruins of Rome, through which he glimpsed the brilliant blue ocean, 'like courtyards paved with mosaic'.[8] They skirted around the edge of the pack, past penguins and fur seals basking on floes. Occasionally they shot a sea leopard to feed to the dogs. Several sheep carcasses hung from the rigging. They sighted a whale, and Antarctic petrels *(Thallasoica antarctica)* hovered above the sails. On 2 January they were driven further north by the pack and Douglas became increasingly anxious. The sea seemed to stretch interminably and he worried they would never sight land. With each passing day they drifted further in longitude from Macquarie Island, narrowing their chances of establishing successful wireless communication. Douglas wrote of his concerns in a letter to Paquita in Adelaide: 'Things looked so bad last night that I could do nothing but just roll over and over on the settee on which I have been sleeping and wish that I could fall into oblivion without affecting you, darling'.[9] On 3 January 1912, 'a great turn of events took place'[10] when, at noon on 8 January, land was sighted by one of the crew.

Sailing southwards towards Oates Land, along the new stretch of coastline, Douglas named it George V Land before reaching a site where he was to make his base. He took Wild with him in the whaleboat to a rocky outcrop they named Cape Denison after Sir Hugh Denison who had donated £1000 to the expedition, and into what they had already named Commonwealth Bay. They were the first to set foot on this part of the continent, which was more or less one long, flat expanse of ice. It lacked the impressive mountains of the Ross Dependency where Scott had landed and where Douglas had gone with Shackleton a few years before. Apart from two bare rocks poking out of the plateau that surrounded the bay, there was nothing but ice that stretched as far as the eye could see. A fresh water lake, then frozen, lay nearby and there were many Adélie penguin (*Pygoscelis adeliae*) rookeries and Weddell seals (*Leptonychotes weddelli*), the latter named after the British sealer, James Weddell who first sighted them in the 1820s. However, they soon discovered that the calm, sunny day of their landing was a rarity and that the severe weather was the reason why Emperor penguins (*Aptenodytes forsteri*) rarely graced the shores of Adélie Land.

Camping temporarily in tents and in a room constructed from benzine packing cases, the men reassembled a hut in ten days, from parts which had been made and numbered in Sydney. They were very fortunate that the weather held out. In the absence of soil they found that guano from the penguin rookeries worked well as tamping material. The Hut comprised of one room 18 feet by 18 feet, surrounded by a veranda where they kept the dogs and housed the food and equipment and scientific materials. There was a darkroom in one corner of the main living area, bunk beds lined three of the walls and the kitchen occupied the fourth. The dining room table was placed in the middle of the room and, near it, a small area was partitioned off to serve as Douglas's bedroom and library. Four skylights were installed to let in light and they became the only means of entry and exit once the winter snow virtually buried the Hut and blocked off the only door.

Due to the difficulties they had encountered in finding suitable landing sites, Douglas had, by then, decided against a fourth base at Gaussberg, approximately 1200 miles to the west, the establishment of which was to have completed his plan of mapping the entire coastline to Cape Adare. In a letter just prior to their landing he had explained this change of plans in a letter to Paquita: 'After our experience I have now arranged to consolidate parties 1 and 3 and make a stronger base at Adélie Land…I have decided to rule Murphy out and to strengthen Wild's and my own parties. Murphy I will place in charge of my hut in my absence.'[11] It was probably just as well. He had elected twenty-three year old Herbert Dyce Murphy from Melbourne to run this base. Murphy was one of only two members of the expedition, apart from Douglas, who had any relevant exploratory experience, having visited the Arctic and Russia. However, once in Antarctica, Douglas confided to his diary, 'Murphy is quite unsafe to send on any journey'.[12] While it is not entirely clear what he meant by this, it is evident that Douglas had decided that Murphy was not suited to a leadership role.

The men who would have formed the fourth party remained at Cape Denison with Douglas. The third base party, comprising of seven men under Wild's command, left in the *Aurora* on the evening of 19 January. In recalling the difficult landing at Cape Denison, and looking back at the harbour through dense fog, Wild was less than optimistic about the future. In a letter to a friend, sent back with Davis that year, he described his feelings as they steamed away from Douglas and his men:

> I for one could not help thinking that our goodbyes were to some of them forever. It is a fearful country where they are landed. Except for less than a mile around the winter quarters, the coastline is a perpendicular ice wall from 100-300 ft high, and it rises back rapidly to about 2000 ft—we cannot see beyond that. From the base there is a fairly clear track leading up to the slope about 200 yards wide. Even that is not free from crevasses, and on either side of this track the ice is so horribly broken up that nothing but a bird could cross it; and, except Mawson himself none of the party has had the least experience.[13]

As it turned out Wild was landed in an even more precarious position, on a huge ice shelf 1500 miles further west. Davis was forced to sail this far, by which time the coal supply was rapidly dwindling. Driven north by the heavy pack-ice, they weathered storms and dense fog and the miserable prospect that they might have to return to Australia without landing before an anchorage was finally found on 14 February, almost a month after leaving the Main Base Party at Commonwealth Bay. One hundred and fifty miles wide and projecting 180 miles out from the coast, the site was named the Shackleton Ice Shelf because it happened that it was discovered on Shackleton's birthday. For their base, they decided on a spot one and a half miles inland and had to hope that the ice didn't break away for the year they were to spend there. Wild was convinced they were on a glacier as opposed to a barrier, which he deemed safe enough. It took five days to haul all their equipment up a thirty-metre ice cliff with the aid of a flying fox. After Davis had left on 21 February, Wild's party began assembling a hut based on the same design as the one at the Main Base. Soon after it was erected it became even more deeply buried than

Douglas's Hut and was forever afterwards referred to as, 'The Grottoes'. To penetrate the twelve feet of ice that collected around it, a shaft had to be dug and a ladder made as a means of entry and exit.

Meanwhile, the *Aurora* sailed back to Tasmania. She entered the Derwent River on 12 March with just nine tonnes of coal to spare, which meant virtually no ballast, passing Amundsen's ship, the *Fram*, along the way. Flags were flying. The Norwegian had attained the South Pole on 14 December 1911. Scott had reached the Pole a month later only to find the Norwegian flag flapping in the wind and paw prints in the snow, as well as a letter inside a silken tent to the King of Norway and one to him. He was bitterly disappointed on realising that he had been beaten. The Pole had meant so much to him and apparently so little to Amundsen who had always been fascinated by the Arctic and not the Antarctic.

Amundsen confessed as much upon reaching the South Pole: 'I cannot say…that the object of my life was obtained…I have never known a man to be placed in such a diametrically opposite position to the goal of his desires at that moment. The regions around the North Pole…had attracted me from childhood, and here I was at the South Pole. Can anything more topsy-turvy be imagined?'[14] In a sense it was fortunate that Scott, who was then days from death, did not live to hear these words.

a skua gull

8

Winter Pursuits

The desire of explorers to see something new and unknown,
inspired each of us. We are in a place where, until now, no one has
set foot. In the quietness of the evening, I yodelled with joy and
danced on the smooth snow.

From the diary of Mertz, 14 September 1912

Douglas described the first days in Adélie Land in brief diary entries, sometimes only one line per day, such as 'Make bunks', 'The roof on', 'A sea elephant captured', 'Lost dog sledge'.[1] He was too tired to write any more. The entries became longer when he began his third notebook on 28 February, by which time they had finished building the Hut. On that day there were over 160 seals in the bay and the photographer, Frank Hurley, took photographs when the blizzard tapered off in the afternoon.

Paquita was, by this time, on her way to Europe to visit The Netherlands and her Dutch relations for the first time as an adult. Her sister, Carmen, was in Vienna pursuing a career as a violinist and one of her doctor sisters, Mary, was studying at a gynaecological clinic, also in Vienna. Accompanied by her mother, her younger brother, Willy, and elder sister, Lica, she had sailed out of Adelaide in January 1912. Apart from a week with his family in The Netherlands later that year, GDD remained in Australia during his family's fifteen-month sojourn in Europe. He took a flat in Melbourne, the home of BHP's head office and where he was spending much of his time consulting his board over the development of the Newcastle steelworks. Theo, the eldest Delprat sibling, was not with the family. He had married in 1910 and moved to South Africa with his wife, Rene and their baby daughter. While her siblings suffered terribly from seasickness, as well as her mother, who spent most of the voyage confined to her cabin sucking ice, Paquita found she was a good sailor and boasted that she was not even sick in the notoriously rough Australian Bite.

Paquita wrote to Douglas from the ship in Bremen. Her voyage was, by all accounts, luxurious and vastly more so than Douglas's voyage to Adélie Land a few months before, on which he never once brushed his hair or washed. While he had swept ice and dog faeces off the deck of the *Aurora* and fastened ropes in a biting December wind, Paquita now played quoits under a blue sky with a young Frenchman she had befriended. Similarly, her colourful descriptions of the sights she was seeing were in stark contrast to the desolation of Adélie Land, 'Colombo with its exquisite colouring, dirty old Port Said…Messina with its pitiful ruins'.[2]

Envying a young French couple on the ship, who seemed so happy, Paquita wondered if the day would ever come when she and Douglas would be together. She playfully admitted that she would gladly 'help' another passenger overboard if it would mean seeing Douglas for just a few minutes. Her heart leapt whenever she saw someone who looked a little like him from behind. She leant over the side of the ship and saw his face in the water. She loved him to distraction. Reading was impossible. She missed him and longed to be with him again. 'Oh darling we are far apart aren't we?' she wrote. 'Does it ever come to you with a rush? … if only nothing is happening to you but I think I should feel it…it is no use wishing you success because when you get this you will be coming back and it will be nearly over. But I know you have had success'.[3] This letter was to be one of four Douglas would receive upon his return to the Hut from the ill-fated sledging journey, almost a year later.

In Adélie Land, the wireless masts, which were 65 feet high, and the aerial, were erected in high winds on 4 April 1912. However, it was not until September that the first messages were sent out but none were received. In an article for Adelaide paper, the *Register*, the expedition

Celebrating Mid-Winter's Day in the Hut, 12 June 1912. Douglas is seated in the back row in
the middle in coat. Ninnis is to his left. Mertz is seated in front row, third from left
(*Mawson Collection, South Australian Museum*)

secretary, Conrad Eitel, described the faint messages both Macquarie
Island and Australia had received intermittently from Adélie Land as, 'the
voice of a deaf man crying out in the darkness', and like, 'the outermost
ripples caused by a stone thrown into the middle of a pond'.[4]

Douglas didn't know it, because he received no reply, but sometimes,
long messages were getting through. Those listening for his messages
learnt that 'terrific winds' had prevented the main party from going on
reconnaissance journeys and were seriously hindering their efforts to erect
one of the wireless masts. In one message Douglas said, 'It is a good thing
the aeroplane wings were not brought here; we could not have flown at
all up to date, as there is no sea ice to take off from'.[5] He reported that
the sewing machines were going non-stop since there was no chance of
outside work. There was some concern that Douglas would try to meet up

with the Western Base. His original plan of three mainland bases was for the different parties to sledge along the coast and rendezvous somewhere midway but Douglas was unaware that Wild was more than 1000 miles west of him and not 600 miles away as initially planned. This one-way contact with Adélie Land was short-lived. On an October day during dinner, that came to be known as 'Black Sunday', the northern mast was blown down in a blizzard. Due to continuing bad weather it was not reassembled in Adélie Land until five months later, in February 1913 and it was only then that messages were both transmitted and received.

The men spent the winter and spring of 1912 preparing for their summer sledging journeys on which they expected to make the majority of their discoveries. They practised erecting tents in high winds and transported food supplies to Aladdin's Cave, a shelter they excavated out of the ice on the edge of the plateau, five miles from the Hut. On sewing machines they made harnesses for themselves and the dogs, strengthened tents, patched Burberry trousers and mended mitts. Their lives could depend on their sewing expertise. If they fell into a crevasse, a strong, well-made harness would increase their chances of survival.

Much care and thought had to go into the preparation of food and equipment. The sledges had to be as light as possible, and a balanced diet, consisting of as much fresh food as possible, was essential to stave off scurvy, the scourge of so many explorers. Food supplies were divided into colour-coded bags. In Adelaide, in the months leading up to the expedition, Paquita and her mother, Henrietta, had sewn many of these bags and the men affectionately referred to them as 'Paquita bags', each holding one week's sledging rations for three men.

In calmer weather they had skiing lessons with Mertz which were, however, short-lived due to the unsuitable conditions, and hunted for penguins and seals and prepared a supply of ice for the kitchen. When the sea froze and its surface was strong enough to bear their weight, the biologists went out and dredged for sea creatures. They returned with traps full of giant red sea spiders, bright green shrimps, starfish and coral, and then worked through the night to preserve them in jars before the specimens disintegrated. Twenty-five year old Sydneysider, Charles Laseron, the taxidermist, killed penguins with a needle to the brain. It had to be done very carefully. If blood rushed into the eyes it stretched the eyelids and spoilt the shape of the skin. Before long, stuffed penguins, snow petrels and other animals decorated the Hut along with the clothes that hung haphazardly from every rafter in the roof.

On Sundays they held Divine Service, ministered by Douglas, and sang hymns. Sometimes they arranged boxing nights and put on plays. Other evenings were spent reading and discussing the latest literature on polar exploration, smoking and playing the gramophone. Their reading material was as much a preparation for sledging as anything else. CD Mackellar*, one of the London sponsors of the expedition, had donated a library of books, including accounts of other expeditions, which they all read with enthusiasm. The Main Base Surgeon, Leslie Whetter, was teased after he ate some raw seal meat in imitation of his hero, Norwegian Arctic explorer, Fridtjof Nansen, who had learnt from the Inuit the value of eating raw meat to prevent scurvy.

Given that the men were about to embark on adventures of their own in the coming summer, it was fitting that over the winter Douglas read to them *The Trail of '98* by Canadian novelist and poet, Robert Service, which had been published the previous year. It is a novel set in 1898 in the Yukon during the Klondike gold rush and centres around the adventures of a young Scot, Athol Meldrum, a loner and a dreamer who had determined since boyhood to be, 'a frontiersman, a trail-breaker, a treasure-seeker'. Arriving in America from Scotland when eighteen years old, Athol is stirred by talk of the Arctic, 'the great White Land' where fortunes are to be made. He sets off with two other men to join the trail of gold-seekers, which is littered with dead horses. Athol fights against the evils of humanity in his encounters with gamblers, thieves and murderers, and against the harsh conditions of the Arctic. The weak are weeded out. It is the land of the strong. Men flounder in the snow, battle against hunger and frostbite under an ominous sky, a lurking, invisible presence that waits for its moment to strike them down. It was one of the few books that was read right through and, as Laseron recalled, it provoked 'lengthy discussions on the actions of the main characters'.[6] Another favourite was WW Jacobs (1863–1943), an English short story writer who wrote humorous tales of seafaring men.

---

* The islands off the Main Base were named after Mackellar.

On other evenings the 'Adélie Land Band' struck up*, which apart from a mouth organ and a piccolo, involved various improvised instruments. A kerosene tin represented the kettledrums, a spanner on a string, the triangle. Douglas was often on the periphery of these activities, partly because he was leader, and, despite his many interests, he had little appreciation for music. In *Mawson of the Antarctic*, Paquita recalled that, at a concert with her one night, he had counted the pipes in the organ during a moving piece of music. However, in Antarctica the gramophone was a great comfort, even to Douglas. Listening to it made him long to hear Paquita sing again. It helped to 'fill in a gap' in much the same way that the celebration of birthdays did. It was Douglas's on 5 May, though he made little reference to it in his diary, only commenting that Dr Archie McLean (the expedition's medical officer and bacteriologist) and Frank Bickerton (the mechanic), had cooked, and that the 'Aurora Australis' (otherwise known as the Southern Lights), of which he was making a special study, was particularly bright that night.

Meanwhile, in The Hague, in 'a narrow treble-detached house', which the Delprats had made their European base, his birthday was cause for celebration. All the Dutch relations rallied around to comfort Paquita, who was missing him. A party was thrown in his honour. A cake was made with whipped cream, representing a mountain, and a coffee-coloured tent made of nougat. A little figure of Douglas in full Antarctic costume worked in chocolate and pink fondant stood beside it with a marzipan sledge and dogs and the flag of the Southern Cross flying on a pole of angelica. Bouquets of flowers arrived throughout the day and talk of Douglas was on everyone's lips. The kindness and generosity of her relations made a deep impression on Paquita. She confessed in a letter to Douglas that she had grown so attached to her mother that she didn't know how she was ever going to leave her, even for him, and she had begun to fall in love with what she called, 'my Holland'. 'I hope you don't mind but I'm quite Dutch'[7], she warned Douglas.

---

* This tradition of live entertainment continues today at the permanent bases in Antarctica. Other forms of entertainment that were not available to the men of Douglas Mawson's era include watching films, sending emails, going to the gym, and playing sports such as volleyball and basketball. Today approximately eighty people live at each of the four Australian stations during the winter and up to two hundred in the summer.

At Commonwealth Bay, the men, who had been cooped up for months, were eager to embark on their sledging journeys but bad timing could have serious consequences. Two years previously, in his impatience to start for the South Pole, Roald Amundsen had attempted to set off in September, which was far too early in the season. (The Antarctic summer begins in November). He was forced to turn back a week after leaving his base on encountering temperatures around -50° C. Five of his dogs froze to death and he and his sledging companions all suffered badly frostbitten feet. Even when Douglas had gone on a short sledging journey into the August darkness with two of the men, to lay food depots, atrocious weather necessitated their return after having travelled only five miles from the Hut. Caught in a hurricane, they released the dogs from their harnesses in the hope that they would follow but they didn't. It was several days before the storm subsided and a search party was sent out. All the dogs were found alive although one, Grandmother, died soon afterwards due to the long exposure and lack of food.*

an Adelie Penguin

---

* Grandmother's skeleton was found by the Australian National Geographic team sent to Commonwealth Bay to restore Douglas Mawson's Hut in the summer of 2000.

9

Sledging into the Interior

For explorers the uncertainty is a strange magic. All of us are
burning with impatience to move, if possible, hundreds and
hundreds of miles further south. The sun is doing its best, shining
now for hours, but the wind blows like a monster...

From the diary of Mertz, 16 August 1912

At the beginning of the southern summer, in November 1912, six parties
of three set off into the Antarctic interior, each assigned to explore a
different section of uncharted territory. Twenty-two year old Englishman,
Frank Bickerton, was to lead a party west (the Western Party) taking the
air tractor sledge, of which he was in charge. His original appointment to
assist as engineer and motor expert had been altered to that of being in
charge of the wingless aeroplane. Its engine had been attached to a sledge
and the propellers moved it along. It had been used, on several occasions, to
carry supplies to Aladdin's Cave. The plan was to take it as far as the petrol
would allow and then abandon it. A Southern Party led by Lieutenant
Robert Bage, astronomer, assistant magnetician and recorder of tides, and
a Southern Supporting Party under the command of Frank Hurley, official
photographer, were to carry out magnetic research work in the direction
of the South Magnetic Pole. Three parties were to go east. The expedition
geologist, Frank Stillwell, was in charge of the Near-Eastern Party which

was to support both the Coastal Eastern Party led by the meteorologist, Cecil Madigan, and Douglas's Far-Eastern party, so called because he planned to go farthest east. He and his two companions were the only ones to take dogs because they intended to travel much further than the other five parties and were to enter potentially more hazardous terrain.

Sledge dogs are very much like wolves to look at. Like wolves they howl and will chase and taunt penguins and seals if not properly tethered. They often eat their own pups. (One female, Pavlova, had six pups in the Antarctic, five of which she sat on and crushed to death and the last she ate.) They can be violent towards each other in an effort to assert their position in the pack. There were several incidents at the Main Base where the pack turned on one of the dogs and disembowelled it. They have a double coat and long fluffy tails that shield them from the wind and the cold when curled up asleep in the snow. Their webbed paws act as snowshoes and a system of blood vessels in their legs protect them from freezing. On the BAE 1907–09 with Shackleton, Douglas had been impressed by how well and how happily the dogs worked in polar conditions. Professor David also realised the value of dogs when he suggested that the time it took Douglas, Mackay and himself to reach the South Magnetic Pole in 1908 might have been halved had they taken dogs.

The other British alternative was Siberian ponies, which were often favoured over dogs because they were easier to obtain and handling them didn't require the special skill that dog-driving does. On the other hand, ponies, being much heavier than dogs and with a poor weight distribution, are more likely to fall down crevasses and, when they do, the loss is greater in terms of food source. Had Socks, the last remaining pony on Shackleton's 1908 trek to the Pole, not fallen to its death in a crevasse, the party may have had enough horsemeat to last them the distance. Ponies are also less resistant to the cold than dogs. Apart from the fact that Scott's starting point for his Pole journey was more than fifty miles further from the Pole than Amundsen's, he was also disadvantaged in that the commencement of his journey was delayed by two weeks, because he had needed to wait for warmer weather for the ponies. Furthermore, ponies require shelter while dogs can sleep outside and, being herbivores, in the absence of grass,

The air tractor sledge (*Mawson Collection, South Australian Museum*)

they require imported feed whereas dogs can be fed seal and penguin meat and in fact, will eat almost anything.

Amundsen's successful attainment of the South Pole, three days after Douglas sailed from Hobart, was largely due to the travel techniques he had learnt from the Inuit and to his use of dogs, managed by experienced dog drivers. Such an enormous amount of energy is expelled pulling a sledge and Amundsen could see no point in struggling if dogs could do the work for him. He sat on the sledge virtually all the way to the Pole and back.* Scott's insistence on primarily man-hauling, which he considered noble,

---

* Captain Davis had many talks with Amundsen when their ships lay together at Hobart in March, 1912. Davis found Amundsen to be 'an exceptionally well-informed student of polar history' and felt that this may have contributed to his success. The Norwegian had carefully studied the records of explorers dating back seventy years all of which clearly marked the inlet that Scott called Balloon Bight and Shackleton, The Bay of Whales. This convinced him that the inlet was a permanent feature and was the reason why he chose it as a landing site. He was closer to the Pole than Scott and away from the Transantarctic Mountains, the origin of fierce blizzards. In London the previous year, just after Amundsen's unexpected arrival in Antarctica had been announced, a journalist had caught Davis off guard and asked him who he thought would win the race to the Pole. He had named Amundsen. However, he was horrified that his comments were then published, as his loyalty was to Scott. Upon meeting Davis in Hobart, in the wake of his victory, Amundsen produced a crumpled newspaper report containing Davis's prediction, which he took for support.

almost certainly contributed to his failure. Inexperienced in the care and handling of dogs on his first expedition in 1900, the dogs weakened to the point where they had to be killed and Scott put their ineffectiveness down to the fact that they were unpredictable and unreliable. Consequently, the previous year, when still 400 miles from the Pole, he sent all the dogs back to the base. Shackleton also favoured ponies: 'Our experience on the *Discovery* expedition, specially during the long southern journey when we had so much trouble with our mixed crowd of dogs, rather prejudiced me against these animals as a means of traction, and we only took them as a stand-by in the event of the ponies breaking down'.[1] As it turned out, one of the ten ponies he took down to Antarctica in 1907 died on the ship. The others had a rough voyage. Davis noted: 'These poor little animals had suffered terribly when the incessant rolling of the ship had constantly thrown them against the sides of their stalls so that their hides were worn through in many places'.[2] Five more died over the winter as a result of eating sand. Shackleton took the remaining four with him on the South Pole journey. Although there is no indication that Douglas knew any more about dogs than Scott or Shackleton, his dogs were to be instrumental in saving his life.

Accompanying Douglas on his journey on the AAE in 1912, were Mertz and Ninnis, who were the dog handlers. Mertz, at five foot ten inches, was the shortest of the three but the most heavily built. Ninnis was the youngest at twenty-three and also the tallest, standing at six foot four, an inch taller than Douglas. It is obvious why Douglas chose them as sledging companions, given the party's reliance on using dogs, but how Mertz and Ninnis came to be the dog handlers is not entirely clear. There is no evidence that either had any prior experience of dog driving. Mertz was a more obvious choice with his skiing expertise as dogs work better when someone skis ahead of them, even though it turned out that opportunities to ski were rare because it proved very difficult to find a suitable surface and the right conditions. It is likely that Ninnis was given the position, perhaps only because he shared, along with Mertz, the job of looking after the dogs on the ship from London and also when docked at Hobart. Originally there were twenty-one dogs at the Main Base, the others having gone to the Western Base. One called Scott disappeared one day and it was suspected he had fallen down a crevasse. Another, Caruso, had to be shot

Crevasse with lid fallen in (*Mawson Collection, South Australian Museum*)

due to an infected wound in his neck. On their journey, Douglas, Ninnis and Mertz took sixteen dogs.

All the Main Base sledging parties were well-prepared, having tested their equipment on shorter journeys over the spring. The contents of each sledge had been worked out to the last detail. Since everything they needed had to be carried, nothing but the absolute necessities were packed. They were sledging into nothingness. There would be no chance of coming across a caribou or a rippling stream or of being invited to dine with an Inuit. The combined weight of the three sledges taken by Douglas, Ninnis and Mertz, which were all eleven to twelve feet long, amounted to almost a tonne (approximately 1000 kilograms). Since they were on a scientific expedition, their load included surveying instruments, as well as photographic equipment, food for three men for nine weeks, fuel for cooking, weapons and ammunition, a medical kit, a 'repair outfit', which included various tools, camping gear and extra clothing. Careful

Douglas resting by the side of the sledge, about to embark on the
Far-Eastern Sledging Journey (*Mawson Collection, South Australian Museum*)

consideration had gone into making their sledges as light as possible. The overall load had been calculated down to the last ounce. Seal steaks for the dogs had been dried over the stove, but not cooked, because this reduced their weight by fifty per cent. Explorers can become quite obsessive about paring down their load. Amundsen apparently planed down the boxes that were to go on his sledges, making them thirty percent lighter. British explorer, Ranulph Fiennes, didn't even take a toothbrush on his journey across Antarctica in 1981–82.

Douglas was confident their journey would be a success and his optimism is evident in the letter he wrote to Paquita before leaving the Hut on 10 November. In the words of Eleanor Jacka, editor of his diaries, 'fate must have had a very treacherous smile on her lips when he wrote this':[3] 'The weather is fine this morning though the wind still blows—we shall get away in an hour's time. I have two good companions Dr Mertz and Lieut. Ninnis. It is unlikely that any harm will happen to us but should I not return to you in Australia, please know that I truly loved you…'[4].

A few years before, Shackleton had promised his wife Emily, that he would not take any unnecessary risks on his journey to the Pole and he had kept his word, turning back when threatened with starvation. Upon his safe return he said, 'I thought you would rather a live donkey than a dead lion'. Similarly, Douglas was aware that being engaged to Paquita meant that he had to take extra care to avoid danger. No longer the single man he had been when he first went to Antarctica, now, he admitted, he had to consider, 'at every turn what would be the best for Paquita'.[5]

By this time, it was almost a year since Douglas had left Adelaide and yet in the ten months since his landing at Commonwealth Bay he had written only two letters to Paquita. He left them in a box in the Hut little knowing that she would not receive them until he delivered them to her in person sixteen months later. He was busy and perhaps disheartened by the fact that he knew his letters could not be sent to her, but it was to be something he would later regret. Four letters he had written at the beginning of the journey, one from Hobart, one from the ship, another from Macquarie Island and then again upon arrival in Adélie Land, had been taken back to Tasmania by Davis on the *Aurora* and forwarded to Paquita in Europe.

The last letter she had written to him before the Far-Eastern Sledging Journey began was dated 14 October and sent from The Hague. In it she enthused about her travels to Milan, Lucerne and Vienna, where the cold weather had made her feel closer to him, but what excited her most was the thought of his return. 'We shall be very happy when you return with the separation behind us…you promised to come back fatter & better.' In response to his comment (in one of the four letters that had reached her), that he did not feel the cold as keenly as last time, she wrote, 'Of course, it is my love that does it. I warm you every night. You are safer there in a way than many here…I can almost feel your arms around me & involuntarily as I write lift my face to yours. Seventeen months without one caress! We *shall* have something to make up for'.[6] Unaware of the tragedy that awaited him, she wrote: 'Dear I know you have done good work down there in the cold…we are all proud of you. Don't be disappointed if you haven't done all you wanted to…I shall never let you go again & you will have me for the rest of your days'.[7] Paquita did not write again until six months later, when she returned to Adelaide.

The calm weather Douglas described soon turned into a blizzard that lasted for the first six days of their outward journey with winds reaching eighty miles an hour. The dogs slept outside the tent with only their nostrils peeping out of the snow. His party had no backup in terms of food depots. It is the custom, on a sledging journey in Antarctica, to lay food depots along the way in much the same way that mountaineers do. In this case they didn't because, as Douglas later explained in his diary, 'it was our bad fortune to meet such impossible country that we had decided to make a circuit on our return to Winter Quarters sufficiently far inland to avoid the coastal irregularities'.[8] Such a decision was to have fatal consequences.

From the beginning of their journey they encountered appalling conditions and a landscape of never ending snowhills and crevasses, the constant negotiation of which necessitated a zigzag course. For weeks they hauled their sledges, which frequently capsized, over steep ridges of ice that rose to as high as six feet. At other times they waded through soft snow, sinking up to their ankles; the dogs sank up to their stomachs. They spent many hours rescuing the dogs and sledges from crevasses, which usually involved untangling the dogs from their traces and unpacking all the securely roped equipment item by item. Winds of up to seventy miles per hour threatened to blow their tent away. Unused to sleeping on hard ice they had, 'terrible dreams'. During the night, the dogs became buried in thick drift as they slept and had to be dug out. The animals were exhausted and sometimes a handicap rather than an advantage. They hated the wind and walked with their heads bent close to the ground, stopping often to wipe the snow away from their eyes with their paws. One dog, Belti, vanished and Blizzard, Gadget and Japper were in such poor condition that they had to be shot. They were fed to the other dogs, along with Gadget's seven dead pups.

Eerily, in the weeks and days leading up to the event that would turn their trek into a race for survival, there were forewarnings of the disaster that was to befall them. In late November, Ninnis narrowly escaped falling into crevasses three times on three consecutive days. On the third occasion they discovered they had pitched their tent over a deep crevasse fifteen feet wide when Ninnis broke through the lid of it as he was breaking camp. Four days before the catastrophe, a snow petrel flew out of nowhere. Such a sighting was unexpected as they were a long way inland. It circled above them and Mertz noted in his diary that it flew over Ninnis's sledge.

By 14 December, a month into their journey, they believed that the worst country was behind them. For once the weather was excellent, suggesting a good day's travelling. Preparations had been made to cache most of the food within twenty-four hours before beginning the last leg of their journey, a final dash to their 'farthest east' point, after which they planned to turn back for the Hut. The night before, Douglas lanced an abscess on Ninnis's right hand forefinger that had been causing him much pain. Ninnis awoke in good spirits, at last having had a decent night's rest after a week of discomfort and sleeplessness.

As so often happens in the moments preceding a disaster, on that morning nothing seemed amiss. They set off at 9 am under a partly clouded sky. According to Douglas, 'the day was gloriously fine, the best we had experienced on the whole journey'.[9] The warm conditions filled their hearts with hope. Mertz was skiing on ahead of Douglas, blazing a trail for the dogs and singing merrily. The only sounds were snatches of his student song on the wind, the panting of the dogs, the clink and rattle of their harnesses, the swish of the sledges gliding over the snow. Ninnis was driving a second dog team close behind Douglas, nursing his injured finger in a sling. Shortly after midday, Mertz signalled the presence of a crevasse. As he crossed it soon afterwards, Douglas looked down and noticed the faint outline of a crevasse beneath his sledge. He called a warning to Ninnis. Glancing back he was satisfied Ninnis had heard the call as he saw him alter his course accordingly, swinging the dogs around so as to, 'take the crevasse fair across' instead of diagonally as he, Douglas, had done.

Giving no further thought to the moment, Douglas sped on for a quarter of a mile. Suddenly he noticed Mertz had stopped. He was holding up his ski stick, a signal that something was wrong, and he was looking back in anxious bewilderment. Douglas turned around to see only the tracks of his sledge in an otherwise empty landscape. He thought of the crevasse that had seemed so harmless and ran back to it with Mertz. There they found a hole eleven feet wide and sledge marks leading up to one side of it. The snow on the other side was smooth and unmarked. Peering into the blue-black ice, they could make out fragments of sledge and a canvas bag containing food for three men for a fortnight. With the aid of a fishing line and all the rope they had to hand, they tried, unsuccessfully, to reach a husky on a ledge they ascertained was about 150 feet down. It was obviously dead but, another, still alive, lay beside it. Its back was broken and it was moaning in agony as it tried in vain to sit up on the shelf on which it had fallen. Its head twisted and turned while its hindquarters remained limp. After a while it stopped writhing and fell silent. They could see nothing else. A chill air rose up from the depths. They didn't even seriously consider adopting the standard rescue procedure, that of winching a man down into the crevasse, even though Mertz wanted to go in after him. It was too deep, the ropes, even when all tied together, were too short. Instead, they stood by for three hours and called and called. Douglas half-expected to turn and find Ninnis standing behind him. But Ninnis, tall and lanky Ninnis, with slightly protruding ears and a broad smile, whom the men had affectionately called 'Cherub' because of his rosy complexion, had vanished without a sound.

His death had been so completely unexpected on the smooth even surface they were travelling along. It was thought that if either sledge were to meet an accident it would be the one in front on which Douglas was sitting. In his book *Antarctica: A Treatise on the Southern Continent*, the polar historian, Hayes, suggested that Ninnis should have been wearing skis or snowshoes rather than finnesko boots because, he argued, 'ski distribute the weight of the body about ten times more widely than human feet'.[10] At the time neither Douglas nor Mertz, although puzzled that it had happened at all, felt that they could have done anything to prevent it. It was a catastrophe, an accident, a terrible misfortune. Douglas had negotiated many crevasses before and when he had crossed the lid of the crevasse it had not looked any more dangerous than the last. In considering why his sledge had escaped, he came to a similar conclusion to Hayes: 'The explanation appeared to be that Ninnis had walked by the side of his sledge, whereas I had crossed it sitting on the sledge. The whole weight of a man's body bearing on his foot is a formidable load, and no doubt was sufficient to smash the arch of the roof'.[11] Douglas was fortunate, particularly given that the sledges were more or less the same weight.

Ninnis's death left Douglas and Mertz with a very slim chance of making it back to the Hut alive. Douglas wrote that they considered it only 'a possibility' they would make it back. And in saying this, he was being optimistic. Ninnis had taken all the dog food with him, all the powerful huskies: Basilisk, Ginger Bitch, Shackleton, Castor, Franklin and John Bull, as well as many tools and provisions, including the ice axe and the tent poles. This left Mertz and Douglas with six miserable-looking dogs and enough food to last just ten days. This was nowhere near enough, given that they had averaged less than seven miles a day over forty-six days on their outward journey. Now more than 300 miles from the Hut, it would take them at best six weeks to get back and this was not allowing for bad weather, which could delay them for days at a time. Pitching and breaking camp would be more difficult and time consuming with incomplete and inadequate equipment. They would be travelling on severely reduced rations and, once the remaining dogs were dead, they would be completely alone.

Their situation called for immediate action. 'May God help us', Douglas wrote in his diary. The truth, he conceded, would hit them, 'in the dismal days to come' and, as it turned out, in the years to come, in the darkness of his dreams. However, at the time they were forced to shelve their horror at what had happened and begin their journey back to the Hut just nine hours after Ninnis was lost. As British polar explorer, Mike Stroud wrote in his book *Survival of the Fittest*, survival depends partly on having 'a very defective short-term memory'.[12]

After much deliberation they abandoned thoughts of following the coast back to the Hut. Although there was a chance of killing seals for food, the country down to the frozen sea was completely unknown to them. Along the coast, the wind continually broke up the sea ice making it an especially dangerous surface. Madigan, Correll and McLean had sledged east as Douglas's party had but closer to the coast, parallel to the sea, where they had encountered many difficulties. Although Madigan's party did not realise it at the time, for a while they were in fact some seventy miles out to sea as they dragged their sledges through slushy snow and frequently broke through the thin surface, wading up to their thighs in ponds of water. Six miles from a safer surface, Madigan wrote, 'I had never felt more nervous than I did in that ghostly light in the tense silence, surrounded by the horror of fathomless depths'.[13]

By remaining inland, in fact thirty miles further inland than on their outward journey, at least Douglas and Mertz knew what lay ahead of them across the plateau. It was windier and colder and there was no hope of finding a penguin or a seal for food but it was a quicker route and they could avoid the worst terrain. They could make it back on their small food supply if they also ate the dogs, which they started eating the day after Ninnis died. George, as the weakest of the remaining pack, was killed and some of his parts fried for breakfast. His head and entrails were fed to Pavlova, Ginger, Mary, Haldane and Johnson, who were already so scrawny they were swimming in their harnesses.

In preparation for their return journey, the men set about paring down their load. They then sledged on in soft falling snow. Their compass was 'very dead' due to their proximity to the South Magnetic Pole and the sun, their only other guide, was hidden behind an overcast sky, making it impossible to keep on a straight course. Douglas was in agony. Despite regular drops of zinc and cocaine under the eyelids, his snow-blind,[14] bloodshot eyes seared with pain. He was seeing double. One eye was bandaged. It felt like both eyes were full of gravel. Although both Mertz and Douglas were well aware of the dangers of snow blindness, when their goggles fogged up in the cold it became difficult to see where they were going, and on these occasions they took their goggles off.

a Snow petrel

10

The Race Back

Alas, Alas! Life is full of disappointments; as one reaches one ridge there is always another and a higher one beyond which blocks the view.

Fridtjof Nansen (1961–1930), Norwegian explorer and scientist

Despite my growing up with the story of the Far-Eastern Sledging Journey, Ninnis was always an elusive figure. He was just a man who disappeared. Even now I know very little about him. He spoke well. He was tall. He owned beautiful clothes. On cooking duty at the Hut he misread Mrs Beeton's* recipe for salmon kedgeree, adding two ounces of pepper, rendering it inedible to all but a few of the men. Douglas referred to it in his diary, noting that, 'Amongst other effects Bage and Close perspired copiously, but stuck to it'. In his book *South with Mawson*, Laseron described Ninnis as, 'a friendly soul with a simple outlook on life'.[1] Knowing his end, I was struck by the irony of Captain Davis's first impressions of Ninnis as 'one of those people who go through life always depending on someone else to pull him out of difficulties'.[2] Ninnis hadn't stood a chance. In the blink of an eye, he had plunged to his death.

---

* English cookery writer, Isabella Mary Beeton (1836–1865) was the author of *Mrs Beeton's Book of Household Management* (1859–60). It contains recipes, as well as advice on how to run a Victorian household, ranging from the management of servants to poisons, childcare, fashion and animal husbandry.

Mertz would not be so lucky. He would endure a lingering, painful death three weeks later.

On the day Ninnis died, after Douglas read the burial service at the edge of the crevasse, he and Mertz had embarked on their long journey back to Winter Quarters without a word to each other with regard to their chances. 'It was a wild race as we careered along', wrote Douglas:

> We plunged on to the lids of crevasses and thundered across the sunken ways…Twice I was wrenched from the sledge as it shot over the brink on to old deeply sunken crevasse lids; three times, portions of the gear broke away from the sledge straps. On every occasion it was with the greatest possible difficulty that I could secure and hold the dogs to make amends, for the poor animals were almost frenzied with the mad speed, the jarring and rattle of the cooker on the sledge. After all, it was only the pace that saved us. Many of these crevasses were dangerous enough in all conscience, but we plunged across with a tense heart and a grim sense of reality—such was the effect of the day's tragedy upon us.[3]

Their days became a pattern of pitching the tent as best they could with skis and the legs of the theodolite, eating, sleeping, breaking camp and walking on. In the middle of the day the sun melted the surface and they had to wade through soft snow. The ice that gathered on their clothes melted too, making everything damp so they travelled at night (although of course it was summer and there was no darkness). It was cooler then and the ground was harder. It was 'a wretched game' trying to navigate under an almost perpetually overcast sky and in falling snow and with Douglas's vision further impeded by his bandaged eye. They struggled over sastrugi. The light was so bad that they could hardly see their feet and they often fell onto their faces on the ice, which Mertz likened to 'a slippery parquet floor'.[4] It made them anxious. They could not afford to make any unnecessary detours. They looked, Douglas wrote, 'a rather mournful procession'[5] meandering blindly across the ice with five emaciated dogs.

Nine days into their return journey, Douglas noted in his diary that he was unable to sleep due to hunger. Ordinarily their daily food allowance, which was based on the sledging rations taken on the BAE, amounted to

34.25 ounces, approximately a kilogram. Broken down, this constituted 12 ounces of plasmon biscuit (biscuits made of wholemeal flour, gluten and milk protein); 2 ounces of butter; 2 ounces of chocolate; 5 ounces of Glaxo (dried milk); 4 ounces of sugar; 1 ounce of cocoa; .25 ounces of tea and 8 ounces of pemmican, (powdered dried beef containing a high percentage of beef fat, a recipe derived from the American Indians who used buffalo meat and crushed berries). As Douglas later explained in *The Home of the Blizzard*, on sledging journeys, 'the daily ration must be limited to the smallest quantity that will sustain the energies necessary for the undertaking'.[6] Anything less than this absolute minimum meant hunger. They were now down to 14 ounces a day, less than half their usual intake and equivalent, in quantity, to a can of baked beans. Yet, they were expending the same amount of energy and, of course, their rations were far from nourishing. Low in fat, they lacked the high-heat value needed in those conditions.

A desire to eat anything that was vaguely digestible overtook them as it had overtaken the dogs, who, Douglas noted, were seized with, 'a morbid desire to gnaw everything within reach'. They fought over any scraps left on the ground, 'however useless or loathsome'.[7] On the day Ninnis died, having nothing to give them in the way of food, Douglas and Mertz had thrown them some worn-out gloves and other old bits of leather, which they had devoured in an instant. Douglas later wrote: 'I will always remember the wonderful taste that the food had in those days. Acute hunger enhances the taste and smell of food beyond all ordinary conception...cocoa was almost intoxicating and even plain beef suet, such as we had in fragments in our hoosh* mixture, had acquired a sweet and aromatic taste scarcely to be described...'.[8]

Food became an obsession. Such was their hunger, Douglas and Mertz lamented the loss of a two-and-a-half-pound-slab of butter 'Shackleton' had ripped open earlier in the journey out and eaten before being properly tethered. Their minds wandered to all the food that had been lost with Ninnis and they talked of what they would eat on their return to the Hut, Mertz promising to make his specialty dish of penguin omelette. When suffering from hunger on the march to the South Magnetic Pole

---

* like a porridge of pemmican, dry biscuit and water, boiled and served hot

on the BAE in 1909, Douglas, Mackay and Professor David had written out entire menus, which consisted of up to eleven courses matched with wines. They included such dishes as: 'Jugged hare with mashed potato', 'Young duck with apple sauce', 'Grouse baked on toast', 'Sheep's head and trotters garnished with carrots'. Desserts included 'Roly-poly with blackberry bramble and blackberry sauce' and 'Apple and mince pies and German black bread and cream cheese' served with port and liqueurs.[9] One of the men on the Greely expedition the previous century had written out each man's ideal menu in a book. Every year after their return to their home city of Chicago, Greely, and one other survivor, Sergeant Brainard, dined on one of these menus on the anniversary of their rescue and in memory of those who had died. Douglas and Mertz did not put their food fantasies down on paper, perhaps because they only had the strength to talk about them.

Constant hunger and the hardship of sledging induced vivid dreams. Mertz and Douglas slept lightly and fitfully in the cold and, in their weakened state, were continually dogged by snow blindness and frostbite. Ninnis had marched with the dogs in his sleep calling out to them to 'hike, hike'. With empty stomachs, Mertz and Douglas were even less able to sleep. Shivering in their soggy sleeping-bags, they dreamt of sumptuous meals but, cruelly, something always happened to prevent them from eating and they would wake up even hungrier than before. On the rare occasion that they got to eat the meal, the one who had not dreamt it was almost envious of the other's dream.

Douglas had a sweet tooth. On his journey to the South Magnetic Pole in 1908, on the BAE, he had longed for a bowl of cream. Now he dreamt he was in a confectioner's shop and the proprietor took him up a winding staircase to a row of gigantic cakes. He ordered and paid for one but forgot to collect it and, upon realising this, he dashed back to the shop, only to find a sign on the door, which read 'early closing'. Time was their enemy in more ways than one. During the day, as they tramped along in their harnesses, there was ample time to think and their minds inevitably wandered to the torturous subject of food.

It became their custom to let the huskies ride on the sledge when they could no longer walk. As soon as they stopped marching, the exhausted and starving dog was taken behind the tent and shot and then skinned and cut up for food. Its head and internal organs, save the liver, were thrown to the other dogs, who savagely tore at the flesh, crunched the bones and even devoured the teeth. Douglas and Mertz were not much fussier. Extreme hunger had reduced them to contemplating eating almost anything in spite of all their visions of such things as scalloped oysters and gooseberry pie. A favourite meal of Greely's starving men had been mouldy dog biscuit mixed with fox intestines. On his first expedition to the Arctic, Sir John Franklin (who had later disappeared in the Arctic in 1847) was so hungry that he had eaten his boots, including the shoelaces. In the absolute worst case scenario, Douglas conceded they would have to eat their reindeer skin finnesko shoes.

In the meantime, they 'treated' themselves to jellied soup made from dog sinews. After the last dog was killed the next meal consisted of Ginger's skull. They cooked it whole, the contents of which they scooped out with a wooden spoon fashioned from a discarded sledge runner. Having no means of dividing the head into two equal parts, they adopted a tried and tested method known as 'shut eye' to avoid unfairness. One man closed his eyes while the other pointed to one side of the head and asked 'Whose?' Their fierce hunger meant that they ate absolutely everything. The brain, Douglas recalled, 'was certainly the most appreciated and nutritious section' and interestingly he remembered Mertz, who later rejected the dog meat, 'remarking specially upon it'.[10]

Huskies and ponies have been used throughout the history of polar exploration not only to assist travel but as a source of food in case of emergency. There are none in Antarctica now as all non-native species, except humans, were banned by the Madrid Protocol in 1991. Most dogs and ponies were worked to the bone until they virtually dropped dead or were dispatched because they were no longer any use. Very few returned alive.

The act of killing their animals haunted many explorers. The year before, on Scott's final expedition, a team of men led by Henry Bowers, were on their way back to camp with a group of eight ponies when they unknowingly camped on sea ice. They later awoke to find themselves floating out to sea on an ice floe. Three ponies had clearly drowned and the remaining three were stranded on another piece of ice. Surrounded by broken floes and predatory killer whales (*Orcinus orca*), the men moved from floe to floe by using their sledges as bridges in an effort to reach the ponies. On reaching the animals, they tried to persuade them to jump their way to safety. Punch fell into the water and after a vain struggle to get him out, Oates had to kill him with a pick. Bowers had to put an end to his pony, Uncle Bill, in the same gruesome way when it also fell into the sea and he didn't want to leave it to the mercy of the killer whales.

Scott chose not to use dogs on the last leg of his journey to the Pole, not only because he believed in the superiority of man-hauling but also because he hated seeing the animals suffer. Even Amundsen, who was an expert dog handler, could not avoid having to kill many of his huskies. In fact, upon his return from the Pole, at a campsite he subsequently named 'The Butcher's Shop', he slaughtered twenty-four of his dogs, as planned, to be fed to the other dogs. Sitting inside the tent he heard them being killed and tried, unsuccessfully, to deaden the sound of the shots by making as much noise as possible preparing dinner. 'Shot followed upon shot' he recalled '…they had an uncanny sound over the great plain. A trusty servant lost his life each time'.[11]

In his bid for the North Pole in 1888, Nansen killed his dogs when he and his companion, Hjalmar Johansen, ran out of food. They used a knife to save precious bullets. Later, Nansen was to recall with horror, the cruel way in which they had been forced to treat their dogs, beating them mercilessly with thick ash sticks until they stopped from sheer exhaustion. He wrote, 'When I think of all those splendid animals, toiling for us without a murmur, as long as they could strain a muscle, never getting any thanks or even so much as a kind word…When I think of how they were left behind, one by one, up there on those desolate ice fields, which had been witness to their faithfulness and devotion, I have moments of bitter self-reproach'.[12] Such words might just as easily have been written by Douglas or Mertz. The huskies were trusting friends and it felt like cold-blooded murder, especially the killing of Ginger and Pavlova, the last two to die. By that time, about ten days into their homeward journey, the rifle had been discarded to lighten the weight of the load on the sledge and so they had to finish them off with a knife, what Douglas described as, 'a revolting and depressing operation'.[13]

According to my grandmother, Oma, Pavlova was her father's favourite dog. Killed five days before Ginger, she became Douglas and Mertz's

Blizzard the pup (*Mawson Collection, South Australian Museum*)

Christmas dinner. She had been named after Anna Pavlova, the Russian ballet dancer, who had knelt down to pat her while visiting the men on the *Aurora* when it was docked at the Thames. Then just a puppy, she had scampered around the ship's deck as Pavlova, the dancer, christened the *Aurora* with a bottle of champagne. I wonder if Douglas was haunted by this happy image as he reduced her to soup, cracking open her bones with a spade. Oma told me that he was so upset at having to kill the huskies that, although they had work dogs on their farm in the Adelaide Hills, he never wanted a dog as a pet[*].

As a child I remember being horrified at the mention of the dogs names. They broke away from my image of a blurry pack pushing through the fog and took on distinctive faces and individual personalities. I could never look at the picture of the puppy, Blizzard[**], with her sad eyes and her head cocked on one side, without imagining Douglas huddled over a pot brimming with floating paws. Douglas's diary is littered with phrases such as: 'fry dog for breakfast', 'we had to put Mary on sledge at 9 ½ miles. Mertz skinned her at camp', 'Up at 11 pm making dog stew', 'Had a great breakfast off Ginger's skull—thyroids and brain'.[14] Crouched in their makeshift tent, the roof of which was so low, that only one could sit upright in it while the other had to lie down, they spent hours cracking and boiling down bones. There was so little flesh left on the dogs that they needed to be stewed for a long time. These gruesome rituals had become their reality.

Dreaming of sumptuous meals

---

[*] There are two stuffed huskies in the Mawson collection at the South Australian Museum, one of which was purportedly the Mawson's pet. When I asked Oma about this husky she said she could not recall ever having one at home. When newly married, Paquita was pictured in the paper kneeling beside a husky called 'D'Urville', a pure Greenland dog and the son of Ginger. Family correspondence revealed that in 1916 Paquita gave him, as a gift, to the staff of the Mount Kosciusko Hotel when she was there on a skiing holiday.

[**] Blizzard in fact, was not one of the dogs Mertz and Douglas ate. They killed her before Ninnis was lost, on 28 November, after she injured her leg, so she was fed to the dogs.

11

The Loss of Mertz

He sleeps on the eastern slopes of the great glacier that bears his name.

From *South with Mawson* by Charles Laseron

On 30 December, sixteen days into their return march, Douglas noticed the beginnings of Mertz's decline when he mentioned in his diary that he looked 'off-colour' and did not seem his usual cheerful self. They had begun to feel more optimistic about their chances only the day before, after covering a distance of fifteen miles. This was a good march, considering they had been averaging about half this distance and it gave them a sense of hope for the future. Yet, they had also started out in high spirits on the morning of 14 December, the day Ninnis fell to his death. Was hope an ill-omen? So too, that they were again visited by a bird? A small seabird, they thought to be a prion, flew around them as they pitched camp on 24 December, an unexpected sight given that they were more than 100 miles inland.

On 31 December Douglas wrote, 'keeping off dog meat for a day or two as both upset by it'.[1] Neither had any reason to suspect that the flesh of the dogs was harmful to them, even though they conceded that it was not very nutritious. In fact, the meat was so stringy that Douglas remarked, 'It was a happy relief when the liver appeared which, even if little else could be said in its favour, was easily chewed and demolished'.[2] His explanation for the stomach pains that ensued was hunger and he reasoned that, 'the gastric secretions, especially under the influence of food dreams, were so active in search of food as actually to attack the wall of the stomach itself'.[3] He found that frequently altering the position in which he was lying often helped relieve these pains but they were nevertheless continuous. Mertz was suffering from the same pains but it soon became evident that his condition was much more serious. Douglas noticed that he was not assimilating his food.

Lennard Bickel described Mertz as 'a near-vegetarian' in his book, *This Accursed Land* and argued that he 'always tried to avoid eating meat'[4], an argument endorsed by Adrian Caesar, author of *The White*. In a letter of condolence to the Mertz family in 1914, Douglas explained that, 'the actual final cause of his death was that his digestive system, becoming weaker by living on poor food, could not cope with the indigestible and non-nutritious dogs' meat. He told me that he believed my greater capability to deal with that food was probably due to the fact that Swiss people are not used to a large meat diet, whereas English people and especially Australians eat a large proportion of meat'.[5]

However, in his diary, Mertz mentioned, without complaint, eating meat on the voyage from England to Tasmania. Breakfast, he noted, is 'a copious meal with porridge, eggs, meat, tea, jam and butter'.[6] His diaries indicate that what was indigestible to him was not meat so much as English meat dishes which he found too 'spicy', by which he meant too much pepper and salt. In the ten months leading up to the sledging journey he ate a lot of meat, apparently without any ill effect. In the Antarctic, breakfast included bacon, lunch was usually tinned salmon or sardines or locally caught fish and/or boiled ham and meat was served for dinner at least five nights of the week—mutton on Sundays, seal on Tuesdays and Fridays, penguin on Mondays and Thursdays. Mertz commented that, 'some of us couldn't eat this food, but I liked it'. In fact he particularly liked the tongue, brains and liver of seals. However, he added, he didn't like it with 'too much curry'.[7] On Swiss National Day on 1 August 1912, he made a special Swiss dinner, which included foie gras, hare stew and grilled sausages with red cabbage. The sausages 'de Berne' would most likely have been pork, and very meaty and fatty.

When I was a child, I was told that both Mertz and Douglas were poisoned from eating the liver of the huskies which contain an excess of vitamin A, harmful to humans and that this is what killed Mertz. The toxicity of the liver was compounded by the fact that the dogs that were eaten had been fed on other dogs. Oma always said, her father gave Mertz more liver because it was the most palatable and the least taxing on their powers of mastication. She wondered if, in doing so, he had unwittingly helped him to his death.

At the time of Douglas's expedition of 1911–14, very little was known about vitamins. In fact, the word 'vitamin' was only coined in 1912, the very year that Douglas and Mertz were fighting for their lives in Antarctica. The theory that they had been poisoned was not put forward until 1969, eleven years after Douglas died. It was given the name Hypervitaminosis A. Two South Australian scientists, Dr Ronald Vernon Southcott and Professor John Cleland, came to this conclusion when four patients were admitted separately to the Royal Adelaide Hospital complaining of gnawing stomach pains, peeling skin, vomiting and other symptoms similar to those Douglas and Mertz had suffered. It turned out that they had all eaten seal's liver. Dr Southcott claimed that poisoning from polar bear livers, the livers of seals, wolves and other polar animals was 'traditional knowledge to the Eskimos'.[8]

In *This Accursed Land*, published eight years later, in 1977, which tells the story of the Far-Eastern Sledging Journey, Lennard Bickel supports this theory. He claims that four ounces of the liver of a husky is toxic for an adult due to its high content of vitamin A. He calculates, although he does not explain how, that Douglas and Mertz suffered to the extent that they did because they ate sixty times this amount, and because they were existing on a diet deficient in vitamin C. It sounds plausible and is generally accepted as the cause of Mertz's death.

Yet, why didn't Douglas die too, especially given that he continued to eat the livers of the dogs after Mertz's death? Was there something harmful in the thyroids and the brain rather than in the liver? This was a question Mark Pharaoh (curator of the Mawson collection at the South Australian Museum) posed in one of our many Mawson conversations. It wasn't until they killed Ginger, the last of the dogs, that Mertz and Douglas ate brain and thyroids, the head and most innards having always previously been thrown to the surviving dogs. The eating of the contents of Ginger's skull also coincided with the beginning of Mertz's decline, and the first time a connection was made between the dog meat and their poor condition. Ginger was eaten on 29 December. Only two days later, on 31 December, Douglas wrote, 'Keeping off dog meat for a day or two as both upset by it'.[9]

This aside, the alleged symptoms of Hypervitaminosis A are very similar to the effects of starvation and cold exposure. Both Mertz and Douglas suffered from peeling skin, a symptom of frostbite. At one stage, Douglas noted that the skin from one ear had come off in a complete cast. They also suffered from stomach pains, which could have been the result of poisoning or simply hunger. Added to this, not all explorers who ate the livers of polar animals, even in large amounts and over long periods of time, experienced ill effects. Douglas and his two companions, Professor David and Dr Mackay, ate the livers of seals and Emperor penguins over many days on their return from the South Magnetic Pole in 1909 without suffering any of the symptoms of Hypervitaminosis A. Douglas obviously experimented enough to learn how best to prepare them as he even ventured to write out a recipe for 'minced seal meat', adding that the livers of adults were 'very good' but that the livers of calves were 'useless'.[10]

In *South with Mawson*, Laseron suggested that part of the reason why Douglas fared better than Mertz lay in their different physiques: 'Physically Mawson and Mertz were in striking contrast. Mertz was stockily built, a man of immense strength and restless activity. As a high-powered machine needs ample fuel, so he needed sufficient proper food to maintain strength. Mawson, on the other hand, was tall and wiry, and even at the Hut ate very sparingly. His type, under the strain of insufficient and indigestible food, was likely to last much longer'.[11] (Interestingly, Douglas later revealed that he believed Ninnis, who was tall and thin compared to Mertz, would have pulled through.) However, while a leaner person has greater powers of endurance, if one thinks of marathon runners, in Antarctic conditions it is an advantage to have extra body fat for insulation. The Inuit, for example, are short and stocky. In preparation for their march across Antarctica in 1992–93, Mike Stroud and Ranulph Fiennes deliberately put on weight with the idea that extra fat stores would help counter the cold and increase their powers of endurance.

Whether or not Mertz and Douglas were poisoned, and whether or not Douglas had a stronger constitution, it seems there were other contributing factors to Mertz's decline. He was at a distinct disadvantage in that he had lost his waterproof trousers. They had fallen into the crevasse with Ninnis. Despite using a spare pair of trousers, these were not Burberry, and could not keep him as dry. He was therefore, continually damp, the snow penetrating to his underpants. It is a wonder he didn't catch pneumonia but, perhaps, more significantly, he was struggling with depression.

On New Year's Day 1912, the sun gleamed weakly and then disappeared behind cloud so, unable to determine their direction, they remained in their sleeping-bags. It was a good opportunity to rest, especially for Mertz who had not responded to the change of diet and had not been himself since 30 December. The following day the sky cleared in the evening and they set off but stopped after five miles even though the conditions were good. Mertz's fingers were badly frostbitten. By 4 January, the conditions for sledging were 'very good' but Mertz was not well enough to travel and Douglas 'doctored him' for part of the day. On 5 January, Douglas tried to persuade him to move, strongly advocating doing a few miles when the wind had died down but Mertz 'practically refused'. By this stage, psychologically, Mertz had more or less shut down. Douglas was mystified by his spiritual decline even more than by his physical deterioration and could not quite fathom it. He could not discern what exactly was wrong beyond exhaustion and the depressing effect of their 'continued bad fortune in the matter of weather'.[12] Mertz, who was usually so communicative and demonstrative had become quiet and listless. His heart, Douglas wrote, 'seems to have gone'.[13]

Was Mertz grieving? It is very likely that he never recovered from the death of Ninnis, to whom he was particularly close. It was a terrible shock. Ninnis, alive and jovial one minute, had disappeared almost without a sound and literally fallen off the face of the earth. Mertz had lingered at the scene of his death because it was hard to accept that he had truly gone. Yet there had been no time to reflect on the tragedy.

This broken shovel, earlier discarded, was retrieved and
repaired after Ninnis was lost. It is now an exhibit in the
Mawson Collection at the South Australian Museum.
(*Mawson Collection, South Australian Museum*)

Prior to this journey, Douglas and Mertz had spent a whole winter in
Antarctica with sixteen other men in very close quarters. Ninnis and Mertz
had formed a friendship through working together as the dog handlers
and because they were two of only three Europeans in the Hut. They
bonded under very unusual circumstances, the isolation and confinement
making for a very intense friendship that had begun in England, months
before the expedition had got underway. In Hobart they had spent days
at the beach together, swimming and sailing. Mertz, warmhearted and
affectionate, had almost mothered Ninnis, who he described as, 'my best
friend on the whole expedition'.[14] Then, the day after losing him, Mertz
had to begin killing and eating the dogs he had reared from pups. As the
dog handler, he had given them all names and over the long winter he
had sewed and fitted harnesses for each dog. They had their own distinctive personalities and had loyally pulled the sledges, only to be butchered
when they were no longer any use. This undoubtedly had a profound
effect on him. Douglas, on the other hand, in his position as leader,

and by dint of his more aloof character, was naturally more emotionally removed from both Ninnis and the dogs.

On 5 January, three weeks into their return journey, Mertz flatly refused to rise from his sleeping-bag and Douglas felt frustrated at not being able to coax him into moving and at not being able to lift him out of his depression. He expressed surprise in his diary at how quickly Mertz gave up.

In describing the planning and preparation of this expedition, a few years later in *The Home of the Blizzard*, he wrote, 'In no department can a leader spend time more profitably than in the selection of the men who are to accomplish the work. For a polar campaign the great desideratum is tempered youth. It is the vigour, the dash and the recuperative power of youth that is so necessary to cope with the extreme discomforts and trials of such exploration…'.[15] Yet, beyond choosing men he thought would thrive, there was nothing more Douglas could do. Until they were in Antarctica there was no way of knowing how the men would bear up under the tough conditions.

During the winter of 1912, he had observed his staff closely and come to the conclusion that the men, 'on such expeditions as this', fell into four categories. They were: 'the accomplished and painstaking stickers who are the backbone of things'; the 'mediocre people who are not really good at anything but can assist under supervision'; those who 'require winding up to keep them going happily' and, finally, those who are, 'not fit for anything and don't belong on an expedition'.[16] He did not venture to say who belonged to which category but, in the same diary entry, he made special mention of both Ninnis and Mertz as being among the men who were always willing to help. This is quite significant given that Douglas seldom praised.

In his autobiography, *High Latitude*, Captain Davis claimed that both Ninnis and Mertz regarded the expedition as 'the supreme adventure' of their lives, 'the test of manhood that the best and the bravest are eager to face'.[17] In fact, of all the hundreds of applicants, they were the keenest to join and the most worried they would be rejected. Clearly Mertz thought he would cope better than he did. The fact that he applied to go on the expedition in the first place suggests that he saw himself as a 'sticker'. He had always been so resistant to the cold and had not suffered from frostbite previously. He could 'scarcely believe it' when his fingers became badly frostbitten. To convince himself, 'he bit a considerable piece of the fleshy part off the end of one of them.'[18] It seems he became overwhelmed with depression when he recognised he'd been beaten, that it was too late to fight. It was as if death had crept up on him.

There is every indication that Douglas had also picked Mertz as a survivor. Yet, now that Mertz was being put to the test, he was crumbling before his very eyes. It puzzled him that this strong, twenty-eight-year-old man, who was so hardworking and cheerful, had lost the will to go on and he was unprepared for Mertz's sudden decline. Even as late as the day before Mertz died, Douglas was still in a state of disbelief. Despite all the signs that death was imminent, it was not until Mertz started to have fits that Douglas realised the seriousness of his condition. His own description, that it hit him like 'a thunderbolt' suggests that he had, up until then, been in a state of denial.

Two days before Mertz's death, Douglas offered to pull him on the sledge. It took some persuading and I have often wondered whether his initial reluctance to get on the sledge was because he was afraid that, by doing so, he was signing his own death warrant. After all, this was the pattern with the dogs. It was the end for them once their legs stopped working and they were lifted on to the sledge. They were doomed to die at the next campsite. In his irrational, delusional state, did Mertz think Douglas would kill him? After covering a distance of barely two miles, he was so cold from inactivity that he refused to go any further and they stopped and camped. By the following day, Mertz had completely lost control of his bowels and, in a delirium, was raving incoherently and having fits.

Douglas confided to his diary, 'Things are in a most serious state for both of us—if he cannot go on 8 or 10m a day, in a day or two we are doomed'. As the leader of the expedition, Douglas had no choice but to stay with Mertz even though he felt he could 'pull through' himself with the provisions they had. 'It is very hard for me', he wrote, 'to be within 100m of the hut and in such a position is awful'.[19] They lay in their sleeping-bags eating into their food supplies and fighting the cold, made worse by their inaction. Their canvas ground sheet for inside the tent had gone down the crevasse with Ninnis and their spare groundsheet was not so effective as they were continually damp. Their sleeping-bags were wet on the outside and soggy on the inside.

Mertz's inability to walk confined both men to their tent and precious travelling time was lost. He had become a liability, just as Oates had on the return journey from the Pole with Scott when his feet became badly frostbitten. Realising that he was slowing the others down, he had hastened his own death by walking out into a blizzard. Although there is some speculation that Oates did not make this decision entirely on his own, that he did so because he was made to feel a burden by the others, Scott noted this courageous and selfless act in his diary and recorded the now famous last words of Oates, who never returned to the tent, 'I am just going outside. I may be some time'.

Ranulph Fiennes argues, in his biography of Scott, in which he draws on his own extensive polar experience to shed further light on the tragedy, that Oates must have received assistance from the others in getting out of the tent, as, 'with useless fingers he would have been unable to untie the lashings of the door tunnel'.[20] With or without help, unlike Oates, Mertz was in no fit mental state to make such a decision. On 7 January, as they prepared to 'go on at all cost' as arranged, Douglas again found him 'in a terrible state having fouled his pants'. He raved long into the night calling out in German and Douglas finally conceded that, 'it would require a miracle to bring him round to a fit travelling companion'.[21] It was only then that Douglas accepted there was no hope of proceeding and became resigned to the task of nursing Mertz and easing his suffering.

Mertz died around 2 am on the morning of 8 January 1913, claimed by the continent he had grown to love. Thriving in the cold and icy conditions, he had often compared it to Switzerland. 'I love this cold area in the same way that I love my Alps, with their natural beauty and dangers', he had confided to his diary the previous May. Ironically, he felt deeply contented: 'Although I am uncertain about the present or the future and I know that Switzerland lies far away, I have never felt such satisfaction and peace in my life'.[22]

He had lost all the skin on his legs and scrotum. For whatever reason— the loss of Ninnis, the trauma of killing and eating the dogs, poisoning from the dog's liver, the cold, the persistent damp and the hunger or a combination of these things, he had finally succumbed. Nothing had prepared him for the appalling circumstances in which he had found himself. Douglas, saddened and perplexed by his demise, later wrote to Mertz's mother in Switzerland: 'I have great admiration for the qualities which your son showed and the admirable way in which he worked both at the hut and on that difficult march where he perished'.[23]

Douglas was now alone, lying beside a corpse in a flimsy tent at the mercy of the elements with no chance of rescue. He later told Davis that when he looked through the entrance of the tent that morning he felt, 'alone in that boundless white plain'[24] and he had the feeling that he was about to enter the unknown. Reflecting on his situation, he wrote: 'For many days now…Xavier's condition has prevented us going on and now I am afraid it has cooked my chances all together'.[25] The delay could cost him his life as it had weakened him considerably. He described his condition in his diary a few days later: 'My whole body is apparently rotting from want of proper nourishment—frostbitten fingertips festering, mucous membrane of nose gone, saliva glands of mouth refusing duty, skin coming off whole body'.[26]

an Emperor Penguin

12

Surviving Alone

Strong winds and heavy drift snow held Douglas up in his tent for a few
days after Mertz died. The cruel weather is one of the biggest threats
to survival in the Antarctic. A blizzard had contributed to the death of
Scott's party, still entombed in their tent. A few months before, while
on a depot-laying journey, a party of five at Wild's Base, had got caught
in a blizzard for a record seventeen days during which time one of their
tents was destroyed. Weakened and on starvation rations, Douglas did
not have seventeen days to spare and he was too far from the Hut to make
a dash for home should his tent get torn to pieces in the wind.

As he sat in the tent mending and adapting his equipment, there was
plenty of time to think about Mertz as a source of food, his body frozen in
its sleeping-bag outside. He buried him at the first opportunity, perhaps
in order to remove this temptation. Douglas was in dire circumstances.
He would eventually return alone to tell a tale his two dead companions

were never able to contest, and for these two reasons there has always been the question of whether he cannibalised Mertz. As far as I know, no one has ever openly challenged his account of the events of the journey but there was, and *is*, absolutely no way of knowing the truth unless one takes his word for it.

It would not have been the first time such a thing has happened in the history of polar exploration. When the six surviving members of the Greely expedition were rescued in the Arctic in 1884, the bodies of those who had died (nineteen in total) were gathered up and taken back for burial in America. The family of one of the dead asked for their son's body to be exhumed following rumours that cannibalism had taken place. Upon examination, it was discovered that the body had been partially eaten. The exhumation of the remaining bodies confirmed that they, too, had been mutilated. It was obvious that it was not the work of animals as the flesh had apparently been cut with 'a surgeon's precision'. Douglas would certainly have known this story and it is more than likely, particularly given the connection with the *Aurora*, that Greely's account of the expedition was among the books that formed the Hut library.

The huge excitement at the rescue and return of the six survivors of the Greely expedition had quickly turned to investigations of cannibalism and, revealingly, *The Times* called it 'The Shame of a Nation'.[1] Greely vehemently denied any knowledge of cannibalism having occurred. The furore eventually died down but it tainted an otherwise heroic story and the message was clear—eating a person was an unforgivable act, even when carried out by men on the brink of starvation. When, some thirty years before the Greely expedition, while engaged in searching for the relics of the missing Franklin party, Dr John Rae had reported having heard stories from the 'Eskimos' of acts of cannibalism among Franklin's starving men. The British public was horrified and refused to believe that civilised Englishmen would resort to such a base means of alleviating their hunger.

Certainly it had no place in a story of heroism. Even as recently as 1992 when a research team recovered hundreds of human bones at a Franklin site on King William Island, which on examination, clearly supported cannibalism, there was still resistance to the idea. When the sixteen survivors of a plane crash in the Andes in 1972 were rescued seventy-two days after the accident, it quickly became evident that they had cannibalised the dead to survive. All sixteen were devout Catholics and they were greeted with revulsion and shock on their return until one survivor, Pancho Delgado, spoke at a press conference on behalf of all the survivors. He defended their actions in a moving speech, in which he claimed they were guided by the hand of God.[2]

Cannibalism, which remains a taboo, was even more inconceivable almost a century ago. Irrespective of whether Douglas cannibalised Mertz, to admit to it would have ruined his reputation and ended his career. It was far more admirable to survive without having to resort to this. In much the same way, had Scott and his men taken their own lives, this would have spoiled the story. They had packed a phial of morphine and opium tablets in case they wished to resort to suicide but the drugs were found untouched alongside their bodies. In declining this option, they died like true English gentlemen with their gallantry intact.

Oma told me quite casually one day that someone once sent her mother a book by Thomas Keneally called *The Survivor*. A novel with obvious parallels with the Far-Eastern Sledging Journey and cannibalism as its central theme, it came out in 1969, by which time Douglas had been dead for nine years and Paquita was an elderly widow. Its connection with the AAE 1911–14 begins with the dust jacket. It is a photograph of Leslie Whetter and John Close, two of the eighteen men based at the Hut with Douglas. It was taken by Frank Hurley, the expedition photographer, and shows Whetter and Close braving a blizzard to collect ice for drinking water. They are holding ice picks and one has been brought to his knees by the force of the wind. It was a picture I was fascinated with as a child. Two unrecognisable figures stumbling blindly through a dark blue world. Although it appears in *The Home of the Blizzard*, I knew it as the cover design for *This Accursed Land*, published in 1977.

The Survivor is about a fictitious scientific expedition to Antarctica in 1925 led by a Doctor Stephen Leeming, a graduate of Sydney University. The main character, Alec Ramsey, is accepted to go on the expedition as the dog handler when the original man chosen falls ill. It is set in the present, forty years have passed and Ramsey is looking back on a sledging journey of which he was the sole survivor. Leeming and a third man, Lloyd, both perished.

In the story, there had always been some suspicion that Ramsey had eaten his companions to survive. The glacier in which Leeming is buried has recently melted and a team goes down to Antarctica to exhume the body. Right up until the end, the reader is led to believe that Ramsey *did* resort to cannibalism, partly because he carries a lot of guilt and dreads the exhumation, and partly because his wife suspects he did. Yet, curiously, Leeming is found and there is no evidence that the body had been cannibalised.

The book upset Paquita. Like Leeming, Douglas was a graduate of Sydney University and his title was 'Dr' at the time the expedition took place. It was a scientific expedition, it was Australian, there were three men and one survivor. It offended her because she felt that the person who gave her the book was clearly intimating that Douglas had cannibalised Mertz. Even though Ramsey is exonerated in *The Survivor*, he lives under a cloud of suspicion for forty years before the body of Leeming is recovered from the ice and found to be intact, and this is what Paquita found upsetting. Perhaps the person who gave Paquita the book thought she was harbouring the truth and, as an elderly woman, might have wanted to relieve her conscience.

Several people, who knew Douglas well, believed that the idea never even occurred to him, that the whole idea of it went against his principles. When the question was put to Eric Webb, chief magnetician at the Main Base, he replied, 'I myself am completely confident that Mawson never contemplated it, never thought it, and to me it was just straight impossible. There was very little to gain by it and Mawson had the sense to appreciate that'. Philip Law was of a similar opinion, 'Mawson was first a sentimentalist, secondly he was a square. He was a conservative man. I think that notion would be beyond his scheme of things altogether'.[3]

In a lecture Douglas gave to an audience in New York in January 1915, he was quoted as saying, 'I thought for two days about eating Mertz...but finally I decided that if I did get back to civilization it would always leave a bad taste in my mouth, so I buried him and went on'.[4] Douglas's choice of words, that had he cannibalised Mertz, it would have left 'a bad taste' in his mouth, had always struck me as odd. Thus I was not surprised to learn, from Mark Pharaoh, that this was a misquote apparently later retracted by the newspaper responsible for printing it, the *New York*

Globe. I then returned to Paquita's scrapbook and found another article printed a few days later in Canada in which Douglas is questioned about this alleged statement. He told the *Toronto Daily Star* that the claim was 'outrageous' and 'the invention of a New York reporter'.[5]

Yet, it is hard to imagine that Douglas didn't consider using Mertz as a source of food, even if only fleetingly, because in a sense it seems a logical and rational idea under the circumstances. In the New Hebrides he had come into direct contact with cannibals and could have learnt something of the preparation of the body for eating. As a scientist he would have known that the human body is high in protein, although the cannibals he encountered ate humans more for religious purposes, as a ceremonial of war, believing that the strength of their slain enemies passed into their own bodies. Mertz was not an enemy or someone unknown to Douglas. Rather, he knew him well. Douglas had grown very close to him and, while it is perhaps too much to suggest that he loved Mertz, he was certainly very fond of him. That Douglas had offered, in fact, promised, to show him Australia when they got back is an indication that they had become firm friends and that they envisaged their friendship lasting.

In his book, *Survival of the Fittest*, in which he considers the qualities needed for survival in extreme circumstances, Mike Stroud includes friendship as an important factor. He argues that, 'the more uncomfortable and dangerous a situation becomes, the more strongly camaraderie is felt' and that, 'to share hardship with another is to forge very strong bonds which will last a lifetime'.[6] To cannibalise Mertz would have been a very difficult thing to do under these circumstances. Added to this, Mertz had died of unknown causes. Eating him might have made Douglas ill.

Yet, Douglas's resourcefulness could have and *would* have extended to using the body of Mertz for food. It seems hard to believe that conservatism was the issue, moral or otherwise, remembering that he was a man who was absolutely determined to survive. Giving up, not cannibalism went against his principles. He was very straight but he was also highly adaptable, and in an extraordinary predicament, miles from civilisation and in the face of death. He was already far removed from everyday life and routine, dining on dog and going for weeks without a bath. Here was a man who wasn't in the least bit squeamish, a man who had eaten all manner of disgusting things from seal blubber to the head of a dog, a man who had proved that he could emotionally detach himself from his appalling circumstances in the name of survival. While I can't imagine cutting someone up and cooking them, Douglas was made of much tougher stuff and I believe that he would have been able to do this, and that he would have coped with the practicalities of preparing the body for eating. The key factor, however, is that he didn't need to.

It is difficult to determine exactly how much food he had left. On the day that Ninnis died we know that what remained to Douglas and Mertz was one-and-a-half-week's rations. Added to this, each man had a bag of personal items, including extra food they called 'perks' (at one point Douglas mentioned finding a biscuit in his bag, which he halved with Mertz, and some chocolate sticks). Precisely what was in these bags is something that has never been ascertained but Douglas calculated that he could get back to Winter Quarters on the provisions he had, remembering also that with Mertz's death there was one less mouth to feed. There is, of course, the possibility that he used Mertz's body as a food source and never admitted it but this is unlikely. The fact that he recorded in his diary exactly where he buried Mertz (approximately 100 miles from the Hut), should anyone be sent to retrieve it for reburial in Switzerland, which, incidentally, they didn't, further erases suspicion.

Alone on the plateau, late on the evening of 8 January 1913, Douglas made a cairn for Mertz. He piled snow blocks up around his body and made a rough cross from some old sledge runners. Then he read the burial service as he had done for Ninnis only a few weeks before. It was an act of respect and I should think this ritual was comforting too. It brought a sense of closure and it was the proper, civilised thing to do. He had grown closer to Mertz in those few weeks they had spent together following the death of Ninnis.

When blizzard-bound in their tent, they had talked for hours about their favourite foods and of all the things they wanted to do in their lives. Douglas had cleaned Mertz when he had suffered bouts of dysentry, gently lifted his head to help him drink beef tea and cocoa, tucked him back into his sleeping-bag when, in a delirious state, he had tried to get out of it. I can picture him doing all of these things. I can imagine him buttoning up Mertz's clothes and all the while trying to encourage him to walk.

View from the living room through into the workshop of 'Main Base Hut'. John Close, Leslie Whetter and Herbert Murphy in foreground (*Mawson Collection, South Australian Museum*)

Returning on the *Aurora*, 1914. **Front row seated left to right:** Alfred Hodgeman, Frank Hurley, Harold Hamilton
Middle row left to right: Frank Bickerton (seated on balustrade), John Hunter, George Ainsworth (leaning against ropes), Cecil Madigan, Robert Bage, Douglas Mawson, Charles Sandell, Percy Correll
Back row left to right: Leslie Blake, Archie McLean (*Mawson Collection, South Australian Museum*)

Douglas Mawson

Captain John King Davis

Frank Hurley

John Close

Robert Bage

John Hunter

Eric Webb

Xavier Mertz

George Ainsworth

Percy Correll

Charles Laseron

Alfred Hodgeman

Walter Hannam

Herbert Murphy

Lieutenant Belgrave Ninnis

Frank Stillwell

Leslie Whetter

Archie McLean

Cecil Madigan

Frank Bickerton

Frank Wild

(All photographs courtesy Mawson Collection, South Australian Museum)

A young Paquita in the garden of the Delprat's home, Broken Hill, circa 1900s (*Gareth Thomas Collection*)

Paquita aged 11, at Robe, South Australia, 1902 (*Gareth Thomas Collection*)

Paquita in Holland, 1912. This photograph was delivered to the Main Base by Captain Davis in 1913 and Douglas hung it above his pillow in the Hut (*Gareth Thomas Collection*)

Wedding, 31 March 1914 ***Front row, left to right:*** Hester Berry (bridesmaid), Douglas and Paquita Mawson, Carmen Delprat (Paquita's sister and bridesmaid), Willy Delprat (Paquita's brother and groomsman) ***Standing behind, left to right:*** Captain John Davis (best man), William Mawson (Douglas's brother), Guillaume Delprat (Paquita's father), Henrietta Delprat (Paquita's mother), Professor Edgeworth David (*Gareth Thomas Collection*)

There was something very paternal about Douglas, who was always very caring when someone was ill. He was like that with his students at the university. On their geology camps, they had a sense of being looked after by him. The hardships endured on the South Magnetic Pole journey on the BAE brought out the worst in Dr Mackay. He lost his humanity and turned into a bully. Frustrated by Professor David's slow progress, Dr Mackay kicked him while, Douglas, by contrast, never lost his compassion. He stopped to help the Professor by taking off his boots for him and warming his semi-gangrenous toes and, in refusing to assume the leadership of the party, despite the Professor's pleas that he accept his written authority, was an act of support. Although irritated by the Professor's many eccentricities, he softened towards him as their journey progressed as he realised that the Professor was doing his very best.

Standing on the ice beside Mertz's grave, Douglas must have wondered if there was any chance of making it back alive. If he was to die, he knew no one would perform the same ritual for him. There would be no one to mark his grave. He would probably just crumple up in the snow, drop dead in his harness as the poor dogs had done. A blizzard would cover him with snow, gradually his body would be carried to the coast and out to sea and no one would ever find him.

sooty albatross

13

Defying Death

Death hath a thousand doors to let out life.
I shall find one.

Philip Massinger (1583–1639/40), English dramatist, *A Very Woman* V, iv

On 11 January 1913, news of the deaths of Scott and his four companions reached London. Three of the men, including Scott, had been found in their tent, which was still standing after an Antarctic winter. The body of Oates was never found. A memorial service was held three days later at St Paul's Cathedral. The congregation sang Rock of Ages, 'While I draw this fleeting breath/ When my eyelids close in death/ When I soar through tracts unknown,/ See thee on thy judgement throne,/ Rock of Ages, cleft for me,/ Let me hide myself in thee'.[1] It was Douglas's favourite hymn and would be sung at his own funeral but that was years away. At the age of thirty-two, he wasn't ready to die. He realised this when, a few days later, snow piled up on the tent half-burying him and he dug himself out, shuddering at the thought of death in his coffin-shaped sleeping-bag. He wanted to live. The 'tracts unknown' were very much of this world and they were waiting for him outside the tent.

On that day, he waited until 8.30 am before he got up because it was warmer then. Outside, the sun was shining and it was almost calm. After paying 'farewell respects to dear Xavier's remains'[2], he got away a little before 11 am but he had walked only two miles when his feet started to feel very painful and strangely lumpy. When he stopped to inspect them, he found, to his horror, that the soles had almost completely come away. With so little food, he couldn't afford to rest. If he were to have any chance of covering the 100 miles back to the Hut, he would have to average at least five miles a day. There was nothing for it but to smother the raw skin with lanolin, bandage the old skin casts back onto his feet and put on several pairs of socks for extra protection.

Paquita described him as having, 'absolutely no sense of pain',[3] and that when his thumb was almost completely torn off in an accident at the university years later, he had had it sewn up without an anaesthetic. He also found inaction impossible to bear. Oma told me that she once said to her father, in reference to the ill-fated Scott expedition, 'They couldn't have done anything else'. Douglas had strongly disagreed. Although he had great admiration for Scott, it frustrated him that he and his men lay in their tent and accepted defeat; that they did not make some attempt to move on, especially when they were at a distinct advantage in that there were three of them to egg one another on and they were only eleven miles from the nearest food depot. It is tempting to wonder whether Douglas would have got them all moving, had he accepted Scott's offer and been a member of the Pole party.

The Latin mottos he jotted down in his diary on the BAE 1907–09 offer us some insight into his moral aspirations. They included *Factus non Verbus* (Deeds not words), *Omnia Desuper* (All things are from above) and *Viribus Unitis* (With united strength).[4] Among the books that he lent to the expedition from his personal library was *Meditations* by Roman emperor and philosopher, Marcus Aurelius (121–180 AD). A series of philosophies on life, it is divided into books and what might be termed lessons. Douglas's approach to the situation in which he found himself on this journey was very much in keeping with the fundamental teachings of Aurelius.

According to Aurelius, we are a small part of the universe in the context of all beings and of all time. Alone in the vastness of Antarctica, Douglas could not have failed to feel humbled in the face of nature. Aurelius advises the practice of rationality, humility and self-discipline. Essentially, he advocates that we are at the mercy of the gods. We are all part of a divine order of things and our destinies are predetermined although he advises we must make the most of 'Providence' if and when she favours us. He argues we are not entirely powerless and are responsible for our own actions. For example, one lesson reads, 'What is the very best that can be said or done with the materials at your disposal? Be it what it may, you have the power to say it or do it; let there be no pretence that you are not a free agent'.[5] In another, Aurelius writes, 'Shame on the soul, to falter on the road of life while the body still perseveres'[6] and 'Nothing can happen to any man that nature has not fitted him to endure'.[7] On pain, he says, 'If it is past bearing, it makes an end of us; if it lasts, it can be borne. The mind, holding itself aloof from the body, retains its calm, and the master-reason remains unaffected.'[8]

Douglas put these lessons into practice, not only on the plateau, but in the way he managed the scientific programme and domestic roster at the Main Base. Afraid of nothing and hard on himself, he also expected a lot from other people. In his diary the preceding winter, he made it very clear that he had no tolerance for laziness, lack of stamina or lack of initiative. It was sinful to waste time, to take longer to do a job than was necessary, to not finish a job properly, to work in an ineffective manner or to avoid work. To not even try was absolutely unforgivable. He was particularly unimpressed with twenty-nine year old New Zealander, Dr Leslie Whetter, who frequently angered him. Lazy and a drinker (it was discovered he had been drinking the expedition's store of port), Whetter also appeared to be suffering from various health problems. His dizzy spells and bouts of diarrhoea failed to win Douglas's sympathy. In June Douglas noted in his diary, 'Whetter is not fit for a polar expedition. I wish I had minded his mother's cablegram warning me...of late he has complained of overwork, and he only does an honest 2 hours work per day'.[9] His official role was surgeon but he was not assigned to any specific scientific tasks at the Hut. His only responsibility, apart from rostered jobs, was to collect twelve boxes of ice each day, a task he seemed to take all day to achieve but one which, Douglas noticed, Laseron accomplished in an hour when Whetter was absent on a sledging journey.

Whetter was uncooperative and often blatantly disobeyed Douglas's orders. When asked to dig out some penguins from the freezer, he made an excuse not to. When, a few weeks later, Douglas asked him to join everyone else in sewing clothes for sledging, he took no notice and retired to bed at 4.30 pm. Others had also not worked hard enough. John Close, Douglas noted, 'gets tired before the day is out and has a nap at intervals'[10] and Stillwell is, 'slow in getting a move on'.[11] These criticisms sound petty and harsh but it no doubt concerned him that he had to nag some of the men to do things and run around after them. Douglas must have been worried about how some of the men might fare out on the sledging journeys, given that some couldn't even cook a basic meal without disastrous results and grew tired after a few hours' work.

Douglas placed a lot of importance on being physically active. Although he was a reader, he regarded reading, in the context of the expedition and of Hut life, as a pastime that could only be justified if all other tasks had been completed. Under any other circumstances it was self-indulgent and not brotherly. For instance, he noted in his diary that three of the men were reading when they could have been writing an article for the Hut newspaper, the *Blizzard*, as none had previously made a contribution. Douglas was not afraid of expressing his dissatisfaction as his diaries reveal that he often confronted his men on these issues. In early October, 1912 he had given them 'quite a long address' and, 'ended by saying that the united efforts of all are required to make the expedition successful'.[12]

In speaking of the united efforts of all, he included himself. He led by example in that he was not exempt from any domestic chore. Like everyone else on the expedition, he took his turn as mess man, cook and night watchman. He worked very hard and he never asked anyone to do anything he wasn't prepared to do himself. Laseron remembered him plunging into icy water to retrieve a box that had fallen into the sea and recalled with shame that it was not before Douglas had gone under a third time that he thought of volunteering himself. Years later, on BANZARE 1929–1931, a scientist refused to peel potatoes because he felt such a job to be beneath him. Douglas immediately started peeling the potatoes himself and the man was so ashamed that he joined him. His geology students recall that he had such an enormous amount of energy and walked so quickly they could barely keep up with him. He was arguably better equipped than anyone on the expedition to get off the plateau alive.

After Mertz died, day after day Douglas broke camp and moved on. When the surface he was travelling along turned to slippery ice, he frequently fell and as he crashed onto the ice he was so thin and emaciated, he almost expected to see his bones burst through his clothing. He staggered on, rewarding himself with little bits of chocolate and a few remaining raisins. It was important to break his journey down and to concentrate on conquering short distances.

Eric Webb recalled that Douglas was 'a marvellous innovator, and improviser, and always very resourceful in the most practical way'.[13] He had always loved *The Swiss Family Robinson* and *Robinson Crusoe* because he enjoyed the way they had to be resourceful and adaptable and think of ways to survive. In these stories the characters exercised qualities he aspired towards.

He had learnt to be frugal as a boy. His mother, Margaret, took in boarders to supplement their income. She allowed Douglas to buy food in large amounts and encouraged him to sell it to her in small quantities to teach him how to run a household and how to manage money. For instance, she would tell him she was having five for dinner and let him work out how many potatoes were needed and what meat to buy. This gave him a good grounding when it came to planning the food for all the men and students who went on his field trips into the outback and on his expeditions to Antarctica. His Spartan childhood meant that he found it hard to tolerate waste. He described Herbert Dyce Murphy, in charge of stores at the Hut, as 'an outrageous cook'[14] for boiling peas and then draining off the buttery water. His frugal ways were not restricted to expeditions. Paquita, who had grown up quite differently, in a far more affluent household, was, by contrast, quite extravagant and Oma recalled her father finding this frustrating. He would try to persuade Paquita not to buy all the best cuts of meat and to try tripe and brains because they were cheaper. Mark Pharaoh made the observation that Douglas was even mindful of waste when it came to his notebooks.* Many of the pages, written in pencil because ink freezes in the cold conditions, are crammed with writing in all the margins.

---

* Mawson's notebooks for the BAE 1907–09, the AAE 1911–14 and BANZARE 1929–31 were transcribed over a period of years and eventually published as *Mawson's Antarctic Diaries* in 1988 by Fred and Eleanor Jacka.

His organisational skills and his ability to make the most of limited resources helped him enormously when he was out there alone on the plateau. Apart from everything else, it kept his mind occupied. He spent hours tossing in his sleeping-bag, racking his brain for ideas on how to make the food last longer and how to make it more palatable; what to discard to lighten his load. Blizzard-bound days were spent mending equipment and weighing up his chances of survival—literally revising calculations for ration units over the remaining days, leaving extra days for poor weather.

When Mertz died, he had immediately set about cutting the sledge* in half with his pocket saw to lighten his load, the full-size sledge being unnecessarily heavy and cumbersome for one man to pull. He made a sail for the sledge by sewing together Mertz's Burberry jacket and a waterproof clothes bag and floor cover. After falling into a crevasse later in the journey, he made a ladder from a length of alpine rope and some of Mertz's clothes with the idea of pulling himself out more easily should he have the misfortune to fall into another, providing the sledge held his weight, as it had before. When he found himself on a slippery surface, he constructed crampons out of the wood from his theodolite** case. His handyman skills or, as he put it, his 'rather gadgety'[15] ways were something Oma often talked about. Despite the fact that his marital home (and Oma's childhood home) was built on sandy soil, he devised a watering system that ensured the garden thrived. He arranged the pipes leading into the bathroom around behind the kitchen range so that the range, which was always burning, kept the pipes warm and ensured a constant supply of hot water. This way it wasn't necessary to light the copper every time they wanted a bath. This aspect of Douglas's character undoubtedly helped to save his life in the Antarctic.

It was also his patience and his calm approach to everything. Paquita claimed that nothing flustered him. In 1929, he sailed from Port Adelaide for Cape Town where he was to meet the *Discovery*, bound for Antarctica on the first BANZARE cruise. On the way to the wharf, the axle of the car in which he was travelling, broke under the weight of his luggage

---

* Originally held at the Royal Geographical Society in London, this half-sledge is now part of the Mawson Collection on permanent display at the South Australian Museum.

** an instrument used in surveying and navigation.

and they only just made it in time. For Paquita it was the last straw but Douglas waved from the deck grinning as if nothing alarming had happened.

He was not generally a rash man and in his diaries he was a man very much in control of his senses. Rather than panic, as so many others might have done, and rush out into the snow unprepared, he kept a clear mind and cooperated with the conditions. He would not have drunk seawater if he were adrift in the ocean. He would not have left his vehicle if he were stranded in the desert because he thought very carefully about everything he did. Douglas is famous for his physical feats but he was also an intellectual. He rose to the challenge of thinking his way out of a difficult situation.

Impatience could lead to disaster and he knew this. Whenever possible, he avoided marching in poor light when the terrain he was traversing was riddled with crevasses. He knew it could cost him his life if he could not see what was lurking beneath. On Scott's first expedition of 1901–04, one of his men, Michael Barne, who was in charge of a sledging party of nine men, made the fatal decision to push on in poor visibility because they were only a few miles from safety. It was a matter of walking along a ridge top and down a ski slope. Little did they know, they were on a cliff edge that dropped down to the sea. One of the men, George Vince, was not wearing snow boots. He slipped and fell into oblivion in his soft finnesko shoes.

Atrocious weather continued to hamper Douglas's progress. With all that time on his hands it must have been very tempting to gorge himself on what remained, but he refrained from eating when he was laid up in his tent because he wasn't expending any energy. Since rations were calculated on a mileage basis, food was only allowed at the end of a day's marching. While Fridtjof Nansen and his sledging companion, Hjalmar Johansen, had survived an Arctic winter by living off polar bear and walrus meat when they got lost on their way to the North Pole in 1896, Douglas, in the Antarctic interior, had almost no chance of finding extra food.

He conserved his energy when he could and looked after his injuries because it was his body that he was depending upon to get him back to the Hut. Every day he spent a considerable amount of time attending to his raw and blackened feet and the numerous boils that broke out all over his face and body. It was hard not to move when the alternative was to just lie in his sleeping-bag, sometimes for days at a time, and wait for the weather to clear, knowing he had many miles to cover and very little food. Patience, not an aversion to walking, kept him inside the tent.

Dreaming of sweet things

14

A Will to Live

For me to have made one soul the better for my birth,
To have added but one flower to the garden of the Earth,
To have struck one blow for truth in the daily fight with lies,
To have done one deed of right in the face of calumnies,
To have sown in the souls of men one thought that will not die,
To have been a link in the chain of life,
Shall be immortality.

Memorial in *Salford Royal Hospital Architectural Review*,
Douglas's diary, 1 February 1914

It was to be more than a month before Douglas reached safety. For many reasons, the most incredible part of his journey was these four weeks. On the day of Mertz's death, he had made the decision, there and then, to put up a determined fight, and there was much to fight for. He was a young man with his life ahead of him and he was already more than halfway there. This was *his* expedition, he was the leader and organiser of it and this was a very important factor in his survival. One doesn't just find oneself in the middle of Antarctica faced with the prospect of starvation and death. Douglas was there because of decisions *he* had made and, although nothing could have prepared him for this, right from the beginning he knew the risks and he never doubted that these risks were worth taking.

People often ask, 'What exactly did Mawson *do* in the Antarctic?'
Many don't even know why he was there in the first place and what he
accomplished because, ironically, the dramatic details of the Far-Eastern
Sledging Journey have almost completely overshadowed the purpose and
the success of this expedition. His objectives were also harder to understand than Scott's and Amundsen's. Even if the meaning of the Pole and
its location was something few could fathom or explain, it was a destination of sorts and a worthy one if only because it was the common goal
of two men engaged in a race to get there first. By 1912, Shackleton
was preparing to cross the whole continent and that was easy enough
to understand, but where was Douglas going? What was he doing 300
miles from his Hut in the middle of nowhere? He wasn't going to the
Pole and he wasn't heading for a mountain or anything as tangible or as
obvious as that. To the average person his aims *were* and *are* obscure and
difficult to grasp. However, *he* knew exactly why he was there. It wasn't
as if he'd caught the wrong train somewhere and ended up in a smashed
up carriage. He knew the territory, he had sledged there himself and his
motivation for being there was an important reason why he survived.

Science had taken him there and the thrill of the unknown. To be out
in the wilds standing where no human had ever stood before was his idea
of bliss. He absolutely revelled in it. It made his heart race. It had been
less than twenty years since the first men had set foot upon mainland
Antarctica and no one had ever before landed where Douglas established
his Winter Quarters. 'What an exultation is ours', he had written to
Paquita upon his arrival in Adélie Land, 'The feeling is magical—young
men whom you would scarce expect would be affected stand half clad
without feeling the cold of the keen blizzard wind and literally dance
from sheer exultation—can you not feel it too as I write—the quickening
of the pulse, the awakening of the mind, the tension of every fibre—this
is joy'.[1]

It was also his refusal to compromise that determined his success.
He had chosen not to go with Scott because it would have meant abandoning his own ambitions. Scott's primary aim, in 1910, was to reach
the Pole by the same route he had first begun to carve out in 1901 on
the Ross Ice Shelf. Shackleton had broadly followed this, carving out a
route onto the plateau almost to the Pole in 1909. In both attempts the

two had failed. One of the reasons why Douglas turned down the offer of a place on Scott's second expedition may well have been because he doubted Scott would succeed, particularly given that Scott did not have a new plan of attack. This aside, Douglas was less interested in the pursuit of national or personal glory. His diaries, in which he presents the bare facts as they are, without embellishment, even when he was aware that he might die, are proof of that. He was first and foremost a scientist. There were twenty-five men carrying out scientific work on his expedition as opposed to only eight on Scott's last expedition in 1910–12. On Scott's first expedition there were only five and only six on Shackleton's BAE. On the AAE 1911–14, only three of the eighteen men at the Main Base did not have some university education. Of the eighteen members of the committee established by the Australian Association for the Advancement of Science to promote and support the expedition, ten were university professors.

Douglas was convinced that the success of the expedition rested on scientific professionalism and was often frustrated that the men he had chosen were not serious enough about their work and were not consistently enthusiastic. There was not enough commitment to excellence, to the finer details. For example, while dredging on the ship on the homeward cruise, he noticed scientists threw away parts of the animals and sea creatures they collected without first checking their organs for parasites. His expectations of his men were incredibly high, considering that most were only young graduates or yet to graduate. In fact, they were the youngest group of men to ever sail for Antarctica (the youngest, Adelaidian Percy Correll, was only nineteen), and because of this there was extra pressure on Douglas to make a success of the expedition. He later confided in a letter to Professor David: 'The men were nearly all very young and without previous extended experience and that meant the utmost drain upon my abilities in order to secure the measure of results that accrued'.[2] With hindsight he wrote, 'If I were choosing another staff I would get specialists for each branch, true scientists capable of assisting with sledging. The long distance sledgers should also have some knowledge of scientific subjects'.[3]

It was this dedication to scientific objectives that drove him to explore and ultimately to reach the safety of the Hut. Upon her mother's death in 1937, Paquita asked Douglas what he thought happened to the soul after death. He replied 'Well Munk (Munk was his nickname for her), no one knows just *what* comes. There is no way at all of finding out. I think we should live so that there is something left in the world after us, that is good because of us, a useful discovery—not necessarily a name but something that remains after you, something worthwhile'.[4] In a letter to her, before setting off on the Far-Eastern Sledging Journey, he wrote, 'How terribly disappointing this land has been. Our only consolation is that we feel that everything has been done that could be done and that on account of the rigour of the climate the information we have obtained will be of special value'.[5]

He was driven by a desire to leave something behind. It might be said that all explorers seek immortality in so far as, the discoveries they make will ensure that their names will survive them and this is undeniably part of the attraction. Douglas knew that dying in the Antarctic would mean that, at best, his work would remain unfinished and, at worst, might be lost forever. (Certainly, 'the agony of leaving his job undone'[6] was something Kathleen Scott was haunted by on learning of her husband's death.) Douglas, though rarely reckless, was nevertheless relentless in the pursuit of his scientific goals and the work he was trying to accomplish went before his own personal safety. An example of this is when on the BAE he fell down a crevasse and, despite his precarious position, he seized the opportunity to collect ice specimens. Hanging in his harness eighteen feet down, while waiting to be rescued, incidentally by Captain Davis, his sledge rope sawed into the ice above him and he slipped, dropping even further into the abyss. Yet, while all this was happening and, while he waited to be rescued, he calmly threw up some ice crystals for later examination. On the Far-Eastern Sledging Journey, he continued to write meteorological logs every day of his return journey, which was quite remarkable under the circumstances. It is a wonder he managed to keep a clear mind. Soon after Mertz died, he wrote: 'As there is little chance of my reaching human aid alive I greatly regret my inability to set out the coastline as surveyed for the 300 miles we travelled and {record} the notes on glaciers and ice formations, etc—the most of which latter is of course committed to my head'.[7] By keeping up the ritual of taking readings and notes he was constantly reminding himself, on a daily basis, of how and why he had come to be where he was.

Douglas later admitted that there had been a moment when he had thought of crawling into his sleeping-bag and of going to sleep and letting go but that he had resisted the temptation when he thought of all the work he'd done going to waste. Perhaps he also dreaded such an end, which would not necessarily be slow. In considering death in the snow in relation to Scott and his men on their return journey from the Pole, Ranulph Fiennes is not convinced that such an option would be painless. 'It might sound beguiling to those who have not tried it,' he wrote, 'but I for one would choose it as a very last resort'.[8] The men who found Scott's body were shocked by its appearance. He looked as though he had suffered terribly. His death had been anything but quick. From the dates of his diary entries, it was evident that he had survived for many days after running out of food and water.

While Scott and his men had been defeated by the cold and a fierce blizzard, Douglas, almost a year later on the same continent, was not in quite such a desperate position. There were still options. He decided that, even if he couldn't make it back to the Hut, he would try to reach a nunatak, (a rocky peak surrounded by ice) he knew of where his corpse might be found by a relief party, together with his notebooks and diaries telling the story of the journey. In the absence of their bodies, the next best thing was to deposit the diaries of Ninnis and Mertz somewhere safe. They had fortunately not gone down the crevasse with Ninnis. It was an added motivation. At least then, none of them would have died in vain.

Thus, the expedition was Douglas's creation. It was *his* vision and it eventuated because of *his* ambition and determination to get it under way. He was the initiator, the promoter and the organiser and had taken a financial risk to his own private account by selling some of his own shares to cover some of the expeditionary costs, and as leader he was and would be, liable for any outstanding debts. One might even go so far as to say that exploring was his whole reason for being in a way that it wasn't for Mertz or for any of the other expedition members. For them it was just an exciting chapter in their lives. Most, apart from Captain Davis, were required to give up a year of their lives and present themselves for duty but anything that happened before or after the expedition was not their

responsibility. As men working under Douglas's command they were not
driven by the same things and they were not there for the same reasons.

a wandering albatross

15

Love and Responsibility

The woods are lovely, dark and deep
But I have promises to keep,
And miles to go before I sleep.

Robert Frost (1874–1963), *Stopping by woods on a snowy evening*

Fred and Eleanor Jacka, who edited Douglas's Antarctic diaries, argued that Douglas became a leader, 'not for the sake of glory or power, or even to set a record, but because of an overpowering conviction…that he could do a better job than most others'.[1] On his first expedition to Antarctica with Shackleton in 1907 he was just twenty-five years old and without experience in the polar regions. Unfortunately his achievements on this expedition were overshadowed by the fact that Shackleton got closer to the South Geographic Pole than anyone previously. This was of far more interest to the public than the successful attainment of the South Magnetic Pole and Shackleton became world famous almost overnight. However, in considering the particulars of this expedition, one can see the makings of Douglas as a future leader and of how invaluable this experience was in terms of his survival on the AAE.

He gained considerable experience of sledging in Antarctic conditions. To a lesser degree, he also endured near-starvation. He climbed Mount Erebus, an active volcano over 13 000 feet, after which he reached the South Magnetic Pole some seventy years after Ross had tried unsuccessfully to attain it. He traversed, with Professor David and with Dr Alistair Forbes Mackay, a tall, solidly built Scotsman, who had been a trooper in South Africa, more than 1200 miles, more than half of which was relay work. They dragged a tonne of supplies spread over three sledges. The relay work was necessary because three men could not pull two heavily laden sledges at the same time. They crossed terrain seamed with crevasses and over hard ridges of ice shaped by the wind that were sometimes as high as six feet and often at right angles to their course. This was no small achievement. They created a record for the longest unsupported journey, which was probably not broken until as recently as the early 1990s by British explorers, Ranulph Fiennes and Mike Stroud who travelled 1350 miles to the South Geographic Pole. This is in so far as such a record can be broken as the circumstances were hardly comparable.

Fiennes and Stroud did not have to do relay work. While they ran short of food, they did not have to eat seal blubber, as Douglas and his companions did, the eating of which caused constant diarrhoea. On the return journey Fiennes and Stroud started to suffer from hypoglycaemia (when blood sugar levels plummet to such an extent that it can lead to unconsciousness), and Fiennes had a badly infected leg. They called for assistance on the satellite telephone and were subsequently rescued, an option that was never open to Douglas's party. In their case it was a matter of walk or die. On the return journey from the South Magnetic Pole in 1909, which they had reached on 15 January, Douglas suffered from a sprained leg. He had never known such agony but nevertheless kept up an average pace of sixteen miles a day, an average they had calculated was necessary if they were to meet the *Nimrod* in time. The skin on his lips peeled off, leaving the raw flesh exposed.

In his account of this trek, Professor David recalled, 'Mawson, particularly, experienced great difficulty every morning in getting his mouth opened, as his lips were firmly glued together by congealed blood'.[2] The hardships of the BAE prepared Douglas physically for the AAE. It also gave him the confidence to consider leading his own expedition. While they were steadily tramping along in their harnesses, there was plenty of time to think and the idea of making a deeper exploration of that part of the continent had begun to form in his mind. While Douglas had been appointed physicist on Shackleton's expedition, he was really a geologist and he longed for an opportunity to work in his chosen field. In his instructions to Douglas, Professor David and Dr Mackay, with regard to their South Magnetic Pole Journey, Shackleton wrote: 'I particularly wish you to be able to work at the geology of the western mountains and for Mawson to spend at least a fortnight at Dry Valley to prospect for minerals of economic value. I consider that the *thorough* investigation of Dry Valley is of supreme importance.'[3] However, in the end they decided to bypass the valley altogether in favour of reaching the South Magnetic Pole when they realised they could not achieve both. Douglas wanted to forgo the Pole but he met with 'great opposition'.[4] Thus, he was denied the opportunity of studying the geology of the region in detail.

As a member of the BAE he was able to put into practice some of the qualities that were to prove so crucial to his survival in 1912–13 and he learnt from this expedition in terms of what supplies were needed and what worked and what didn't. For example, he decided against using Manchurian ponies on the AAE as they didn't appear to thrive in the conditions.

Afraid they wouldn't make it to the Magnetic Pole on the provisions they had, the three men had gone on to half rations, which for many weeks consisted of two plasmon biscuits a day. Plasmon biscuits, from what I can gather, are utterly uninteresting. They are so hard (to prevent them from crumbling on bumpy sledging journeys) that they had to be broken with an axe but in their extreme hunger the men decided they were very nice after all and every crumb was savoured. As the biscuits varied in thickness, they practised 'shut-eye' to ensure that the rations were divided fairly, the method Douglas adopted with Mertz when it came to eating the head of Ginger. 'Grievous was the disappointment of the man to whose lot the thinnest of the three biscuits had fallen', remarked Professor David in his account of this journey.[5] Douglas's culinary skills were most appreciated because he was able to make an interesting meal out of what they had. This was important because, apart from everything else, it boosted morale. David remarked, 'Mawson's cooking experiments continued to be highly successful and entirely satisfactory to the party'.[6]

Douglas's recipe for minced seal meat went as follows:

> Minced seal meat is one of the best forms for expeditions. Best way to prepare
> it: Very finely chop seal blubber in large quantity, fry in fry pan for long time,
> say ½ hour at least, then add a lump of blood in amount up to ¼ the meat to
> be used. Keep this stirring round as it thaws out. After the heat has cooked it
> to setting see that it is in fine state of division by pulverising with spoon, then
> add meat (finer cut better) in about equal amount with original blubber. Add
> pepper and salt if needed. Stir frequently for about 20 min. If biscuit can be
> spared it will greatly improve the dish if added in powdered form to about ¼
> dish or enough to take up the oil.
>
> Calf's kidney good but kidneys of grown-ups useless.[7]

In recalling his interview with Douglas for the position of assistant biologist on the AAE, Laseron remembered being surprised that the first question he was asked was not about his scientific qualifications but whether
or not he could cook. Douglas's students joked that they would only pass
geology if they succeeded in cooking a good Irish stew, which was one of
Douglas's specialties. As Oma explained to me, according to her father's
instructions, it was important that the meat went in first, followed by the
onions and finally the potatoes that weren't to be overdone. In actual fact,
on geology excursions, Douglas did most of the cooking, perhaps partly
to ensure there was no wastage of food for the real cooking test came
when there were limited supplies.

He associated being able to cook with imagination and resourcefulness. It wasn't about being a gourmet chef but about having an ability to
use one's head in terms of making the best out of what was available. This
was a potentially life-saving skill. On the return journey to the Hut with
Mertz, Douglas described half a tin of hoosh and cocoa and half a biscuit
as, 'a rattling good meal'.[8] Of course this was an indication of the extent
of his hunger. However, it was also his inventive preparation of the food
that made the meal enjoyable. Although he used the same ingredients as
the other two men on the BAE, something separated his cooking from
theirs and gave the men a sense of satisfaction, even if it was only an
illusion of satisfaction.

Some way into the journey to the Magnetic Pole, Professor David suffered an attack of snow blindness, severe enough for him to ask Douglas to take the lead in their trekking. He wrote: 'I asked Mawson to take my place at the end of the long rope, the foremost position in the team. Mawson proved himself so remarkably efficient at picking out the best track for our sledges, and steering a good course, that, at my request he occupied this position throughout the rest of the journey'.[9] Professor David praised Douglas's excellent navigational skills that were to prove a great advantage on the Far-Eastern Sledging Journey as he trudged on in thick snow and poor light with an unreliable compass.

The youngest of the BAE group, Douglas was often frustrated that the limitations of the other two men affected the progress of the whole party. He expressed his frustrations in almost every diary entry, which on first reading come across as petty and pedantic. On closer inspection one realises that the things he was complaining about, while ordinarily unimportant, were hugely important under the trying circumstances. Professor David was then fifty years old. He was a gentle, humble man with an excellent mind. A very popular and respected member of the expedition, Davis described him as having 'that rare gift of ennobling all he touched'.[10] He was not a silly old man but he almost turned into one on this journey. He became sloppy and careless in a situation where there was no room for error. He was five foot nine inches tall, slightly built and a little stooped and he struggled to keep up with the younger two men (Dr Mackay was thirty). Douglas noted that, 'The Prof is certainly a fine example of a man for his age—he does more than any other man of his age probably could—but he is a great drag on our progress'.[11] He recited poetry while Douglas and Dr Mackay did all the heavy pulling. He dodged packing the sledges and setting up camp. He spent an inordinate amount of time counting biscuits and dividing rations. He was extravagant with food, in so far as rations did not last as long as they were meant to, and he wasted cooking oil. He broke, lost and sat on things. The numerous layers of clothing he insisted on wearing continually hampered his progress and made him ill, as well as causing great discomfort to Douglas and Dr Mackay, who were forced to the edges of their three-man sleeping-bag when the professor squeezed himself in between them.

Professor David had inspired Douglas's interest in geology and it was through his influence that Douglas had gained a place on Shackleton's expedition. Douglas never forgot this. Before the BAE, in May, 1906, he had discovered a radioactive mineral in the north of South Australia which he called 'Davidite' after the Professor. Despite this, their friendship, which lasted until Professor David's death in 1934, was shaky at times. Yet, although he was very fit, an eminent scientist and a great man in his own right, Professor David was barely up to the rigours of man-hauling sledges over hundreds of miles across Antarctica. He almost didn't make it. When the three men finally made it to safety, Davis described Professor David hobbling on to the *Nimrod* with the aid of two sticks, 'ashen grey with fatigue'.[12]

While Douglas noted that Dr Mackay was good at basic manual labour, he observed that he was sometimes lazy and lacked skill. He concluded that, while he made a good soldier, Dr Mackay would never make a general. Had Douglas been forced to assign him into one of the four categories of men he outlined in his 1911–14 diaries, he would probably have described Dr Mackay as being somewhere between two and three, as a man who could work under supervision but who lacked initiative. Professor David was the leader of the party but when the strain got too much for him, he lost interest in the trek and became listless and morose and 'partially demented'. It was then that Douglas who *did* have the makings of a general, became the driving force in their journey.

Douglas was champing at the bit. If it were possible he would have dragged a sledge to the South Magnetic Pole and back single-handed. He proved later that he could do just that on the Far-Eastern Sledging Journey. Fiercely independent and self-reliant, it would have suited him much better to fight with the elements, to be up against nature rather than up against other men who could not always be relied upon and constantly dictated his pace. It is not surprising that he ended up in a position of leadership. He was versatile. There were very few things he couldn't turn his hand to. He could navigate. He could cook. He was broadly educated in the sciences. He was an excellent shot. He was unafraid of danger and unafraid of responsibility and he had the initiative to begin organising the AAE before he was even thirty years old.

As leader of the AAE, he possessed qualities that explain his survival, among them, a strong work ethic, a highly organised mind, self-confidence, self-motivation, self-sufficiency and self-discipline, qualities that he had revealed from a very young age. And as the originator and commander of the expedition, people were counting on his return, all the members of the expedition and all those who had supported it. He had written in his diary, as he lay in the tent with the dying Mertz, knowing that both their chances were going, 'I don't mind for myself, but it is for Paquita and for all others connected with the expedition that I feel so deeply and sinfully'.[13] This was a huge weight on his mind, a weight that probably anyone in a position of leadership feels. Certainly, the thought of the responsibility her dying husband must have felt, tormented Kathleen Scott. In the days following the news of his death, she wrote: 'How one hopes his brain soon got numbed and the horror of his responsibility left him, for I think never was there a man with such a sense of responsibility and duty…losing the other lives and leaving me uncared for must have been unspeakable'.[14] The deaths of his father and only brother, Archie, had left Scott with the sole responsibility of supporting his mother and his sisters. It was to this and to the families of his dead companions that he was referring when he wrote, 'For God's sake look after our people'.[15]

Interestingly, it seems that at no point on his journey did Douglas write anything that resembled a dying note. One person who was very much counting on his return was Paquita. Being as weak as he was, it was too exhausting to think beyond the moment. He needed to conserve his energy. All his thinking was channelled into the things that were going to help him to survive. It was neither helpful nor constructive to long for Paquita who was at the other end of the world and could not save him. Yet, while she was not in the forefront of his mind at the time, she was nevertheless a huge inspiration. Later, while recovering at the Hut, he wrote with reference to the Far-Eastern Sledging Journey, 'Don't imagine that, even then, you were not a daily visitor pushing your way in amongst the intricacies of my more immediate thoughts'.[16] In another, he admitted, 'My love for you and duty to you was the real incentive which finally availed in my reaching the hut'.[17]

Research has shown that testosterone levels reduce dramatically in men under extreme physical stress who are isolated from women. Thus sex was most likely the last thing on Douglas's mind at the time. He was cold and starving and the skin from his scrotum had come away but he wanted to fulfil his promise to marry Paquita, and a desire to consummate his love was very probably another motivating force. It was perhaps another of life's mysteries he had yet to discover. Of the thirty-seven men on the expedition, only two were married and Douglas and Madigan were the only ones engaged. A man without a woman to return to would perhaps not have fought so hard. (Incidentally, anticipation of meeting a woman is apparently enough to bring testosterone levels back to normal!)[18]

Douglas had boldly declared to his future father-in-law that he had not yet failed in anything he had undertaken. The Delprats were a prestigious and wealthy family and, in wanting to marry Paquita, Douglas was aiming high. He had confessed in his letter to GDD, who was at the time one of the highest paid men in Australia, that he had 'poor means' for supporting his daughter but that he had 'character' and 'honour', he was educated and he had good prospects for the future. In the absence of material wealth, it seems he was advocating that these personal attributes made him worthy of Paquita, bringing him up to her social standing. His letter had exuded the optimism, even the arrogance, of youth. Out there in the ice, he undoubtedly felt he owed it to GDD to fight, to prove that he deserved Paquita's love, and to live up to his promise that the 'dogged grit' he claimed he had inherited as a Mawson, would never forsake him while he was alive.

It was perhaps also very important to Douglas to succeed where his own father had not. By the time Douglas had moved to Adelaide in 1905, Robert Mawson was in New Guinea where he had bought three thousand acres that he planned to develop into a rubber plantation. However, he lacked the capital to fund it and, interestingly, had failed to convince Douglas to invest in this scheme.

While he inherited his father's adventurous spirit, Douglas was far more focused, more single-minded and much more ambitious. There is a sense that, apart from being dogged by bad luck, Robert had his finger in too many pies. When Douglas was on the Far-Eastern Sledging Journey, Robert Mawson lost his life to fever in New Guinea while mapping unknown parts of the country and trying to make scientific observations. At around the time he died, in fact on the very day that Douglas had begun his journey with Ninnis and Mertz, his father had come to him in a dream, which Douglas later interpreted as a premonition of his death. To suggest that Douglas thought of his father as a failure is unlikely but neither was he a great success. In fact, his mother, Margaret, set a better example. It was Margaret who was ambitious for her sons, encouraging them to gain a scientific profession, and I think this is also where Douglas got his determination to succeed.

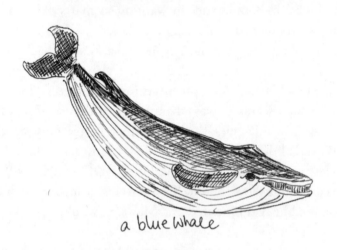

a blue whale

16

A Miraculous Return

Courage is to feel
The daily daggers of relentless steel
And keep on living.

Douglas Malloch (1877–1938), *Courage*, stanza 2

Eric Webb, chief magnetician at the Main Base, described Douglas
Mawson's survival as, 'the outstanding feat of any lone traveller in polar
history'.[1] When Mertz died on 8 January Douglas had traversed, with
Mertz and Ninnis, more than 200 miles of difficult terrain in the most
trying conditions. He was starving. His rations were down to eight ounces
a day, little more than half a tin of baked beans. The shock of Ninnis's
death, the tragedy and anguish of Mertz's end and the killing and eating
of the dogs, had upset his mental equilibrium. And now he was alone,
his chances of survival much reduced. He was to write later, in a letter of
condolence to Mertz's mother, '…nothing was more detrimental to my
prospects of safe return than Mertz's death, it practically eliminated my
last hope of reaching the hut'.[2]

The first thing that had struck him, when Mertz died, was the fact that
he was utterly alone. Even when venturing just a few yards from the Hut
in the months preceding this journey, he had momentarily experienced
a sense of isolation. 'One might be a lone soul standing in Precambrian

times or on Mars', he wrote, '…all is desolation…Life opens up to one as it must to the savage'.[3] In the words of Laseron, loneliness in Antarctica, 'weighs like a giant pall' and, even in company, there is 'an ever-present feeling of a hostile presence, hovering and waiting for a chance to strike' and that, 'one had the impression of fighting, always fighting, a terrible unseen force'.[4] Even the hideous sound of the huskies howling with hunger and the ranting of Mertz in his last hours were signs of life. Once Douglas was alone, it was just the incessant moaning of the wind, the crunch of snow under his feet, the thud of his emaciated body hitting the ice as he slipped and stumbled his way through a maze of crevasses. Even when Mertz died, his body, toggled up in the sleeping-bag beside him, had offered some sense of companionship.

Psychologically, the isolation was hard to endure alone. Apart from everything else, the monotonous landscape was so depressing. Even in the Arctic there is some vegetation but in mainland Antarctica there is nothing but ice. For Douglas there were no landmarks to aspire towards and half the time the snow was so dense that he couldn't see more than a few feet in front of him. Added to this, his cyclometer, a wheel attached to the end of his sledge, which measured the distance covered, critical for navigational purposes if he was to find his way back to the Main Base, frequently jammed with snow, rendering it impossible to calculate, precisely, how far he had travelled.

In his letter of condolence later written to Mertz's mother in which he described Mertz's death as 'detrimental' to his own survival, he was referring, in part, to the difficulty of breaking and pitching camp single-handed, remembering, of course, that he had lost much of his strength. When Mertz died, together with thick drift and falling snow, the wind was blowing at about fifty miles an hour (the average wind velocity for Europe, which has the highest average wind velocity of any other continent, bar Antarctica, is around ten miles an hour). Laseron devoted more than a page to the importance of tents in Antarctica in his account of the expedition, *South with Mawson*. A wind blowing at fifty miles per hour is defined as being somewhere between a strong gale and a whole gale according to the Beaufort Scale*, the classification of winds Douglas used in *The Home of the Blizzard*.

Laseron claimed that, in a stiff gale (and a wind of fifty miles per hour well and truly qualifies as this), erecting a tent required 'the united efforts of three men'. Over the winter and spring of 1912, the men had all practised mastering the necessary technique of erecting their conical-shaped tents and it was quite a complicated process and very difficult in the appalling weather. Laseron explained:

> ...first enough large blocks of ice or hard snow were cut, and placed handy; then the tent was laid down with the apex upwind, and the entrance on top, so that it would be in the lee when the tent was raised; next one man crawled inside and, with the other two hanging on, the tent was lifted, and the man inside spread the three windward legs, one directly upwind, the others far enough apart to keep the material taut, and at the same time give sufficient room for the leeward legs to fall into position. This required a considerable knack as the wind the whole time would be tearing at the structure...[5]

Upon reading this, one appreciates how difficult it must have been for Douglas with no one to help him and without proper tent poles, lost in the crevasse with Ninnis. Fortunately he and Mertz had retrieved an old worn tent cover but they had had to improvise a frame by using the theodolite legs, which were much more difficult to work with considering that normally the poles were sewn into the canvas. (This idea, of sewing the poles in, had occurred to the men over the winter of 1912 after discovering the difficulty of erecting a tent in Adélie Land conditions.) In fact, the day after Mertz died Douglas estimated the wind was blowing at about forty-five to fifty miles per hour and he didn't dare take the tent down for fear of not being able to get it up again by himself. On another occasion, he wrote that, had it not been for the 'delightful evening', he

---

* The Beaufort Scale was named after Sir Francis Beaufort (1774–1857), a British Admiral and Naval Hydrographer who devised, in his private journal, while surveying Montevideo on board the *Woolich*, a scale of numbers from 0 to 12 to denote wind force. The scale, which is still evolving, was officially adopted by the Admiralty in 1838. According to the modern Beaufort Scale of 1906, 4 is classified as 'a moderate breeze' accompanied by the description 'raises dust and loose paper; small branches are moved'. Beaufort also devised a system of letters by which to record weather conditions. For example, 'g' stood for 'gloomy dark weather', 'd' for 'drizzling rain', 'u' for 'ugly threatening appearances'.

would not have found the strength to pitch camp. He sometimes took three hours to erect the tent, which had to be erected every time he took a meal break because the primus stove would not light in the open. Such was the effort required to erect it that he and Mertz had only once set the tent up for lunch. Almost every day, he faced thick falling snow, which severely limited his vision, and winds of up to seventy miles an hour, the velocity of which rates 11 on the Beaufort Scale. (Defined as 'a storm', superseded only by a hurricane, it is described on the scale as 'very rarely experienced; accompanied by widespread damage'.)[6] During the previous spring he had noted in his diary that Ninnis and Mertz took stores to one of the three caves they had built as shelters but could only pull a load of forty pounds as the wind was blowing at fifty-five miles per hour.

In order to better understand the enormous effort it required for Douglas to make a successful return, Eric Webb wrote, 'We have to remember that he had already spent a whole winter in the base hut under the most blistering gales ever experienced by men'[7], these gales being, incidentally, much fiercer than any experienced on the BAE. The wind, usually accompanied by thick, drifting snow, was relentless. It was not for nothing', wrote Davis in *High Latitude*, 'that Mawson subsequently named his book on the work of the expedition *The Home of the Blizzard*.[8] Winter descended upon them, as Davis so colourfully described it, 'with the shriek of a thousand angry witches'.[9] In November 1912, in his last letter to Paquita before setting off with Ninnis and Mertz, after ten months of almost constant hurricanes, he had admitted, in his usual understated way, to finding Adélie Land, 'terribly disappointing'[10]. Soon after landing at Commonwealth Bay in 1911 they had discovered they were in the centre of an area which was the windiest place on earth and they immediately realised the necessity of modifying and improving their equipment to suit it. Ordinary crampons proved 'unserviceable'.[11] Swiss crampons with spikes of an inch and a half were the only ones that gave enough grip. The light drill tents that Scott and Shackleton used on their expeditions in the Ross Sea region were promptly ripped to shreds in the Adélie winds. Madigan, Whetter and Close were forced to make a thirteen-mile dash for safety when their tent was torn to pieces during a reconnaissance journey. Minutes after two of the men had erected a metal depot flag in preparation for the summer sledging journeys, it was completely destroyed. After this they resorted to tents made of japara* sail cloth which was much stronger**.

The katabatic wind was almost unceasing and it dictated their lives and dominated their conversation. They grew so used to it that on the rare occasions that it stopped, the sudden eerie silence sometimes woke them in the night, the echo of it still ringing in their ears. Privately Douglas worried that the wind would totally ruin his hopes for the expedition. Even in the height of summer, 'the climate proved to be little more than one continuous blizzard'.[12] Davis later observed that the violent conditions were 'local in character' and did not generally extend more than fifty miles offshore. Based on this observation, he concluded that, 'Commonwealth Bay and its immediate vicinity form the narrow end of a gigantic funnel and that down this funnel rushed the cold air of the polar plateau.'[13] He deduced that gales and hurricanes resulted when this cold air met with the warmer air on the coast.

Throughout most of the winter and spring, when Douglas and his men were preparing for their summer sledging journeys, the wind had varied from full gale to hurricane force on the Beaufort Scale. They had held sweeps, bidding with chocolate and squares of cake, on the hourly wind velocity for each month, which averaged fifty miles and occasionally even reached speeds of more than 200 miles per hour. This was extraordinary, even by Antarctic standards. In the same year, 1912, an average of twenty-one miles an hour was recorded at Cape Evans where Scott was based. The winds experienced at Cape Denison would flatten any city. For instance, in 2004 'Hurricane Jeanette', which ripped through West Palm Beach on the coast of Florida, reached gusts of 100 miles an hour (not uncommon in Adélie Land), destroying thousands of buildings and tearing out power lines, leaving more than two million homes without power. The same hurricane earlier hit Haiti, killing more than 1600 people.

In Antarctica in 1912 the roof of the Hut bent inwards under the pressure of the wind and only remained standing because it was almost completely buried in snow. The windows were blocked by a sheet of ice five inches thick. The only means of entry and exit was through the roof.

---

* a waterproof cotton used for making tents and oilskins.
** The tents, conical in shape, were at least eight feet high when fully erected, which made them vulnerable to the wind, and the noise of the flapping canvas would have been deafening.

It is more than likely that the wind would have hurtled in and torn off the roof had they been able to open the door. Douglas had confided to his diary, 'We have discussed the possibility of our roof blowing outwards...' but fortunately this did not happen. Any other hut, in Douglas's opinion, would not have withstood the Adélie winds. 'It is impossible to over-estimate the importance of having devised so strong a hut', he wrote. 'Imagine the awful end of any other expedition having come to this spot with the huts provided them. Or even of a ship frozen in the pack off here. Imagine a hut with all in it suddenly blown away into the sea'.[14] In fact, the Hut was so well-designed and so well-built with its pyramid-shaped roof and strong timber that it still stands today, almost 100 years later.

Within a minute of stepping outside the Hut an ice-mask formed around the face, the violence of the wind took one's breath away and Douglas wrote that he was quite sure that anybody who has experienced it for a few minutes would, 'gladly exchange it for hell and chance his luck'.[15] The men had to crawl on hands and knees as they couldn't stand upright unless they had mastered what they called 'hurricane-walking', which involved leaning at an angle and putting one's feet against rocks and ice for support. To master it Douglas wrote, was, 'an accomplishment comparable to skating or skiing'.[16] The electrical effects that accompa-nied the storms were such that rocks, the corners of boxes, the edges of helmets and the ends of mitts glowed with a pale blue light that sometimes induced an electric shock. In a hurricane the sea, was 'literally swept off in a blinding sheet of spray, so that it was impossible to tell where water ended and air began'.[17] The 'awe-inspiring waves',[18] were carried up to 300 feet into the air like small waterspouts and froze the instant they hit the shore. Some fish traps, the whale boat and a sledge were blown away across the frozen sea.

Added to the wind, there was the cold. The temperature can drop to -51° C below freezing. Even in the Hut, where a stove was kept going day and night, they struggled to keep the temperature above freezing point. Douglas and his men were kept busy stuffing paper and cloth into all the cracks and crevices through which the snow continually drifted. They slept with just their noses peeping out of their sleeping-bags. In winter, a layer of ice formed on their bedding and their mattresses froze to the walls. Everything liquid, except petrol, turned to ice, including writing ink. It took hours to extract the evening meal from the store, a natural freezer under the veranda. As Douglas observed, 'several crowbars were bent on the mutton'.[19] The tide gauge clocks and other measuring instruments stopped working in very low temperatures and had to be dried in the oven and oiled with chronometer oil*. Outside the dogs froze to the ground and whined piteously because they couldn't move. An ice-axe was needed to set them free.

Three of Scott's men, Edward 'Birdie' Bowers, Edward Wilson and Apsley Cherry-Garrard, had experienced the coldest temperatures imaginable when, in June 1910, they had embarked on a winter sledging journey to an Emperor penguin rookery at Cape Crozier to collect eggs in incubation (they are laid in the winter) with the aim of discovering a link between penguins and dinosaurs. They probably only survived because the journey was short by sledging standards. Temperatures dropped to -60° C. Their clothes froze into straitjackets. So glorious was the effect of drinking something warm in those climes that Wilson described it to be, 'like putting a hot-water bottle against your heart'.[20]

Douglas had not even contemplated a sledging journey in winter. With the winds as they were at Cape Denison, it would have been suicide. It was necessary to venture outside on a daily basis, at least for the meteorologist, Madigan, who took regular readings from the Magnetograph House, which was some distance from the Hut. Whetter (surgeon) and Close (assistant collector) were the two in charge of collecting ice every day for the kitchen. Men got lost at one time or another for up to two hours when just yards from the Hut.

On the whole of the main continent the temperature never rises above freezing point in winter. It is never warm enough for rain during this intense season. The snow that has fallen over the centuries has covered the land with a thick sheet of ice that literally covers mountains, creating an average elevation of 2300 metres. It is the highest continent, more than three times higher than North America, the second-highest, and this is one of the reasons why it is so cold. While the site of Douglas's Hut was barely above sea level, it is vulnerable to the winds from the plateau.

---

* Today the inside temperature is kept at around 18° C at the stations in Antarctica where people live and work all year round. This means that inside ordinary clothes can be worn, such as t-shirts and jeans.

In the months leading up to the summer of 1912, Douglas and his men had soon realised they would get nothing done at all if they waited for a good day but the weather posed all sorts of problems. For the photographer, Frank Hurley, negatives froze in their solutions. His camera sometimes filled with ice and it was a constant battle to prevent his fingers from becoming frostbitten and to find a moment of calm to erect the tripod. For the scientists, dredging for sea specimens was a frustrating business. If they froze on the way back to the Hut, delicate organisms were destroyed. Collecting became impossible when the winter set in and the sea floor turned to ice. When Douglas plunged into the sea to retrieve a case of food that had fallen into about six feet of water, even as he hurried to the Hut to dry himself, ice was forming on his body.

Apsley Cherry-Garrard, a member of the 1910–12 Scott expedition, wrote that going to the Antarctic was 'the only form of adventure in which you put on your clothes at Michaelmas and keep them on until Christmas...'.[21] Like all polar explorers, when sledging, Douglas and his men wore the same clothes day and night for weeks on end. It was simply too cold to undress and it was a waste of energy. In the Hut washing was kept to a minimum. No one shaved and each man had a bath every eighteen days in a folding canvas arrangement. This was mainly because water, as opposed to its frozen state of ice, was such a precious commodity and was not easily procured.* It took a long time to fill a box with ice, which would then have to be melted, using precious energy. The wind and the hindrance of gloves made swinging the pick with any degree of accuracy almost impossible and even then, often the chips were small and were swept away before they could be caught. At other times, a half-full box of ice was wrenched out of the collector's hands and blown out to sea.

When Douglas, Mackay and Professor David were rescued by the *Nimrod* in February, 1909, they had not washed or changed their clothes for four months and their stench was overwhelming. In 1916, a few years after the AAE, when Shackleton, Worsley and Crean arrived at the whaling station after their epic crossing of South Georgia, their beards were long,

---

* Even today in Antarctica, obtaining water is difficult and time-consuming. Ice has to be collected and then melted down. The people living at the stations are restricted to three-minute showers and can only shower every three days when supplies are short.

their hair matted and they were in clothes they had not changed for a year. The first man they saw ran off in fright!

Evidently, in polar conditions at that time, men sometimes didn't even undo their trousers when they needed to go to the toilet. They just did it as they walked along and it froze on its way out. In blizzards they made a latrine inside the tent so that they didn't have to venture outside. Tim Jarvis, who wrote *The Unforgiving Minute*, about his Arctic and Antarctic adventures, said that, 'How do you go to the toilet?' is a question he is often asked. His stock answer is 'quickly'.

Douglas had noted that by March of 1912, eight months before he set off with Ninnis and Mertz, that there were very few animals around. 'Seals suddenly became very scarce' he wrote, 'no doubt disgusted by the continuous winds'.[22] The Antarctic is a harsh environment for any animal. The Weddell seal, unlike other sea animals, doesn't return to the open sea in the winter. Instead it swims around in warmer waters below the ice but as a mammal it has to come up for air. It makes breathing holes by breaking through the frozen surface of the sea. They suffocate to death when they lose their strength and teeth in old age and can no longer bite through the ice. Emperor penguin eggs freeze in less than two minutes if they roll out from underneath the fold of feathers and skin above the adults' feet. Their hatching season takes place in the winter months where temperatures drop as low as ninety degrees of frost. The male stands on the ice for three months withstanding blizzards to protect their eggs. They are the only Antarctic animals that don't migrate for the winter. I am inclined to agree with Cherry-Garrard, that no one on earth has a worse time than an Emperor penguin. In Adélie Land, where Douglas was based, there were no permanent inhabitants as Emperor penguins rarely visit this part of the coast, a fact Douglas put down to the impossible winds. The smaller Adélie penguin is a common sight but it stays on the continent for a bare six months of the year before migrating onto the pack-ice.

an Adelie on its belly

17

Providence

Count your blessings, name
them one by one,
Count your blessings, see what God
hath done!
Count your blessings, name
them one by one,
And it will surprise you what the Lord hath done.

Hymn: 'Count Your Blessings', words by Johnson Oatman, Junior, and
music by Edwin O Excell, 1897

Extreme cold can be life-threatening for many reasons, not least of all because it debilitates movement. Ten days after Mertz died, Douglas nearly lost his life in a crevasse. If he had hesitated too long the cold that was fast chilling his fingers would have made it impossible for him to pull himself up the rope to solid ground. He was blundering blindly through dangerous terrain in poor light and falling snow when he suddenly fell and found himself swinging freely on the end of a fourteen-foot rope. In describing this scene in his diary, he wrote, '...I was dangling on end of rope in crevasse, sledge creeping to mouth. I had time to say to myself "So this is the end", expecting every moment the sledge to crash on my head and both of us to go to the bottom unseen below'.[1]

He had often wondered when the end would come and how it would come and it was a relief to now know. Yet, miraculously, the sledge held fast in the snow above him. It was his closest encounter with death and it was a turning point. His life was, for the first time, seriously threatened; he had to make a conscious and a spontaneous decision to live. It was tempting to end it all. There was a knife in his pocket within easy reach. He could cut the rope and it would all be over in an instant or he could simply wriggle out of the harness. For a moment, the thought of what lay beyond almost excited him. It was a temptation he so very nearly yielded to. Upon learning of Scott's death a few weeks later, he wrote to Scott's wife, Kathleen, and confessed, 'My own case has enlightened me in the secret feelings of the soul, the willingness to pass into oblivion…'.[2]

In pulling himself out of that crevasse, Douglas chose life but it was a Herculean effort and more than once he fell back at least half the length of the rope. Because it had been a warm day, he had taken off his outer clothing, and, added to this, the clothes he *was* wearing filled with snow when he fell. Fourteen feet is a long way up, higher than the average ceiling, and his fingers were badly frostbitten, the nails blackened and falling away. He told an audience at a lecture in America two years later that it had taken him four and a half hours to climb out.[3] This is a remarkable feat considering how weak he was by this stage of the journey and given that muscles cool down very quickly in the cold, making any movement slow and difficult. Stroud discovered upon his return to England after his trek across Antarctica with Fiennes in 1992, that he had lost so much muscle mass that he could not climb stairs without holding onto the banisters and could not even lift his small children. Stroud concluded that, 'the internal structure and mechanisms of our muscles had literally been burned in order to survive'.[4]

One thing that spurred Douglas on to fight was the thought of all the food that lay on the snow above him, the food he had so carefully rationed and he couldn't bear to think of it lying uneaten. Had he known he was going to die, he would have had a feast. He also feared that he wouldn't be killed outright but suffer a broken leg and be worse off than before. Although he and Mertz had felt comforted in the knowledge that Ninnis had met an instant death, there was no way of knowing the particulars of his last moments in that abyss.

Perhaps even more interesting was his faith in Providence. Many explorers attributed good fortune and the things they could not explain, to what they called Providence. A few years after the AAE, following the sinking of his ship, *Endurance*, Shackleton and a select party sailed 800 miles from Elephant Island to seek help. They landed on South Georgia where they knew there was a whaling station. However, the station was on the opposite side of the island to where they landed and they had to cross a mountain range to get to it. Shackleton took two men with him but, he later said, he felt a fourth person beside them, whom he associated with Providence, helping them on their journey. TS Eliot made reference to Shackleton's experience in *The Waste Land*, though he wrote of a third man and not a fourth:

> Who is the third who walks always beside you
> When I count, there are only you and I together
> But when I look up the white road
> There is always another one walking beside you
> Gliding wrapt in a brown mantle, hooded
> I do not know whether a man or a woman
> —But who is that on the other side of you?[5]

Douglas mentioned Providence many times in his diary and attributed his luck up to that moment to some higher being that was helping him through. In both his first two letters to Paquita, at the beginning of the expedition, he had thanked Providence for, 'coming through at the eleventh hour'[6] during their voyage and saving the ship from destruction. It explained every bit of good fortune on the sledging journey. His luck had begun on 14 December when Ninnis was swallowed by the crevasse that theoretically should have taken him. On several later occasions he attributed Providence as having saved him from falling into crevasses when he could not see where he was going. It had helped him out of the crevasse that had almost claimed him. That his sledge didn't fall down on him, was, he believed, Providence giving him another chance. The fact that he couldn't recall how he had managed to get out and couldn't remember anything until he found himself sprawled on the snow led him to believe that something had assisted him, something other than his own bodily strength. When the days were calm and when the sun came out, it was Providence smiling on him.

Eric Webb claimed that Mawson had told him that, 'there was some other power he had borrowed on that journey which was superior to the willpower that pulled him through'.[7] In fact, he carried a Bible on this journey and it comforted him to read passages from it. Douglas wasn't religious in the ordinary sense of the word. He once kept his daughters at home from school and wrote a letter to the head mistress explaining that they were studying at home because he did not agree that so many hours of the week should be devoted to religious studies. Yet, he certainly approved of the church. He paid pew rent at his local church, St Jude's in Brighton and, although the Mawsons hardly ever went as a family, he upheld the notion that something had made this world.

Douglas's commitment to science was not contradicted by his private sense of a God. Oma studied first-year geology under her father. She remembered that, in his geology lectures at the University of Adelaide, he acknowledged that a superior power had created the earth and, that the description of the creation in Genesis made sense scientifically, in terms of the sequence in which things were made. Darkness was followed by light, the seas were formed before the land, plants preceded animals. The specifics of his beliefs were vague but his faith in Providence was a tremendous help on this journey. In fact, it was hugely significant in that he more or less believed that the intervention of a benevolent presence was the main, if not the sole reason, for his ultimate survival. On 8 February, the day on which he staggered towards the Hut and to safety, he wrote in his diary, 'What a feeling of gratitude to Providence for such a deliverance.'[8] Some time later he said, 'How I reached the hut I do not know. I was delirious.'[9]

Although Paquita did not call it Providence (she was a self-proclaimed agnostic), she was convinced Douglas was meant to survive when she heard of his safe return. 'A life is not spared like that for nothing',[10] she wrote from Adelaide while he was recovering at the Hut. In fact, Douglas's survival has been described as a miracle and really it was when one considers the number of coincidences that contributed to his successful return.

His was the only party to take dogs and without them he would certainly have perished. Ginger (as distinct from Ginger Bitch who went down the crevasse with Ninnis) ran away during their journey and later returned to them and she was to prove the best at pulling, outlasted all the other dogs and subsequently became a vital addition to their food supply. Douglas traversed terrain peppered with crevasses as it was the shortest route back, and, despite falling into one on more than one occasion, his sledge held his weight and he was able to haul himself to the surface. The first time this happened, Douglas wrote, 'Never have I come so near to an end; never has anyone more miraculously escaped'.[11] Even with an unreliable compass and stumbling through a maze of serac* ice with no light, he managed to find his way back.

On 29 January, during his last days alone, he stumbled upon a food cairn left by three of the expeditioners. At the time he had only two pounds of food left, which amounts to about two and a half cans of baked beans. He was then about twenty-six miles from the Hut, an easy run for a fit man but a long way for a man in Douglas's condition. For several days leading up to the discovery of the food cairn he had been averaging three to four miles a day, the weather having greatly hampered his progress. It is possible that the appearance of the food cairn at this particular moment saved his life. If he thought he had a strong chance of reaching safety by that stage, the food virtually guaranteed his survival. He wrote, 'As I left the depot there appeared to be nothing on earth that could prevent me reaching the Hut within a couple of days'.[12]

It was an extraordinary stroke of good luck as he realised that, 'a few hundred yards to either side and it would have been lost to sight in the drift'.[13] Laseron was amazed that Douglas found it and later wrote, 'To appreciate the one chance in a thousand that had led his steps to this spot, it might be likened to finding a buoy in a fog at sea when even its existence was unsuspected'.[14] Bage's party had missed a food depot on their return journey from attempting to attain the South Magnetic Pole, which they didn't quite reach. Forced to turn back when a little more than 100 miles from the point Douglas, Dr Mackay and Professor David had reached on Shackleton's expedition a few years before, due to

---

* a field of broken, ridged or pinnacled glacier ice

shortage of rations, they failed to find a depot containing five days' food. They spent two days looking for it until they had to concede defeat. The flag and mound had obviously been covered over by drift snow. They marched fifty-seven miles on just one day's ration.

The colour-coded calico food bags that Paquita and her mother had sewed for the expedition were bright red, orange and yellow as Paquita had the idea that this would cheer the men up in their world of white. When Douglas reached the cairn, inside it he found a red Paquita bag and it was a wonderful reminder of her love.

With the food was a note from Hurley, Hodgeman (cartographer and artist) and McLean, telling Douglas that they had deposited it that very morning and that Aladdin's Cave was only twenty-one miles away. Douglas had excavated Aladdin's Cave out of the ice the previous year with Madigan and Ninnis because, he thought, 'this will save us a lot of wear and tear on tents and be of advantage in other ways'.[15] They had named it Aladdin's Cave because it was 'a truly magical cave'. The walls sparkled like diamonds just as in the story, Aladdin's palace shone with rich jewels. The sound of the roaring wind was completely blocked out. Douglas arrived at the cave two days after finding the cairn. It saved him from having to erect the tent, and without the continual flapping of the canvas, he was able to sleep in peace after more than ninety days out on the plateau.

A blizzard blew continuously for a week, which prevented him from moving. It was an agonising few days, which he spent constructing crampons out of a dog harness and benzine cases to get him across the five miles of slippery ice that led back to the Hut. (He had earlier abandoned his finnesko crampons to lighten his load in preparation for a climb of 3000 feet out of the Mertz Glacier.) In describing these last days in *The Home of the Blizzard*, Douglas wrote: 'Think of my feelings as I sat within the cave, so near and yet so far from the Hut, impatient and anxious, ready to spring out and take the trail at a moment's notice…I tried the makeshift crampons on the ice outside, but was disappointed to find that they had not sufficient grip to face the wind, so had to abandon the idea of attempting the descent during the continuance of the blizzard'.[16]

Given that 'ordinary crampons' were useless in this part of Antarctica, it is easy to imagine the impossibility of trying to walk, in the midst of

Douglas's half-sledge on return from the Far-Eastern Sledging Journey, now on permanent
display in the Mawson exhibition at the South Australian Museum
(*Mawson Collection, South Australian Museum*)

a fierce blizzard, with home-made ones that pinched his feet, the nails
driving up into his soles. Yet, despite this perfectly acceptable reason for
his delay in returning to the Hut, it is nevertheless tempting to ask, albeit
from the comfort of my living room almost 100 years into the future
with zero experience of Antarctica, why a man, who had just completed
a six-hundred-mile round trip in the most appalling conditions, couldn't
manage a measly five miles that meant so much. Fresh fruit in the cave,
a pineapple and some oranges, was an indication that the *Aurora* had
returned. If Douglas could get back to the ship in time, he could go
home to civilization and to Paquita but the ship would not wait forever.
Taking everything into account, not least of all his aversion to inaction
and the fact that he could hardly be accused of cowardice or weakness, in
all probability he would have made this final dash earlier had it been at

all possible. He was alive. He had food and shelter. It wasn't worth risking his life unnecessarily. It would have been terrible, pathetic even, for a man who had so carefully negotiated his way back to safety, to rush out into the storm in a reckless dash for safety only to die, like a fool, a few miles from the Hut. And when that few miles was all that he had achieved on some days, the distance was still considerable for him, even after resting and supplementing his rations with those left at the cave. Rather, waiting for the blizzard to subside was entirely in keeping with his character, so too, busying himself in fashioning two pairs of crampons from some found at the cave, one as an emergency pair, and fitting his sledge with 'a patent anti-crevasse bar'.[17]

The *Aurora* had crept into Commonwealth Bay on 14 January having lost her best anchor in a gale the day before. Some of the crew had gone ashore in the launch and discovered that half the men of the Main Base had returned from sledging and that there were still nine men out on the plateau. The previous year the six parties had agreed to be back at the Hut by 15 January. All had returned by 18 January, except Douglas's. The last to trudge in was Bickerton's Western Party and, seeing them approaching from a distance, a worried Davis, in charge as second-in-command of the expedition, felt relieved when someone mentioned sighting dogs. It turned out to be a mirage. His anxiety increased when the Far-Eastern Party was a week overdue. Ironically, Davis did not imagine the 'doctor', by whom he meant Douglas, was starving; 'He has plenty of grub, that is a great comfort',[18] he wrote. He was closer to the truth than he realised when he wondered if the cause of the delay was because one of the men had 'met with an accident'.[19] Oddly, he didn't think of crevasses given that they were a constant threat to the men's safety. Men had frequently fallen down them on all of the sledging journeys and there had been many close calls. On average, Douglas fell down a crevasse every third or fourth day during the final month alone. Madigan fell eight times in the space of four miles when re-crossing a glacier that was subsequently named the Mertz Glacier, which Douglas had also crossed on his return, once even dropping twenty-four feet down a crevasse. In the light of this, it is a wonder that throughout the expedition, only one man fell to his death and none on other expeditions in the Heroic Age.

On 29 January, a period of bad weather had passed and Davis sailed along the coast in search of the missing party following instructions left by Douglas in the Hut. He did so again the following day, the day that Douglas reached Aladdin's Cave. This was not the first time that Davis had attempted to rescue Douglas from Antarctica. Four years before it was Davis's ingenuity on the BAE that had saved Douglas, Professor David and Dr Mackay from the Drygalski Ice Tongue on another part of the coast. Only a day late and within sight of the spot at which they were to meet the ship, Douglas and his companions took three days to walk around an ice ravine that stood in their way. Convinced that an inlet lay hidden behind a group of icebergs he had seen during a blizzard, Davis had managed to persuade the less than pleased Captain Frederick Pryce Evans, to return to the Ice Tongue by which time they were low on coal and on the verge of abandoning their search. There they found the three exhausted men who had covered 1260 miles in 122 days. Ironically, had they been able to see the depot when they had passed the area the first time, the crew of the *Nimrod* would not have seen the men who were then engaged in getting around the ravine that barred their way to the coast.

In February 1913, Davis held out little hope of another happy ending. Even as he steamed along firing distress signals and flying a huge kite, he felt certain that the party would not have had a hope of reaching the coast due to the heavily crevassed land leading to the sea and the steep ice cliffs. In his pencilled instructions, Douglas had suggested a point along the coast where they might meet in the event of his party not reaching the Hut but they passed it without seeing a flag or any sign of him. Those who kept watch from the Hut had agreed, in the event of Douglas's return, to fly the Union Jack from the wireless mast, which had finally been erected during the days of waiting for the return of Douglas and his party. However, the bare mast seen from those on board the *Aurora* only compounded their fears for their leader's safety. 'What can we do to help him?' asked Davis. 'God help a man adrift in this cursed country…'.[20]

The increasing hours of darkness, the heavy drift, the icebergs that had started to drift into the bay were all signs of the approaching winter. Strong gales made the *Aurora* almost unmanageable. The barometer was registering wildly. The ship was burning tonnes of coal a day. Hard flakes of driving snow flew into Davis's eyes and made them sting. An anxious Davis knew that it was imperative they leave for Wild's base as soon as possible. 'From the accounts of the gales here in March', he confided to his diary, 'it seems we should certainly have great difficulty in getting back, and I am a bit afraid that we might get caught in one of them in the darkness and ice and lose the ship and all hands'.[21] One evening, he walked out on to the plateau, little knowing that Douglas was then only forty miles away, and looked to the south over the icy slope and wished he could march out there himself and find out where the Far-Eastern Party was. The scene of desolation did little to relieve his anxiety. 'From less than a mile, the Winter Quarters looked like a heap of stones' he wrote. 'All around to the Southward, the boundless ice sloping up to the sky line, dreary beyond description. To the North, the dark water broken by the snow, or rather ice, covered Mackellar Islands and a berg here and there on the horizon…On a fine day it looks beautiful and little shows what a terrible vast solitude it is, reaching back to the other side of the world, and constantly swept by violent winds and drift.'[22]

On 8 February the weather cleared. Ironically, both Davis and Douglas saw it as an opportunity to make tracks, unfortunately in different directions, departing for their different destinations within an hour of each other. Just before noon, Captain Davis sailed out of Commonwealth Bay bound for Wild's Party at the Western Base. At 1 pm, five miles inland, Douglas emerged from Aladdin's Cave and began making his way to the Hut on his improvised crampons. He could not have left earlier because the wind, which had already subsided on the coast, was still howling where he was, high on the plateau.

When a mile from the Hut, his heart sank because he could see that the *Aurora* was not in the harbour and his eye caught a speck that looked like a ship on the horizon and he knew then that this meant another year in Antarctica and another year without Paquita. He must surely have thought back to the Shackleton expedition only four years before when he had been saved by Davis and of how it had been a much happier ending. He was sitting in the tent with Professor David and Dr Mackay when he heard a shot. It was the *Nimrod* come to rescue them. He had flown out of the tent and seen its bow peeping out from around the inlet. Professor David described the experience to be like passing from death into life.[23] This time, however, there was no ship and instead of three survivors, there was only one and he wasn't going home.

18

A Shadow of Himself

Could ye come back to me, Douglas,
Douglas!
In the old likeness that I knew
I would be so faithful, so loving,
Douglas,
Douglas, Douglas, tender and true

From *Too late* by Dinah Maria Craik (1826–1887)

While Douglas was making his way to the Hut, slipping and sliding on his improvised crampons, unsteady on his legs after a week of refuge in the cave, Paquita was in Italy, soon to sail back to Australia. The four letters she had forwarded to Douglas, written in Europe between February and October of 1912 were by then at the Hut, having been delivered by Davis. In all of them she expressed her excitement at the prospect of seeing him again. 'You will have a warm welcome on your return', she assured him. 'My arms are open for you already as I think of it…Don't I long for the first quiet hours together. I make no promises to meet you as I can only answer for myself & not my family on whom it depends. But my heart will be there if not in flesh in spirit'.[1] Throughout 1912 she had been busy collecting things for their home—pewter, old Dutch brass, silver spoons, bed linen and table linen. Her family had been angelic; her sisters were all 'ducks'. They had all tried to make up for his absence but, she confessed, 'I had no idea I should miss you like this'. 'Don't go and stay away another year! You're under contract to return less than a year from now' she had joked.[2]

Naturally, the possibility that something might go wrong had crossed her mind. 'If only nothing is happening to you but I think I should feel it'[3], she had written in her first letter from Europe in February 1912. It was a fear she partly attributed to having too much time to think about him. 'When I start studying again it will be better' she added. (In The Hague she had studied French and German and continued singing lessons and playing the piano.) In her second letter, a few months later, she revealed that the fear for his safety never entirely left her: 'I am thinking of you hard every night & wondering whether you are hungry or cold or lonely…mother is an angel & whenever I feel worried about your wellbeing tells me earnestly she would feel it if anything was wrong with you'.[4] With the recent sinking of the *Titanic* and the outbreak of the first Balkan War, Paquita had consoled herself by reasoning that he was safer in the Antarctic than anywhere else. She knew, at the end of 1911, when Douglas was on his way to Adélie Land, that Amundsen had reached the South Pole. She calculated, in May 1912, that Scott would return at 'about the same time' as Douglas, and anticipated the Englishman's disappointment at not being first to the Pole. She did not then know of Scott's death but, curiously, something had compelled her to write, 'How thankful we are that you aren't bound for there'.[5]

Initially, Paquita had little concept of the kinds of dangers Douglas would be up against in Antarctica, particularly given that, in 1911, he had set off for an unknown part of the continent. In some ways Adélie Land was more perilous than where Scott was in that it was riddled with glaciers but even then, neither Davis, nor any of the men at the Hut, had guessed what had happened to the Far-Eastern Sledging Party. It is unlikely Paquita had thought to consider the particulars of crevasses—how numerous or how big they were; what the odds were of getting out alive if one fell down one and what the chances were of falling down one in the first place. She knew of two incidents involving crevasses that occurred on the BAE. Both had been translated into funny stories she repeated years later at dinner parties and in *Mawson of the Antarctic*.

The first involved Professor David. One day, on the journey to the South Magnetic Pole in 1908, Douglas was changing photographic plates in his sleeping-bag (it was the darkest and warmest place in which to do this), when he heard Professor David calling him. The Professor was painfully polite. 'Mawson, are you busy?' he called timidly from somewhere outside. Douglas replied that he was. Before long the Professor called out again and received the same reply. Minutes passed, after which he again called out, this time adding that he was hanging over a crevasse. He was sorry to be a bother but he didn't think he could hold on for much longer. When Douglas rushed out of the tent, all he could see were two hands clutching onto the ice.

The other involved Douglas on the day he, Mackay and Professor David were rescued by the *Nimrod* in 1909. Douglas was so excited to see the ship and anxious that it might pass without seeing them, that he didn't look where he was going and promptly fell eighteen feet into a crevasse, nearly breaking his back. 'Fortunately for Mawson, and for the subsequent history of Antarctic exploration, the crevasse was not a very deep one', wrote Davis in his own account of this accident in his autobiography, *High Latitude*.[6] In fact, Davis had to be lowered down on a rope to save Douglas from the ledge he had been fortunate enough to land on. That it was so very nearly a fatal accident was downplayed and made into an amusing story of momentary clumsiness no more serious than falling into a large puddle of water. That Douglas, ever the scientist, was industriously collecting ice crystals, of which he was making a study, while his life hung in the balance, became the focus of the story. Similarly, the incident involving David became less a story of a lucky escape from serious injury or death, than a supreme example of the lengths to which the professor would extend his politeness. Neither revealed anything much about the perils of crevasses.

Thus, at least for a while, Paquita was spared a lot of anxiety due to ignorance of the real dangers of Antarctica. She did not know for example, that on average, Douglas had fallen into crevasses regularly in the last one hundred miles back to the Hut. It was not until she learnt of the deaths of Ninnis and Mertz and of Scott, and of Douglas's narrow escape from death that she was alerted to them. Before that, love and ignorance had filled her with hope and optimism and certainty of Douglas's success.

Her father, on the other hand, was always more aware of the risks and could consider the situation objectively. He had worried that such a dangerous trip would permanently injure Douglas's health or, worse still, claim his life, hence his attempt to persuade Douglas to give up the expedition. And GDD was right. There is no question that the hardships Douglas endured on the sledging journey had a profound and far-reaching effect on his health. By the time he reached Aladdin's Cave he suspected he was suffering from scurvy. His joints were very sore and he was bleeding from the nose and from 'outbursts' on his fingers. A few days later he began to feel the, 'whole weight of the privations endured'.[7] A great tiredness overcame him, his legs swelled up and his internal organs were severely disrupted.

Four days after arriving back at the Hut he wrote, 'I have shaken to pieces somewhat, and I anticipate it will take some time to pull me up to anything like I was physically before that awful journey home'.[8] He had, as he put it, 'sounded to the lowest depths of starvation without actually perishing' and this had so disrupted his system that it was two months before his 'internal arrangements' were again in order and 'several weeks before normal sleep returned'.[9] A year later, on the *Aurora*, on the voyage back to Australia he noted that, 'my nerves, damaged by the sledging adventure, are starting to play up again'.[10] Even after he was married, Paquita quietly mixed eggs into his cocoa at night as he was 'still very far from being himself' and 'slept badly and restlessly'.[11]

Normally fifteen stone (95 kilograms) and, by Paquita's calculations, 'six foot three in his socks',[12] he purportedly weighed something less than eight stone (50 kilograms) when he staggered back to the Hut. It seems astonishingly thin for a man of his height (I am shorter and a much smaller frame and weigh more than this). Yet, it seems quite plausible when considering that Ranulph Fiennes, who had weighed ninety-five kilograms when he set out to cross the Antarctic continent in 1992, weighed sixty-four kilograms when he was rescued in February 1993, some 337 miles short of his objective. His travelling companion, Mike Stroud, dropped from seventy-two to fifty-one kilograms, and, although low on food, presumably what little they had was more appetising and nutritious than dog flesh. Stroud took urine and blood samples throughout the journey to test the physiological effects of such an undertaking. Before

Douglas on return from the Far-Eastern Sledging Journey
(*Mawson Collection, South Australian Museum*)

setting out, he had estimated that they would lose half the weight they did and upon their return, tests revealed their body fat had reduced to almost nothing.[13]

Years after the AAE, in describing his first meeting with Douglas, Eric Webb recalled being struck by his enormous physical strength as he watched him lift boxes 'heavier than lead' on to the back of a lorry in Broken Hill. When he saw Douglas again, several years after the AAE, he noticed that he had aged, even though he was then still a young man. He feared that Douglas was, 'never again the same iron man who started on that fateful journey'[14] and even went so far as to suggest that the experience had shortened his life. It very probably explains his recurring boils, as well as the acute arthritis he suffered in old age, the latter of which he endured with the same courage and stoicism he had shown on the Far-Eastern Sledging Journey. In the last years of his life, he would fly to Melbourne for Antarctic meetings and fly back on the same day to avoid having to dress himself the following morning because he could rarely manage without Paquita's help.

When Douglas reached the top of the slope leading down to the boat harbour on the afternoon of 8 February 1913, he was virtually unrecognisable. Davis had nominated six men to stay to look for the Far-Eastern Party and he had left Madigan in charge. Five of the six men, Bickerton, Hodgeman, McLean, Bage and Madigan, were working in the harbour when they noticed a figure in the distance waving at them. Douglas, anxious to know who would be his companions for another year in isolation, was only able to identify the first man when he got within fifty yards of him. It was Bickerton. In recognition of his own emaciated state, Douglas conceded that, 'it must have been more difficult for him to decipher my identity'.[15]

The men took his sledge from him. In brilliant sunshine and in a light, northerly wind, they slowly made their way to the Hut as Douglas described what had happened to Ninnis and Mertz. Amazed at his own survival, he wrote of his feelings at this moment:

> What a grand relief! To have reached civilization after what appeared utterly impossible. What a feeling of gratitude to Providence for such a deliverance. I had intended to push on to the utmost in the hope of reaching a point where my remains would be likely to be found by a relief expedition, but I had always hoped against hope for more. Now I had arrived at the goal of my utmost hopes. The outlook was so different that I was overcome with a soft and smooth feeling of thanksgiving.[16]

Yet, as he later wrote, '…that wonderful occasion was robbed of complete joy'[17] by the absence of Ninnis and Mertz.

Upon his return to the Hut, Douglas found Paquita's letters, as well as some gifts, including a picture of her for which he later made a frame and hung above his pillow. He discovered that the men had been hard at work laying stores for the winter. The freezer was filled with seal steaks and penguin breasts. The Hut exterior had been secured for the coming year with canvas and bags and the wireless station, which they had been unable to establish the previous year, owing to the winds, had been successfully erected. Left behind to operate it, in place of the original wireless operator, Walter Hannam, was the sixth man and a newcomer to the expedition, Sidney Jeffryes. Although he did not acknowledge it in his diary, Douglas already knew Jeffryes. He had rejected him when he applied for a position on the expedition in 1911, evidently deeming him unsuitable, testament to Douglas's ability to judge character, for the engagement of Jeffryes was to have disastrous consequences. Jeffryes had omitted to mention his unsuccessful application to Conrad Eitel, the Australian manager who had accepted him when he applied in Melbourne, to go down with Davis on this third voyage.

However, on 8 February, Douglas had other things on his mind apart from Jeffryes. His main priority was to recall the ship, which had only been gone a few hours. The *Aurora* was equipped with a receiving set and it had been agreed that Hannam would listen each evening on the *Aurora* between 8 pm and 1 am. A telegram was sent that evening. It read: Arrived safely at hut. Mertz and Ninnis dead. Return and pick up all hands. Mawson.[18]

a Southern Giant Petrel nesting

19

The Aborted Rescue

True is it that we have seen better days

Shakespeare, *As You Like It*

The men at the Hut started to pack in anticipation of rescue as Davis, who had just reached the pack-ice, began to steam back to Common-wealth Bay in 'thick, dark' weather. As he neared the shore five hours later he noted that, although the weather was clearing, the wind was 'freshening'.[1] By 8 am it had developed into a gale ('dangerous for sailing vessels' according to the Beaufort Scale) and in the morning the men on shore emerged from the Hut to discover the previous day of calm had turned into a hurricane. The ship was seen beating up and down in the bay. They sent another message saying that they were anxious to get away and that they hoped Davis could wait a few days more. They retreated inside. The following morning the ship had gone. It had slipped off unobserved by all in the Hut, the flag announcing Douglas's return still flying from the wireless mast.

Davis had decided it was too dangerous to remain any longer in the bay. Many ships had been beset in the frozen ocean before. The most recent had been the *Gauss* in 1902 on 22 February, in the very waters he was bound for, and it was a risk he wasn't prepared to take. The *Aurora* was not provisioned for a winter in the ice, as most spare supplies had been left at the Main Base. Yet, did Davis do all he could? His diary entries at the time reveal that he was annoyed at being asked to turn back and, from the outset, reluctant to return to the Hut. 'Why did they recall us?' he asked. 'It simply means that we are going to lose Wild for the sake of taking off a party who are in perfect safety'.[2] He was overtired. He admitted to being 'worn out and a heap of nerves' to such a degree, it seems that he had lost compassion for a party of men who had all, apart from Jeffryes, spent more than a year in the harshest climate in the world. Safe or not, they were in no hurry to extend their stay unless absolutely necessary.

Davis claimed that, after explaining to all on board the ship that he was going to leave Commonwealth Bay without having collected the Main Base Party, that all were 'unanimous in declaring that we had done everything possible'.[3] He wrote twice in the same diary entry, as if needing to justify his decision, and as if it were some consolation for being abandoned, that the Main Base Party was, 'in perfect safety and have everything they want'.[4] According to Davis it had not been safe to put a boat out, although several men had volunteered.

David Madigan, son of Madigan claims, that his father, 'was certain that they could have got off, but that, "a falling barometer must have scared the ever-cautious Davis".'[5] It does seem strange Davis had waited three weeks longer than planned and yet could not wait another day. Davis was the first to admit the sudden changes in the weather, how within a few hours a fierce gale could dissolve into 'light airs' and a calm sea. Had he waited, the wind might have died off completely but he had just endured a week-long hurricane. Davis was in an unenviable position. Emotions were running high and in such an atmosphere, everyone was quick to judge. As Davis explained in his autobiography, *High Latitude*: 'The Captain of a ship…is of necessity a lonely individual who must make most of his decisions in the light of his own knowledge and experience. Before his decision is made he is generally precluded from discussing it with anyone if he wishes to retain his authority over those under his command…'.[6]

It was generally considered that Davis was a cautious man. In his diary on the voyage in the *Aurora* from Cardiff to Hobart in 1911, Mertz's opinion of Davis had been that, 'he thinks too much about how to keep to the route, and about all his duties'.[7] Fifteen years into the future, on the first voyage of BANZARE, 1929–30, Douglas felt that Davis was over-cautious in his navigation and the two men argued continuously. However, in February 1913, he appreciated that Davis had just spent three very trying weeks waiting for him and fully supported his decision to leave when he did. Of course I did not like commanding him to remain', wrote Douglas, 'as he was responsible for Wild's party, which he had left in a difficult situation'.[8] Davis, who later described the voyage to relieve Wild as 'one long continuous battle with the elements'[9], had only just managed to land the Western Party the year before, well over 1000 miles west of the Main Base on an ice floe which could have, meanwhile, broken away from the shore.

Douglas sent a last message to Davis informing him that he was leaving it up to his, Davis's, discretion. Davis, however, did not receive this, which would have given him peace of mind. He learnt of it only when he and Douglas were comparing notes the following year. When Paquita met Davis in Australia soon afterwards, she confided to Douglas: 'I certainly always have the feeling that I must cheer Capt. up & say he did the best. It was a blow to have to leave you'.[10]

There must have been some cursing on the beach the day the *Aurora* sailed out and talk of all the 'what ifs' but, like Davis, Douglas was alone as leader and had to keep his feelings and his opinions in check. His diaries reveal no trace of the crushing disappointment he must have felt when he awoke on the morning of 10 February to find 'no ship in view'. It seems he held out hope that Davis might be able to pick them up on the way back after collecting Wild's party from the Shackleton Ice Shelf. On hearing that the *Aurora* and Wild's party had arrived safely at Port Esperence a month later, they were relieved but also disappointed as Douglas explained: 'We had always a lingering ray of hope that there might be sufficient coal to bring the vessel back to Adélie Land. Later on we learned that on account of the shortage of funds the ship was to be laid up at Hobart until the following summer'.[11]*

---

* Davis and his crew had a very difficult voyage to the Western Base and on several occasions they feared the *Aurora* would be destroyed. Davis successfully navigated his way through the icebergs despite not being able to see more than a short distance ahead, impeded by thick driving snow and darkness. The day before reaching

It was characteristic of Douglas to be resigned to his position. In an instant he turned from the sea and the vanishing ship back to the Hut, which would soon be lost in snow and darkness. In his customary matter-of-fact way, the very next line of his diary reads, 'the fellows went ahead with covering the hut etc'.[12] Davis had brought an old sail down with him, which was secured over the roof of the Hut to make it more windproof. The wind had completely dropped by the afternoon and they could have got away had the ship waited but he did not dwell on this.

It was this ability to look forward and make the best of a situation that was one of the qualities that ensured his survival, both on the sledging journey and during this second season at the Hut. 'I have a saving quality' he later told Paquita, 'and that is of never being discontented'.[13] And it was perhaps a blessing to have been left behind. Possibly Davis had unwittingly saved his life for a second time, as Douglas later reflected that, had he sailed back to Australia in 1913 in such a poor state of health, he doubted he would have survived the voyage. In saying this he probably also took into consideration that he always suffered severely from seasickness.

A weddell Seal swimming

Wild, Davis wrote: 'The next seven hours were the most anxious I have ever spent at sea. Although the wind blew hard from the south-east, we passed through the sea of bergs without mishap, guided and protected by a Higher Power'.

20

Telegram from Antarctica

Love is not love which alters when it alteration finds

Shakespeare, Sonnet 116

It was not until 24 February, three weeks after Douglas's return, after battling against appalling weather, that Jeffryes succeeded in sending the first official wireless ever from the Antarctic continent. He relayed to the world, even before the *Aurora* had reached Hobart, the story of Douglas's survival and of the deaths of Mertz and Ninnis. A message was sent to the King asking for permission to name the territory they had discovered and explored, between Adélie Land and Oates Land, 'King George V Land' which covered an area of more than 2500 miles. A long account of the tragedy was sent to Professor David in Sydney due to his being a leading member of the committee of eighteen scientists established to promote and support the AAE. Madigan sent his fiancée, Wynnis Wollaston, a message and she replied, becoming the first woman to send a telegram to Antarctica. Many messages were also received, of sympathy and congratulation, from all over the world.

An anxious Douglas, knowing that Paquita was still at sea and out of reach, sent her father a cable on 7 March. GDD replied, 'Heartfelt sympathy with your terrible experience stop take good care of yourself stop all my family well stop arriving Adelaide next month'.[1] GDD then forwarded the news of the deaths of Ninnis and Mertz and of Douglas's extended stay in Antarctica on to Paquita who had boarded the *Roon* at Naples on 26 February and was, by then, in the Indian Ocean, in the Gulf of Aden. Fifty years later, she described this moment in *Mawson of the Antarctic*:

> The captain of our ship had had the news by cable and sent a copy down to my mother's cabin, which I shared. When I awoke I saw these sheets lying on her empty bunk bed below and wondered what they were. My mother had gone into my sister's cabin for some moral support. She had hesitated to wake me, but I saw on her face when she came in that it was bad news. Quietly she handed me the papers: 'You must be thankful' she said, and left me to it…Later when I met Mrs Ninnis and the Mertz family I realized how fortunate I had been.[2]

At around this time Kathleen Scott was also at sea, on Scott's expedition ship, the *Terra Nova* on her way to Lyttleton, New Zealand, to meet her husband upon his return. On 19 February, somewhere between Tahiti and New Zealand, she had been called into the captain's cabin where she learnt, a month after the rest of the world that, along with four others, her husband had perished in a blizzard. Scott had been dead for nearly a year but there had been no wireless station at Terra Nova Bay, hence the delayed announcement. In a way she had expected it, perhaps because Scott had been once before and she knew it was a perilous journey to the Pole. Curiously, one morning the previous September, after she had awoken from a bad dream about him, her three-year old son, Peter, had turned to her and announced that his father wouldn't come back. Had Douglas joined Scott's expedition, and Scott kept his verbal promise to Douglas of a place in the Pole Party, he would almost certainly have died too.

News of the Scott tragedy was the first Douglas received by wireless in Adélie Land. Acknowledging this in his diary he wrote, 'I know what this means as I have been so near it myself recently'.[3] From the Hut he wrote a letter of sympathy to Kathleen Scott of her husband's death:

...is it not the height of being to accomplish great things against great
odds—to sacrifice one's self to a noble cause! You cannot be the loser though
you may feel the loss. It is not the thing of a day but for all time: a temporal
loss and a permanent gain. Believe me, yours is the hardest part, but indeed
the British Heart will pulse with your own and the years, as they roll on, will
be mellowed by the knowledge of having done something for Our England
which will inspire further generations to win an honourable passage through
the battlefield of Life.[4]

Scott's party had left behind valuable scientific records and almost thirty-
five pounds of rock specimens and fossils. They had died for king and
country and would be remembered, perhaps forever. Yet, however much
Douglas believed, as a fellow explorer, that Scott had died for a worthy
cause, the fact remained that the Englishman had lost his life and left a
wife and a young child behind. In acknowledgement of this, Douglas
concluded, 'I cannot lose sight of the fact that there is in these human
frames of ours a something which a presence can only satisfy, and for this
I grieve with you'.[5] Kathleen Scott was alone and, had Douglas died, as
he so very nearly did, Paquita would now be alone too. The possibility of
this far graver outcome and the effect it would have had on her life and
happiness was not something he had seriously considered before.

As well as the four letters from Paquita, Douglas had received letters
from her sister, Lica, and her mother, Henrietta, also written in Europe
the previous year. Henrietta confided to him that, although Paquita had
been, 'always bright and cheerful as usual, I know she missed you very, very
much'.[6] Lica similarly confessed that while her sister had, 'not changed a
bit outwardly', she was suffering in silence. She told him that Paquita had
hung a picture of him in her room that everyone had felt compelled to
say nice things about and to assure her she was right when she said there
was, 'only one Douglas in the world'.[7] He later wrote to Paquita's sister,
Carmen, the concert violinist, expressing his gratitude that the family
had been there for Paquita throughout 'a very unhappy year' and that he
hoped it would never be her, Carmen's, misfortune to place her future in
the hands of 'a vagrant such as I'.[8]

In asking Paquita to wait for him while he went off exploring and
putting his life at risk, Douglas had, he realised, introduced into her life

'anxieties and uncertainties which must haunt each day with fretful fore-bodings'. 'If only I could chase it all away—If that I could breathe a word in your ear', he wrote remorsefully.[9] It is significant that he made no refer-ence to the deaths of Scott and his party in his letters to her throughout 1913, and it was not until August of that year that he mentioned Mertz and Ninnis. Even then it was only in passing, to say that Bickerton and Hodgeman were making them a memorial cross out of broken wireless masts.*

Physically weakened by his experience, and believing he had selfishly expected Paquita to continue to love him against an uncertain future, Douglas initially felt undeserving of her love. This is evident in the first telegram he sent her upon her arrival in Adelaide in April, a month after she had received the wireless on the ship. He offered to release her from the engagement. It was sent to her home in Tynte Street. It read: 'Deeply regret delay stop only just managed to reach hut stop effects now gone but lost most my hair stop you are free to consider your contract but trust you will not abandon your second hand Douglas'.[10]

Although it was half done in jest, he was concerned that Paquita might be disappointed to find he had deteriorated with the strain of his ordeal. He worried enough to try and encourage some of his thinning hair to grow back as he later revealed in a telegram that, McLean was 'producing quite good results' with a 'new hair restorer'.[11] While the playful nature of his telegram serves as a protection against rejection, it also imparts confidence in Paquita's love for him. Her most recent letters had reassured him of this. 'I have no doubt of your love', he wrote, 'you speak eloquently of it'.[12] Yet he was wise enough to realise the importance of physical appearance in the early stages of a relationship, and to a young woman barely out of her teens and nine years his junior. He acknowledged that she had 'a magnificent opinion'[13] of him. Perhaps it was well she did not see him on that afternoon of his return to the Hut on 8 February; that he had time to regain his looks and his health before they reunited. Years later

* This cross was erected on Azimuth Hill overlooking Commonwealth Bay. A tablet at its base is inscribed with the words 'Erected to commemorate supreme sacrifice made by B.E.S. Ninnis R.F. and Dr X. Mertz in the cause of science A.A.E. 1913. The parts were 'bolted together and bound with heavy strips of brass'. Douglas noted that it 'appeared solid enough to last for a hundred years even in that strenuous climate'. It still stands today, ninety-three years later.

Paquita wrote: 'The strongest feeling I had, after thankfulness was a sense of love and gratitude to the men who stayed to look for Douglas—not only because they did stay, but because of the wonderfully understanding manner in which they tended him when they found him—an emaciated worn and sorrowing shadow of his former energetic and inspiring self'.[14] However, in 1913, having not seen him in the flesh since his departure, her abiding memory of him was not of an emaciated, balding man but of the strong, ambitious man who had set off for new lands more than a year before.

Tall with clean, wholesome, boyish features, Douglas had left for Antarctica 'a gallant explorer' and 'an intrepid leader', and when the story of his lone survival reached Australia it only served to further his heroic status. Cinematography was still a new phenomenon and Hurley's film of the AAE, of which Paquita was given a sneak preview in April 1913, before its release a few months later, brought the Antarctic alive and showed the men going about their daily tasks in inhospitable surrounds. Scott had died in a blizzard and Hurley had managed to capture a blizzard in full force. There was also footage of heavy drift snow passing the Hut, Madigan's frostbitten face, Douglas, Mertz and Ninnis packing their sledges in swirling snow in preparation for the Far-Eastern Sledging Journey, images which gave the public a greater appreciation of the perils that men were up against in Antarctica.

Conrad Eitel, the expedition secretary, had gone down with Davis in the *Aurora* to collect the men late in 1912. His impressions of the voyage through the roughest seas in the world were printed in the Adelaide *Register* and further enlightened the public of the dangers of polar exploration. It was no 'yachting cruise' explained Eitel, and, 'sometimes it is really more like a nightmare…Rarely could you open two eyes at once for the wind hurled the hard, gritty snow at you with such force that it felt like gravel thrown in handfuls at short distance'. He described pounding through the ice, being surrounded by enormous icebergs, sometimes miles in length and as dangerous to strike as solid rock, backtracking sometimes as far as fifty miles to find a 'lead'*. 'The discomfort of the voyage alone would destroy any foolish notions that Antarctic exploration is in the

---

* A passage of open water in the pack-ice.

nature of a beautiful picnic',[15] he concluded. Drawing on this first-hand experience of Antarctica, Eitel declared Douglas Mawson 'an iron man' for surviving the sledging journey.

In February 1913, Douglas fell far short of this description and, while struggling to regain his health and strength, his instinct was to protect Paquita from disappointment. In letters following his initial telegram, he warned her that he had been 'roughly used' on the Far-Eastern Sledging Journey, that he had 'all the faults of everybody else and a few original ones besides', and added, 'do not think you are about to marry a saint'.[16] In reference to this telegram in a letter to Paquita a month later, he admitted that his low physical and mental state in the immediate aftermath of the journey had impelled him to write this. 'Though this demonstrated my physical ability at the time', he explained, 'it was a great shock to my system and the effects of it left me more than ever convinced that I did not merit your appropriation'.[17]

He need not have worried. By her own admission, Paquita had grown from a girl into a woman and her love for him had deepened and matured. She replied immediately on arrival in Adelaide on 1 April 1913: 'Deeply thankful you are safe stop warmest welcome awaiting your hairless return stop regarding contract same as ever only more so stop thoughts always with you stop all well here months soon pass stop take things easier this winter stop speak as often as possible'.[18] Later that month, in her first letter to him since October 1912, she wrote, 'The disappointment of your non-return counts as nothing against the gratefulness that you are safe & well....my heart is full of thankfulness'.[19] However, these last were brave words. Paquita was only at the beginning of what was to be a long and trying year. 'The winter of 1913 was for Douglas, and the men who had stayed behind to look for him, one of their hardest, as it was also for me',[20] she later wrote. As Douglas noted, '...last year everything was prearranged and one resigned ones self to the inevitable...how different this year—this unexpected happening having put a deeply grudged interval upon our happiness'.[21]

Out on the plateau, Douglas had battled against the cold, atrocious weather, lack of food, loneliness and physical weakness. Now he was faced with a completely different survival test, as was Paquita. Limited communication, the sheer passing of time and all that this brought with it—separate experiences which could potentially lead to a change in feelings and in expectations, threatened the survival of his relationship with Paquita. In growing up away from him, there was always the chance that Paquita would grow apart from him and Douglas was aware of this. The risk of this happening was even greater because she hadn't mooned around Adelaide waiting for him to come back. Instead, for almost the whole of 1912, she had travelled around Europe. He had hoped she would come back still wanting him. 'You will be quite a woman of the world then—perhaps quite too fine for me?'[22], he had written prior to setting off on the sledging journey. Now a year later, her love for him had not cooled but she was being asked to wait again and this put further strain on their relationship: 'Douglas I have grown so much older in these months & I came back from Europe with my head full of things to discuss with you. And now everything has to wait,' she wrote, when the reality had sunk in. 'I feel the need of you now—am at a sort of turning point…I do want you so badly'.[23]

In 1912 Douglas had worried that Paquita was 'harassed by a multitude of doubts' about the 'non-fulfilment' of the wireless messages that had been expected to commence in the first few months of the expedition and about the safe return of the *Aurora* to Hobart. It could have easily been caught in the pack-ice or sunk after leaving the Main Base. He had looked forward to making up for this 'offence', believing he would never have cause to incur such anxiety in the future, never imagining the tragedy that was to befall his party.[24]

Paquita had literally counted the days to his expected return early in 1913, and planned her life around it. She had visited a number of countries with her family but had left London and Paris to his 'guidance' and she looked forward to showing him The Netherlands. She had borne the separation because she was prepared for it. She was not, however, prepared for another year without him and adjusting to and enduring the prolonged separation was, in many ways, much harder for her. She was always, throughout the expedition, in a more disadvantaged position. Powerless to help Douglas and often powerless to even communicate with him, she could do little but wait and hope. Until she received the telegram at sea she had absolutely no notion that anything was wrong.

It was different for Douglas, from the day Ninnis was killed in the crevasse. He had more time to adjust. He knew then that the return journey with Mertz could end in their deaths. When he eventually made it back to the Hut, his relief at having survived outweighed, if only temporarily, his disappointment in missing the ship. It was not the shock it was for Paquita, remembering of course that he was almost a month overdue and, with winter approaching, he knew the ship could not wait indefinitely. Staying meant that he would have time to recover, and time to start writing up the story of the expedition. He could picture Paquita in her house in North Adelaide, on the sofa where they had often sat together on the veranda of El Rincon, the Delprats holiday house, and know that she was 'in the best of keeping'. He could draw comfort from the receipt of her 'delightful letters'.[25] Meanwhile, Paquita was left to languish in Adelaide after the thrills of Europe and the distractions of ship life and without even a recent letter to keep her going. It had been more than a year since she had last received mail from Douglas and the only two letters he had written since that time were on the *Aurora*. Due to an apparent oversight, they were not delivered to her and she would not receive them until Douglas gave them to her in person in 1914.

a Dutch spoon
for Paquita's trousseau

21

Lost Letters of Love

Love comforteth like sunshine after rain

Shakespeare, *The Two Gentlemen of Verona*

While waiting at the Hut for Douglas and Mertz and Ninnis to return at the beginning of 1913, Davis had found a box in Douglas's room containing papers. He noted in his diary that he had 'carefully gone through the papers'[1] and found a rough draft of instructions to him regarding what to do in the event of Douglas's non-return. It is inexplicable that he didn't find two letters to Paquita, which lay in this same box. He might have felt reluctant to rifle through Douglas's personal correspondence, but under the circumstances it is unlikely that he would have been concerned about future accusations of nosiness. As the weeks passed and the likelihood of finding the party alive began to diminish, would he not have been actively looking for something to give Paquita? Would not the men have been looking for something too? Did it not occur to any of them that over a period of twelve months, during which time he was to undertake a dangerous journey, that Douglas would have written something to his fiancée? It was Douglas's nature to be organised, to plan ahead. It is more than likely, given the open plan of the Hut, that he wrote the letters under their very eyes at the dining room table. One of these resembled a will, written on the morning of his departure with Ninnis and Mertz.

Yet, incredibly, Davis had sailed away from six men he knew he was leaving in isolation for another year, knowing that the party he had left them to look for, was probably dead. The men had already started to talk of Ninnis, Douglas and Mertz in the past tense. He was carrying letters to the wives and girlfriends of the men left at the Hut, including, presumably, letters to Wynnis from Madigan, but with apparently nothing to give Douglas's fiancée. Douglas's box, containing the two letters to Paquita, was brought onto the *Aurora*. It was stored somewhere on the ship by someone, possibly by Davis himself, but it was not delivered to Paquita.

In August 1913, the Delprats sold their house in North Adelaide and moved to Melbourne, where Paquita met Davis in September. No record survives of what she made of the fact that he came to her empty-handed. The *Aurora* was in Melbourne in dry dock from March until October 1913. She had afternoon tea with Davis, Murphy and Harrisson in the *Aurora* wardroom, little knowing that somewhere on the vessel the letters lay undiscovered. Of course she can't have known then, that Douglas had written her anything at all, but throughout the expedition she had received just four letters from him, written between December 1911 and January 1912, when Davis returned on the *Aurora* from the first voyage to the Antarctic to land all three parties. Given that more than a year had passed since then, it is extremely unlikely that she didn't find the absence of any further correspondence, strange, or at the very least, disappointing. Although she made no direct reference to this fact in subsequent letters to Douglas, it might have been at the root of her increasing frustration at the lack of communication as the year 1913 progressed.

The comfort that Paquita's four letters of 1912 brought Douglas over the second long winter in the Hut made him realise how wrong he had been in dismissing the importance of correspondence. 'If only you knew how valuable is each piece of paper from you', he wrote. He re-read her letters 'on the occasion of each celebration'[2] throughout the subsequent months and it is not too much to say that they saved him from despair. 'I am never alone now;' he wrote to Paquita, 'for if the immediate present does not occupy my mind you are there having little talks with me'.[3] 'I simply love these hours that are devoted to writing to you. You are divinely sent to me to make life happy and your influence is a power even here...Your fresh and healthy girlhood—your trust— your love—your tenderness—All these things are ever before me, and in this frozen, austere solitude loom up as giant angels'.[4]

In the first year he had told her he would be too busy to read her letters. Her concerns that she was writing too often, 'Is four letters too much?'[5] she had asked, and her admissions that she had sometimes written him letters only to tear them up, afraid of encumbering him with correspondence, reminded him of his words and he admitted that he now 'bitterly rued'[6] saying them. He also regretted not writing to her more often for the same reason. He had not placed enough importance on her need for private words from him. His letters of the year before were short and thin in detail. 'The general reports are in the newspapers and I need not repeat'[7], he had written casually, by way of justifying this.

Somehow sensing her anxiety, by June 1913, Douglas began to suspect that his two letters of November 1912 had not been delivered. 'I hope and hope that you are not worrying', he wrote. 'Have often wondered whether Captain Davis posted several letters I had written and locked up in my box'.[8] The box, he recalled, also contained letters to his father, of whose death he had since been informed, his brother, Will, Professor David, and his mother, then in failing health.*

'Had I known what lay ahead how I should have devoted myself to writing to you last year'[9], professed Douglas. The two undelivered letters, the only ones he had written from January to November 1912, would have been all that remained to Paquita had she lost Douglas and they hardly qualified as letters but were rather, by his own description, 'short notes'. Neither contained any detail about his feelings or doings over the ten months preceding the sledging journey. Neither would have offered much consolation to a bereaved fiancée. Douglas immediately set about making up for this by writing regularly and answering Paquita's news, item by item, however outdated and, despite knowing that every time he sat down to write, there was no letterbox in which to post them. She would not receive these letters until he was safely back in Australia but, as

---

* Paquita visited Margaret Mawson in Campbelltown, New South Wales in October 1913. It seems she had suffered a stroke as Paquita reported that she had 'not yet regained her memory'. She would not recover sufficiently to attend Douglas and Paquita's wedding in March 1914 and she died a few years later, in 1917, at the relatively young age of 58. At the time of her death, Douglas and Paquita were living in England.

a record of his life in the Hut, of his love for her, of his responses to all her questions and fears, they would be a kind of solace if anything happened to prevent his return.

an iceberg

22

Descent into Darkness

I wake and feel the fell of dark, not day.
What hours, O what black hours we have spent
This night.

Gerard Manley Hopkins (1844–1889), *Carrion Comfort*

Writing became a welcome diversion in a place where, 'time hangs heavily'. Douglas and his men had arrived a year before to a completely new land but in 1913, as Douglas later explained in *The Home of the Blizzard*, 'the field of work which once stretched to the west, east and south had no longer the mystery of the unknown'.[1] The first year had been so busy that there had been, as he later noted in *The Home of the Blizzard*, 'few moments for reflection'.[2] There had been eighteen men, including Hurley and Murphy, both of whom had kept everyone entertained with their amusing stories and antics, and Mertz and Ninnis, whose empty bunk beds and the echo of their laughter and song were now a constant reminder of their deaths. According to Madigan's son, David, his father heard Bickerton 'sobbing under his blanket' at night.[3] Now there were only seven. Even the atrocious weather had been a novelty at first but without summer sledging journeys to prepare for, there was little to look forward to. 'The prospects', as Douglas put it, were 'decidedly duller'[4], especially in the knowledge that they had so very nearly been rescued from what promised to be a dreary and difficult year, and, as it turned out, an even windier winter with particularly heavy snows and dense drifts. While the winter had not begun until March in 1912, the winter of 1913 began in February and the July winds were to surpass all previous records. On 16 April they witnessed the last vestige of summer, a lone penguin perched on a rocky ledge overhanging an icy cove to the east.

In the first few weeks back at the Hut Douglas claimed he did, 'little else than potter about, eat and doze, with frequent interruptions from internal disorders'[5] while the men vied with one another to make his life as comfortable as possible. Yet, by March, barely a month after his return, he had resumed a substantial work load, and was tackling *The History of War and Peace* by GH Perris. He was again taking his turn at night watch, now every seven days as opposed to every eighteen days in 1912. By May, he had resumed Divine Service on Sundays. In fact, it is remarkable how much he achieved during this year considering all that he had endured. With editorial assistance from McLean, he began writing up what would become *The Home of the Blizzard* and, gathering from his diaries, he got as far as chapter seven by the end of the year. Chapter seven in his published account of the expedition is entitled 'The Blizzard' and is devoted to the nature and effects of the relentless and violent winds he had again found himself in the thick of. The manuscript came to include accounts by other members of the expedition, and the chapter numbers may well have altered in the editing process. Yet, even allowing for this, it is unlikely that Douglas got as far as The Far-Eastern Sledging Journey over the winter of 1913. The events of it are not described until some way into the book, in chapters twelve, thirteen and fourteen. Writing about it so soon after his return and under the circumstances would have been difficult. As it was, writing at all was a strain, not so much physically, but mentally. By mid-July he wrote, 'cannot pull myself together to go on with expedition narrative'.[6] He did, however, map the sledging journey and write up the meteorological records of the trek. The previous year he had made a special study of the auroras and he also worked on getting his notes for this up to date.

Magnetic research was continued. Bage was not only magnetician and astronomer but also took on the role of storeman, formerly Murphy's job. He was kept busy stacking boxes of penguin eggs, as well as continuing as meteorologist, while Madigan, who assisted in this, also took charge of the twenty-one dogs, donated to the expedition by Amundsen and taken down south by Davis on the *Aurora*.

Some of these dogs had taken Amundsen and his party to the Pole. Although they provided some welcome company, they were nevertheless quite a responsibility to maintain. Despite being well-trained to pull sledges, they were barely domesticated and sometimes so difficult to control that Madigan found it necessary to beat them for their violent behaviour. More than half died in one way or another before the end of the year. One, 'Laseron', was 'ripped up' in April by the others and had to be shot. Three set upon another, George, the following month. Peary was attacked in July, and Mary had to be operated on due to injuries in August. On fine days Madigan took them down to the boat harbour where he stored several seal carcasses, which he hacked into with an axe sending chips of frozen meat in all directions for them to catch in their mouths. Bickerton was wireless engineer and general mechanic, Hodgeman continued as cartographer while also serving as assistant meteorologist. Apart from nursing Douglas back to health, McLean collected and preserved parasites from birds and fish and took on the role of editor of the *Adélie Blizzard*, their monthly magazine which they started again in April. Douglas had been editor in 1912 but no issue was produced, partly because the men were then busy preparing for their summer sledging journeys. The first issue of the magazine was completed by the end of April 1913 and four more issues followed, which included some contributions from 1912 and consisted of a wide range of writing from plays, stories, poetry and book reviews to scientific articles. Although not the first Antarctic publication, it was unique in being the first to have a column of news of the day received by radio. McLean typed the one and only copy of the magazine, the total five issues of which amounted to more than two hundred pages, and, as each issue was ready, it was passed around the Hut. Later, in England, Douglas and McLean tried, unsuccessfully, to publish the magazine as a way of paying off the expedition debt.

They all took their turn at cooking and each mastered a particular dish, Hodgeman, tapioca pudding, Jeffryes, milk scones, Madigan, puff pastry; Bickerton, 'mixed-spiced pudding', a dessert that had evolved from the inclusion of a surprise ingredient. From a mixture of stout, flour, sugar and dried fruit, the men managed to successfully grow a culture of yeast and thenceforward made bread, a welcome change from bread made from baking soda, and McLean became adept at making yeast waffles. Douglas was known for his excellent scones. Paquita was told by some of the expeditioners, who had returned from Adélie Land on the *Aurora*, that Douglas cooked 'the best'.[7]

To create variety in their routine, they made any excuse to celebrate with a special dinner. On Empire Day, on 24 May, they hoisted the Union Jack and gave three cheers to the King. On Mid-Winter's Day, 21 June, Bage and Bickerton 'dressed up in coloured togs'.[8] The year before they had woken up with hangovers after beginning birthday celebrations at midnight, for Ninnis, who had turned 24 on 22 June. Swiss Confederation Day on 1 August, which had been celebrated and hosted by Mertz, who had cooked special Swiss dishes the previous year, passed uneventfully, so too Mertz's birthday on 6 October. Douglas made no reference to it in his diary for that day though he could not have failed to remember how the occasion had been celebrated the year before. Douglas had given him a collection of English poems and produced a 'special plum pudding' made by Paquita, which Mertz had clearly appreciated, commenting in his diary, 'the lady seems to have talent for cooking'.[9] The men had written Mertz a song, good-naturedly making fun of his broken English. Douglas had noted down the lyrics in his scrapbook. It ended with the following words:

Come give a cheer, for it is here,
Our old roundhead's birthday.
So here's to long life, Und a good vife,
To fill him mit delight,
Now chaps you'll all mit me agree,
SAPRISTI! SAPRISTI!, Old X is "quite all right".[10]

As expected, the weather gave them few opportunities to exercise. They seldom left the Hut except for the routine meteorological and magnetic observations. Rare occasions (when the wind blew less than fifty miles an hour) allowed for skiing practice and for short walks along the shore to watch the birds. Douglas made light of the battle with monotony upon his return to Australia. At his lectures he enjoyed telling his audiences of how they eventually exhausted their reading supply and began reading the Encyclopaedia Britannia from A to Z. Some persevered for longer than others, he joked, but no one got further than 'O'. It was a story that always produced a laugh but in truth, boredom could easily lead to depression and no one was invulnerable to it.

The depressing isolation and tedium of a polar winter in confined circumstances had threatened the morale and mental health of men on previous expeditions to polar regions, both north and south. Fifteen years previously, Fridtjof Nansen had struggled to maintain his sanity when his ship, the *Fram*, was frozen in the ice off the north-east coast of Siberia and drifted for two and a half years.* 'I long to return to life', he wrote: 'At times this inactivity crushes one's very soul; one's life seems as dark as the winter night outside…I feel I must break through this deadness and inertia and find some outlet for my energies…'.[11]

When stranded in the Arctic in 1883, Greely had realised the importance of keeping his men busy. Although on the brink of starvation for most of the winter, he had insisted they all kept a regular diary and arranged evening talks, which involved each man talking about a different state of America. More recently and closer to home, from February to September 1912, Scott's six-man Northern Party had been forced to live in an ice cave on Inexpressible Island after the *Terra Nova*, unable to penetrate a belt of ice, had failed to reach them. They excavated the cave for shelter, their tents having been torn to shreds in the wind, and with only summer sledging gear they were almost completely confined to it. It was difficult, and even more so when they began to suffer from dysentery. They survived for seven months on six weeks sledging rations supplemented by penguin and seal meat. Their entertainment consisted of a handful of novels and a copy of the Bible, which they read by the weak light of seal blubber lamps. They remained remarkably in tact both physically and psychologically despite their confined circumstances and

---

* It was Nansen's intention to allow his ship to drift. The discovery of relics off the coast of Greenland from the *Jeanette* which had sunk near Wrangle Island in June 1881, indicated a current had carried them. Nansen believed if he left his ship to the mercy of the winds, this same current would carry it across the North Pole. He calculated correctly that it would drift into the North Atlantic. On 14 August 1896 the *Fram* reached Danes Island, Spitsbergen having achieved a Farthest North of 85°55'N at 66°31'E.

poor diet.* However, Petty Officer, Frank Browning succumbed to 'a fit of hysterical depression'[12] just before the party escaped across the Drygalski Barrier to the hut at Cape Evans in September and Petty Officer, George Abbot, suffered a nervous breakdown on the voyage home to England.

The previous winter at the Hut Douglas had read *Through the First Antarctic Night* by Frederick Cook,** surgeon and anthropologist on the Belgian Antarctic Expedition under Adrien de Gerlache in 1897 and had confided to his diary that he was 'shocked' by the account.

Trapped in the ice for a year, Cook wrote of the terrible melancholy that descended on the whole party in the *Belgica* when the sun disappeared for seventy days. Except for a murky yellow haze on the horizon at midday twilight, the men were enveloped in darkness in their stranded ship. With the same icy wilderness for a view and with no change in the sky to divide morning from night, they struggled to keep up their morale. On a moving sea of ice there was no prospect of long land journeys to break the monotony. Lethargy and an attitude of indifference settled in. They wavered between insomnia and the desire to sleep all the time and wondered how many of them would be there to greet the returning sun. They developed a pale, greenish complexion. Their skin grew oily, their faces puffed up and their hearts were weak, their pulses irregular. They lost all interest in food. Their organs were sluggish and they were unable to concentrate and to focus their thoughts. Even mild exercise left them breathless. Cook described it as polar anaemia, the cause of which he attributed to the low temperatures, the constant darkness, the isolation and the tinned foods. Even Nansen, the ship's cat, appeared to succumb to depression before it eventually disappeared. The magnetician, Emile Danco, reputedly died from a heart condition but the darkness claimed him long before that. Danco seemed destined to die the moment the sun vanished. Despite there being no shortage of food, Cook claimed that the canned food was to blame for their ill-health. This was 'rot' in Douglas's

---

* Douglas, when starving on the plateau, had dreamt of visiting a cake shop and walking away empty-handed, only to return to find it had closed early. The Northern Party all experienced a recurring dream almost identical to this, of crawling out of their cave to find either a butcher's shop or a confectioners. Like Douglas, they never made a purchase as it was always early closing day.

** Cook later mounted an Arctic expedition (1907–1909) on which he claimed to have reached the North Pole ahead of Peary. Controversy followed but Cook's claim was later officially rejected by the University of Copenhagen.

The Hut and wireless masts at Commonwealth Bay
(*Mawson Collection, South Australian Museum*)

opinion. According to him, inactivity was the sole cause of their lethargy and loss of appetite.

In the Hut he advocated regular exercise and going outdoors at every opportunity. As Cherry-Garrard wrote in his account of the first winter with Scott in 1911: 'The importance of plenty of outdoor exercise was generally recognised, and our experience showed us that the happiest and healthiest members of our party...were those who spent the longest period in the fresh air'.[13] In late March 1913, after only six weeks of confinement, Douglas confessed to his diary, 'I find my nerves are in a very serious state, and from the feeling I have in the base of my head I {have} suspicion that I may go off my rocker very soon'. He concluded that, 'too much writing today brought this on'. He resolved to 'take more exercise and less study, hoping for a beneficial return'.[14] Two months later, he was not much better. 'I have a boil on left temple forming', he wrote, adding, 'Am quite down in general health. Too much concentrated writing on top of sledging trials and no outdoor exercise'.[15] Of course, he was still in very frail health after the sledging journey, but there were other concerns plaguing his mind.

He would be ultimately responsible for the debt incurred due to the unexpected extension of the expedition. He was, as he confessed in a letter to Paquita, 'entirely ignorant of the state of the funds'.[16] In Australia, the Antarctic Committee was busy raising the money needed for a third voyage to Antarctica to collect the seven men at the Hut. Davis sailed to England early in 1913 to seek further support from there, the result being that contributions to the required £8000 were made by the Commonwealth government, the British government, as well as private individuals, including Kathleen Scott. The expedition secretary, Conrad Eitel, had not left a bank statement at the Hut and it had evidently been decided that it was unwise to disclose the financial details of the expedition by telegraph. Once back in Australia, Douglas discovered that Eitel had paid himself too much, written cheques he was unable to explain and withdrawn cash from the expedition account he could not account for, which was very probably the reason why a statement was not provided. Douglas gathered, from 'hints received', that the committee had spent more than they ought to have in 1912 and this made him uneasy and, marooned at Commonwealth Bay, he was powerless to do anything. Putting his trust in other people was not something he felt comfortable with. With reference to the committee, he wrote to Paquita: 'They should have made a strong appeal to the governments *now* whilst we are down here and got every penny necessary which I believe I would have no difficulty in doing had I been there—however. I have discovered once again that an expedition lies in one man only and I can't expect to hear much to my advantage on return'.[17] (Of course, *had* he been there, and not trapped as he was for a second season in Antarctica, it would not have been necessary to raise the funds for another voyage.)

He did not reveal to Paquita what had happened, to trigger this realisation 'once again' but his doubts, were not ill-founded. The unpaid debts of the expedition, which amounted to £5000, would have to be met by him personally over a period of years. Yet Douglas would not know any of this until much later. Throughout 1913, this uncertainty put him under huge strain. Lack of communication and limited information was a common source of anxiety for all polar parties. For Scott's Northern Party, it was not knowing what had happened to Scott, whether anyone would be at *Terra Nova Bay* when they got there and whether the *Terra Nova* was ever going to come back for them that had caused them the most distress.

As leader, it was Douglas's responsibility to keep the men motivated and inspired in an atmosphere of disillusionment. He did this by continuing to set a high standard of work despite his own precarious health. Still a hard taskmaster, he observed that, 'Bickerton likes doing things he likes to do', that McLean was, 'not too ready to skin animals' and that Madigan, who liked to read all day on Sundays, 'unfortunately does not work such long hours at other times as he might to make up for it'.[18] He wrote in his diary of having to 'galvanise' them into action. Although the men were still carrying out valuable work, which would contribute to the final results of the expedition, they lacked focus as essentially they were creating work to pass the time until the ship came back. Madigan's son, David, described how, 'a state of slackness fell upon the Hut, a sort of resignation. They crawled out of bed at times varying from 9–11 am and staggered to the breakfast table. Everyone did what he liked, which was often nothing, and there was no regular housekeeping schedule. But in time some sort of routine was established'.[19] Did the men resent sacrificing another year of their lives to the expedition? David Madigan claims his father, who had postponed his marriage and a Rhodes scholarship, certainly did, and he claims the others did as well. If this was true, this was yet another strain on Douglas.

The highlight of their day was receiving wireless messages which, Douglas wrote, 'took the place of a morning paper'. They would wake up in the morning and find 'quite a budget of wireless messages', which they discussed 'from every possible point of view'.[20] Jeffryes worked hard at the wireless every night. In May, Douglas noted 'Jeffryes good so far'[21], as if anticipating trouble. Only a few days later Jeffryes retired to bed early just when conditions for sending had improved, and Douglas felt frustrated that he couldn't get him or Bickerton, (engineer for the wireless), to 'take the subject up scientifically'.[22]

Theoretically, the wireless, which had failed in 1912, should have been the highest achievement of the expedition in 1913. Douglas later wrote, 'the wireless proved a success and a boon throughout the year, though temporary stoppages occurred, owing to unusual difficulties arising chiefly from the constant hurricane'.[23] Hurricanes carried the mast away and loosened the stays, but there were other obstacles to contend with, such as the muffled sound of the wind, the auroras, and the crackling of St Elmo's Fire, (a build up of electricity in the air brought on by storms). There was the howling of the dogs in the veranda, signals were picked up from ships on the south coast of Australia and along the shores of New Zealand and, even when conditions were good, they were frequently 'jammed out' by Australian stations.

Yet, something else, far more difficult to overcome, became the main source of interference as the year progressed. Wireless messages were sent and received almost daily for the first two months. On 25 February the aerial was carried away by the wind but Bickerton managed to repair it almost immediately and communication continued. On 8 June, however, the top section of the mast was blown away and the middle section shattered 'bringing everything to earth'.[24] They were completely cut off from the world for the next two months as record winds prevented them from repairing the damaged equipment. It was not until 5 August that repairs were completed and the wireless work resumed. From then on conditions for sending were often favourable but by then a more ominous problem became apparent. Jeffryes, who was operating the wireless, was incapable of working it with any degree of consistency, as, at times, he lost his mind.

Krill, the bottom of the food chain

23

Madness and Misunderstanding

My dear I only hope I will do you credit—and would be glad to be back in civilization, for this place can only sere my body and mind making them less fit for an offering to your imperial love.

Douglas to Paquita, 15 July 1913

In May Douglas had noted the first signs that Jeffryes was not well. He observed that he went on long tiring walks during the day and was then unfit to man the wireless at night, frequently falling asleep at the controls. Douglas conceded that listening at the wireless receiver was 'very tedious work', that it required ignoring a multitude of interfering sounds and that Jeffryes 'would sometimes spend whole evenings trying to transmit a single message, or conversely, trying to receive one'.[1] Yet, despite the intensity of the work, Jeffryes's apathy soon angered Douglas who was very unsympathetic towards anyone who did not have the interests of the expedition at heart. He felt like 'skinning' Jeffryes for taking the crystal out of the setting each evening so that nobody else could use the instruments.

In early July in the depths of winter, Jeffryes, an ex-boxer, challenged Madigan to a fight and Douglas deduced that his 'touchy temperament' was being very 'hard tested with bad weather and indoor life'. He diagnosed it as 'a case of polar depression' but he concluded 'I trust it will go now'.[2] However, Jeffryes's alarming behaviour continued. He muttered in the dark on his bunk, 'ate ravenously' and walked around glaring. He began to say peculiar things, often interjecting conversations with irrelevant remarks and laughing uproariously at inappropriate moments. Douglas wrote, in reference to his cooking one night, 'The pudding he made was a revelation in rotten egg and grease'.[3] On another occasion, incidentally, on Paquita's birthday on 19 August, he *sat* in the pudding. Several times tins of tongue exploded in the oven when he forgot he had put them there to thaw. He refused to wash until Douglas eventually turned the darkroom into 'a temporary washing chamber' to encourage him to do so. However, by the time Jeffryes finally washed, his personal hygiene had been so neglected that Douglas talked of having to disinfect the canvas bath before anyone else could use it. Worse still, Jeffryes would not even take out his own 'waste'.

Douglas had experienced delusion with Mertz as he met his end. To a lesser degree, he had encountered it with Professor David, who had shown symptoms of a mental breakdown on the BAE, on their journey to the South Magnetic Pole. On that journey Douglas had noted the professor's memory was 'fainter' and described him as 'demented'.[4] Mackay had threatened to certify Professor David insane if he did not hand over the leadership to Douglas. However, the professor's breakdown proved temporary and circumstantial and it did not extend beyond the expedition. Jeffryes, however, was seriously mentally ill and was committed to an asylum immediately upon his return to Australia. According to Davis, 'he never properly recovered'.[5]

Jeffryes became paranoid, violent and irrational and had to be watched at all times. Believing that everyone was sitting in judgement over him, when Madigan mentioned having just finished reading *The Hound of the Baskervilles*, Jeffryes interpreted it as a reference to him. He suspected he was the subject of articles the men were writing for their magazine, *The Blizzard*, and accused them all of conspiring against him and of plotting to murder him, and threatened that they would all be thrown into gaol on their return to Australia.

It was absolutely essential for the welfare and sanity of everyone else to somehow get Jeffryes under control. Douglas noted that he seemed to respond when spoken harshly to. However, it was a delicate situation. 'I would certainly expel him from the expedition', wrote Douglas (which he incidentally did, temporarily, towards the end of the year, in so far as he absolved him of all expeditionary duties), 'but for the fact that we could then no longer call upon him to operate the wireless. No one else is proficient at "sending" '.[6]

Wireless operation was a very new skill. Jeffryes was evidently very adept at operating the wireless, gathering from Douglas's comment in a letter to Paquita, that, 'he sends too quickly for any of us amateurs to read him', and by the fact that after a brief period at the controls, Bickerton wanted Jeffryes to be reinstated despite Jeffryes's unstable condition.

The strain of looking after a mentally ill man in confined circumstances further contributed to Douglas's poor health. He felt his brain was 'on the point of bursting' with 'all the worries and the indoor life, want of exercise and Jeffryes's trouble on top'.[7] Later in the month he noted that 'some teeth need attending to' and that he had contracted a bladder infection and 'a large deep-seated inflammation'[8] over the right side of his face. Furthermore, he knew that Paquita would be wondering why his wireless messages were as rare as his letters and he was powerless to explain any of it to her except in undeliverable letters. In these he told her that Jeffryes had 'lost his reason' and that this was having a very depressing effect on everyone in the Hut. They could never be sure when or if messages were being sent. Jeffryes, in one of his worst moments, had admitted to trying to send a message to the effect that five of the men were insane and trying to murder him.

Even when the wireless was working, Jeffryes failed to take advantage of favourable conditions and communication diminished. Up until the day the wireless mast was destroyed in the June winds, Douglas calculated that he had sent Paquita four messages, 'one of my escape—one in gratitude of your love—one sending *much* love—and another thanks for birthday greetings'.[9] (His birthday was 5 May.) As the months passed with the wireless still out of action, he became frantic. In October he revealed that he had been wandering around for a fortnight 'feeling wretched', unable to settle to writing or any other work because he could not get a message through to her. A month later, he wrote:

I hope that it is only that I am wracked by anxious thoughts—I trust that you are well—that you are enjoying health and life—I cannot however help feeling anxious, most anxious. A wretched fit seizes me; sets the imagination running in a doleful tune; figures you unwell, cast down by worry—or piqued and hurt by my seeming unconcern—these wretched scraps of information that have passed to you. Ah! Did you but know how difficult to send news. Could you be here but for one moment, how all this would be spared you.[10]

Exactly what information was reaching her ears, in the absence of news from him, was also a source of concern to him. He realised that, 'much that is untrue and exaggerated gets into the papers, even regarding expeditions. Editors are not particular and are often misled.'[11] One newspaper article wrongly reported that the Australian Government had sent a steamship to relieve Douglas and his men because they had run out of food and were surviving on the hearts and tongues of sea elephants. This was, in fact, an exaggerated description of the situation on Macquarie Island, where the team there was also spending a second season.

On 7 March 1913, two weeks after two-way wireless communication had been successfully made between Macquarie Island and Adélie Land, Douglas had sent a message asking Ainsworth and his men if they would agree to stay on the island until the end of 1913 to keep the wireless station going as without them wireless contact could not be maintained between Adélie Land and Australia. The party had consented to stay, and had had to contend with Jeffryes's erratic contact and censure some of his irrational messages. However, the delayed arrival of extra supplies on the *Rachel Cohen* meant that they ran very low on food and commodities. When the kerosene ran out, they resorted to lighting their slush lamps with sea-elephant oil. For food, they caught rabbits and wekas (Mother Cary's chickens) but by the time another ship, the *Tutanekai*, finally arrived in August (the *Rachel Cohen* meanwhile having ended up in New Zealand, badly damaged), they were living on sea-elephant meat, sago and French beans. Sawyer, one of the wireless operators, had apparently fallen ill and it had been arranged for him to return to Hobart with the ship. His farewell dinner had included sea-elephant tongue, which had led to a misconstrued article, which Paquita had pasted into her scrapbook. Presumably she had had the sense to realise it wasn't true. When she came to write *Mawson of the Antarctic*, she commented that she was pleased to have the opportunity to print 'the real text' as the wireless messages Douglas sent her were, 'picked up and quoted in the Press in various parts of the world with remarkable variations'.[12] However, for a woman anxiously awaiting the safe return of her fiancé, false reports of a rescue or successful return are potentially devastating. Cruelly, before learning of her husband's true fate, Kathleen Scott had been swamped with messages of congratulation following false reports that, according to Amundsen, Scott had reached the Pole.

It seems that Paquita was under the impression that she would have regular wireless contact with Douglas throughout 1913. When months passed with no word from him and with the added pressure of everyone asking her if she heard from him every week, she began to worry. As Douglas feared, she interpreted the long silences as a lack of interest on his part at keeping in touch and it began to push her love and patience to the limit. 'You know my feelings for you are stronger & warmer because in my letters last year & in these I can assure you of that', she wrote. 'I have only the three or four wires. And oh I can't help saying it—I would have been so much happier if I had been able to think that your need to send word to me, however little, more often than four times in a year, was greater than your dislike to use the wireless for private use.'[13]

While Paquita was not confined and isolated in the way that Douglas was, she was in limbo like him and struggling to keep busy and positive. She missed 'the music and movement' of Europe and felt the 'emptiness of Adelaide' without him.[14] Later in the year she wrote, 'You can explain it all when you return I know...I know you can't send every week that would be nonsense but none since last May until the other day. Shall I tear up this? Perhaps I shouldn't say this to you. I should wait calmly till your return & not worry you'.[15]

a leopard seal

24

Anxiety about the Future

Doubts are more cruel than the worst of truths

Moliere (1622–1673), *Le Misanthrope*

Without the reassurance she so craved and having had to survive without Douglas's love for so long, Paquita began to lose confidence in the future. Her contemporaries, Emily Shackleton and Kathleen Scott, were both married when their men went to Antarctica. When Kathleen Scott heard of her husband's death, the knowledge that they had shared thirteen years of marriage was some consolation and some comfort. She confided to her diary: 'Had he died before I knew his gloriousness, or before he had been the father of my son, I might have felt a loss. Now I have felt none for myself'.[1] Paquita, on the other hand, was only engaged. While in one sense it might be said that she had less to lose, on the other hand, her situation was far less certain. She had only Douglas's word, which was fast becoming a dim memory, and it was extremely difficult to maintain her love when she felt as though she was writing to a stone wall. The long silence was driving her to despair. 'What wouldn't I give for just one fat bulgy love letter' she wrote. 'I feel quite equal to copying your handwriting & writing myself a love letter'.[2]

How easy it was to let her mind wander and imagine, for example, that his promise of love and marriage was something he might renege on upon his return. Prior to his departure for Antarctica with Captain Cook in 1768, Joseph Banks had proposed to Harriet Blosset. He had kept her waiting three long years and then returned only to announce that he was 'not the marrying kind'. What if this happened to Paquita? Her letters indicate that this was something she sometimes feared. How could she be sure he was telling the truth in his rare wireless messages, how could she be sure that he wasn't waiting to break off their engagement in person? After all, rejecting her via a wireless message he knew would pass through many hands before reaching hers would be a cruel thing to do in much the same way that now it would be heartless and cowardly to break off a relationship via an email or a text message. She was opening up her heart to him and it frightened her that he might not love her as she loved him. 'Are you frozen?' she asked him. 'Am I pouring out a little of what is in my heart to an iceberg? …Can a person remain in such cold and lonely regions, however beautiful & still love warmly?' 'Oh for a few private dear words' she implored. She tried hard not to let paranoia set in, 'There is no reason why you shouldn't like me as much as before'[3], she reasoned.

Of course she did not know that Douglas was busy writing to her of his continued love, of how he would never regret the struggle through which the sledging journey had dragged him. 'Had I been really incapacitated to be your Husband, I should not have reached the Hut', he assured her. 'My love you had to trust—*that* you need never fear for unless miracles happen to yourself…I know of no reason why our horizon should be clouded'.[4] 'My own darling there is heaps and heaps of love for you frozen up down here'.[5]

But not knowing any of this, by September, serious doubts, of a different kind, began to creep into Paquita's mind. Along what lines was Douglas thinking? She admitted that she was afraid of 'the fascination of the South'.[6] She knew that Shackleton was 'off again' and, all the members of the AAE she had met since their return from the Antarctic in 1913, Murphy, Hurley, Correll and Harrisson, had told her that, given the opportunity, they would go again. Meanwhile, another expedition, the Canadian Arctic Expedition 1913–18 under the command of North American explorer, Vilhjalmur Stefansson, had begun. Among its members was Dr Mackay, who had trekked with Douglas and Professor

David to the South Magnetic Pole a few years before, and James Murray, who had been the biologist on the BAE. Stefansson's party had set off ill-prepared with inadequate supplies in an unsuitable ship, such was the lure of the ice.

Was Douglas harbouring thoughts of a return expedition, of a future that did not include her, she wondered: 'I have seen unhappiness where I thought all was well. Calm homes also have skeletons in a cupboard it seems. I want you to reassure me that all will go well with us & our love'.[7] Douglas had spent much of his adult life in tents and boarding houses, exploring the world. Paquita was anxious to know if he was ready to settle down. 'Will a calm life ever satisfy you?'[8], she asked. 'It will be a glorious day when you return', she wrote. 'I shall not be a bit jealous of the expedition but when everything is over—you will be happy to live quietly & not dash off again, won't you?'[9] In another, she asked: 'You will not go again, will you? I know you will not. It isn't anything for married men to do'.[10] What she was really wondering was, what possible miseries lay in store for her as the wife of an explorer? Would she be left at home alone for long periods of time raising a tribe of children single-handedly, forever expecting a telegram bearing the news of his death? So many explorers had died leaving grieving widows in their wake.

Thirty years before, American naval officer, George Washington De Long had died in the Arctic on a quest to reach the North Pole via the Bering Strait in what had become one of the great polar tragedies. De Long's ship, the *Jeanette*, had eventually sunk in June 1881 after becoming beset near Herald Island in September 1879 and drifting for two years. He had left behind a wife, Emma, and a young child, Silvie. Like GDD, Emma's father had initially been opposed to the marriage. He did not want his daughter to marry a naval officer. 'He thought that the continual separations would not make for happiness'[11], wrote Emma in her autobiography, *Explorer's Wife*.

De Long's first experience of the Arctic had come about when he was appointed by the US government to lead a relief expedition to find *Polaris*, a missing Arctic exploring vessel.* His first impressions of the Arctic were

---

* The *Polaris* was reported missing in the Arctic when nineteen of its crew members were rescued at Baffin Bay by a whaler, *Ravenscraig*, in May 1873.

far from enthusiastic; 'I never in my life saw such a dreary land of desolation and I hope I may never find myself cast away in such a perfectly God-forsaken land',[12] he wrote in a letter to Emma. Yet he nevertheless fell under the spell of the Arctic. Despite dreaming of a peaceful life and a home with Emma this never happened because, as Emma explained, 'the polar virus was in George's blood and would not let him rest'.[13] De Long died in the Lena Delta on his way to Siberia. When his body was found at his final campsite by a search party, in March 1882, along with five of his men, he was buried and a cairn erected.

Emma was left to defend his reputation in court when a man named Collins claimed De Long had persecuted his brother, Jerome, the expedition's meteorologist, who had died alongside De Long. She had to bear the painful news that her husband's coffin had been raided, his corpse dragged out and sketched for intended publication in newspaper articles. Emma spent years arranging for his body to be relocated to America. This involved obtaining permission from the Russian Government to transport it almost 5000 miles across Siberia, Russia and northern Germany and then across the sea to New York in 1884. She would never be free of the Arctic. She would write of the *Jeanette* expedition at the age of eighty-seven, sixty years after De Long's death. In her opening paragraph she wrote, 'That long period has not dimmed the recollection of my husband who gave his life for Arctic exploration while I waited vainly at home for him to come back'.[14]

Was this to be Paquita's lot? Would she end up like Emma De Long or like Kathleen Scott? Both women had been robbed of a future with their husbands. While waiting for Scott to return, Kathleen Scott had allowed herself to fantasise about growing old with him. She planted bulbs in the garden. 'Isn't that comic?', she wrote in her diary, written as a record for him of her life and thoughts during his absence, 'I shall settle down into the most conventional of middle-aged matrons with immaculate house linen and polished silver and stair rods'.[15] And yet it was not to be.

Would Douglas go on exploring and one day disappear without trace like John Franklin? She did not know Douglas well enough to know to what lengths he would go in his quest for adventure and knowledge; whether for him the AAE was just the beginning of a long string of expeditions. He had been so determined to go in 1911 that he had claimed he would sail there in a whaleboat. Although Adélie Land was disappointing in so many ways, the discovery of it had made his heart race. He called it 'a wonderful, terrible place'.[16] Did this constitute polar fever? And he was still a young man in the world of exploration. Scott was forty-three and Amundsen, thirty-eight. The hapless Franklin had embarked on his third and final expedition, minus several toes, which he had lost to frostbite, at the age of almost sixty. Robert Peary was over fifty when he claimed to have reached the North Pole in 1909 (at his fourth attempt), by which time he had lost all of his toes to frostbite.

Every time an explorer went on another expedition, the risk of injury or death increased, partly because experience of the conditions led men to underestimate the dangers. Paquita did not know it then but both James Murray and Dr Mackay (together with a third man), overconfident as a result of their experiences on the BAE 1907–09, would die on Stefansson's expedition and their remains would never be found. They left the main camp, established after the ship had sunk, with the intention of reaching Wrangle Island in the Arctic Ocean, north of Siberia. Dr Mackay 'practically mutinied' Douglas later explained in a letter to a friend after learning of Scot's fate. He probably wasn't surprised as Dr Mackay had revealed mutinous tendencies on the BAE in his attempts to depose Professor David in favour of Mawson.

Shackleton was about to go south for the third time. There is every likelihood that Paquita knew something of the Shackletons' marriage and she would not have wished for Emily's life. Shackleton was seldom home because being at home made him feel suffocated and restless to be away again. He was an erratic father and an unfaithful husband. On the BAE he had had an affair with a woman on the voyage out and named a mountain in Antarctica after her. The lives of other explorers' wives were no less comforting. The first wife of French explorer, Jean-Baptiste Charcot, had divorced him for desertion, the second was made to promise never to oppose his expeditions. When Josephine Peary went to the Arctic in search of her husband, she arrived at his base to learn that he was not there. She waited nine months for him to return, wintering with the 'Eskimos', one of whom she learned was Peary's mistress and pregnant with his child, one of two illegitimate sons he is believed to have fathered in the Arctic.

Franklin, driven by reckless ambition, embarked on his first expedition even though his wife of seventeen months was dying of tuberculosis. His second wife, Jane, spent years organising expeditions to the Arctic to find out what had happened to him after 1845, in the meantime enduring rumours of cannibalism. His body was never found. When Captain Cook was violently murdered in Tahiti, his wife, Elizabeth, was just thirty-eight years old. Her husband had been home for a mere four of their sixteen years of marriage. Her only daughter and two of her sons died in early childhood and all at times when Cook was away. After his death, the remaining three sons had all died by the time Elizabeth was fifty-two. She spent the last forty years of her long life utterly alone, dressed in black, clutching her Bible for comfort.

Douglas had kept from Paquita the details of his physical condition, which explains why she thought he might soon want to go to Antarctica again. It was hardly true that he was 'very fit' as he claimed in the wireless message sent her only a little more than a month after reaching the Hut but he didn't want to cause her any more anxiety. There was no prospect of further explaining his condition or circumstances beyond a few sentences by wireless, often tacked on to the end of business telegrams, which had to take precedence over personal messages. Thus it was unlikely that he was going to send her a message saying, 'gravely ill'.

While it had always been his hope that wireless contact to and from Antarctica would include regular updates on the progress of the expedition, he saw little benefit in worrying people unnecessarily. In fact, when he finally got a message through to Paquita at the end of September he reported, 'everything splendid here',[17] which was not in the least bit true. He had stressed in an interview in Sydney, a year before he set sail from Hobart, that the news sent through from the Antarctic would have to be 'tactfully censored'. 'For instance', he went on to say, unwittingly portending Ninnis's end, 'it would never do to send through such news as "John Smith fell down a crevasse today. Little hope of recovery".'[18]

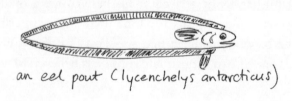

an eel pout (lycenchelys antarcticus)

25

Thoughts of Reunion

Ever the wide world over, lass,
Ever the trail held true,
Over the world and under the world,
And back at the last to you.

Rudyard Kipling (1865–1936), *The Gipsy Trail*

While Paquita's fears were understandable, as she could not know the trend of his thoughts, another expedition was the last thing on Douglas's mind at the time. Rather, he was feeling just as homely as she was. He enjoyed reading, and indeed re-reading, in the four letters she had written the previous year, of all the things she had collected for her trousseau and of her dream of having the finest house in Adelaide. It comforted him to read, in the relative discomfort of the Hut, where he regularly scraped ice from the walls, and where a bath was an occasional luxury that involved squatting in a chilly 'canvas arrangement', that she longed to provide him with a comfortable home. 'No more boarding houses for my man', she assured him. 'No more nasty dinners and having to go away every night'.[1]

For Douglas, the idea of a home with Paquita as 'presiding deity', his head resting on her breast 'all care forgotten', had never seemed so sweet. By his calculations he had spent four of the last thirteen years out of 'a proper house', six months of which he was camped in the New Hebrides. Settling down would be a new adventure he was anxious to begin. He was tired of sleeping with 'one eye open' and, having spent most of his life in male company, he liked the thought of life under her 'domestic eye'.[2] 'You do not want me to go away again!', he wrote, 'Well I hope it will always be like that'.[3]

On the subject of their future home, he conceded that he was far too fussy to ever find a house he liked and instead wrote of building their own. He came to the conclusion that there was 'a good deal' to learn about house design and even found, to his surprise, that he was interested in looking at the furniture pages of the magazines and newspapers they had at the Hut. On the Far-Eastern Sledging Journey, he had survived by focusing on the practicalities of rationing his food and calculating the distances he needed to cover. In 1913, his practical nature was, once again, something that helped him to survive and to stave off depression in the confusion of the Hut. In a place where the days were almost indistinguishable from each other, it was now necessary to focus on psychological landmarks as it had been on the featureless plateau. Over the long hours as night watchman, by the warmth of the stove, he busied himself with drawing up plans for his ideal house, which he described to Paquita. It would be one storey as this would be easier to maintain and more attractive to maids. It would have high windows to stop people from peering in. It would have a veranda and a long driveway. He amused himself by calculating how much it would cost them to furnish their house; what money might be left over for their own pursuits after he had paid all the expedition expenses.

These plans would eventually be used in the building of Jerbii at Brighton, a few blocks from El Rincon, the Delprats' house, upon the veranda of which Douglas had proposed to Paquita. The site was attractive for this reason and perhaps also because, after two months locked in the interior, the sea had come to represent freedom and the way to civilisation, to Australia and to Paquita. Of his eventual sighting of the sea as he neared the Hut the previous February, he had written, 'It was like meeting an old friend and I longed to be down near it'.[4] And even though Paquita claimed to prefer the cooler climate of the Adelaide Hills, for her the sea was also a friendly presence separating Douglas from her while also connecting him to her. Throughout the expedition she wrote several times of how she felt closer to him when she was at sea. In one of her last letters to him before his return, she asked him to transmit his love to her across the ocean, to lean over the *Aurora's* side and whisper it to the breeze.

It is significant that Douglas was absolutely certain they would marry and find happiness. His letters do not reveal the same doubts as Paquita's, most certainly because he had more recent confirmation of her love and because she was not the wandering explorer. She would wait for him, of this he seemed sure. And despite her uneasiness about the future, Paquita's love for him had grown stronger and she continued to write warmly. 'I loved you then as a girl who knows nothing at all of life', she confessed, '& now—as a woman…I never understood when you said that at 25 one loved more than at 20'.[5] She was keen to show him how she had changed. She had attended a course in typing and shorthand with a view to helping him type up the story of the expedition. She had gone to see some of his geological specimens at the university and was proud to admit that she had 'understood quite a lot'.[6] She had seen 'Scott's pictures', the film of his last expedition, and read *The South Pole*, Roald Amundsen's account of his journey to the Pole. She had learnt more about Antarctica and the AAE through members, Murphy and Davis, Correll, Hurley and Harrisson.

She was no longer afraid of what she mysteriously referred to as 'the dark side of life' and 'such things'[7] that she thought only happened to other people. Allusions were made to her being frigid in the past. In one of his letters to her, Douglas wrote, 'don't come to me as ivory as you sometimes do'.[8] As if in answer to this, she confessed, 'I own I was rather cold before you left through ignorance of everything'.[9] Certainly she was naïve and had led a protected childhood. 'In our family we had been very strictly brought up and until I married Douglas at twenty-two had never been out by myself after dusk'[10], she later revealed in *Mawson of the Antarctic*. When her sisters, Lica and Mary, were studying medicine at the University of Adelaide, GDD had forbidden them to leave their anatomy books lying around the house in case their younger brother and sisters, including Paquita, found them and read them. It apparently worked. Paquita purportedly feared she might be pregnant after Douglas kissed her one night. However, that was all before he went away. She assured

Jerbii, the Mawson's home, Brighton, South Australia (*Gareth Thomas Collection*)

him she was now 'much warmer' and no longer the 'young and silly' girl he had left behind in 1911. In fact, it seems she couldn't wait to prove it, 'Oh dear, let's get to business!'[11] she wrote.

However, in the midst of all her professions of love, in a 'faint way'[12] Paquita dreaded their impending reunion. She wondered if Douglas would like all the ways in which she had changed and whether or not he had accounted for the fact that she *had* changed, stressing in one of her last letters to him before his return that she hoped he understood he was not coming back to the 'Paquita of 1911'.[13] She anticipated that they would feel 'almost estranged'.[14] 'Heaven give that we won't be disappointed in each other. Our wants are different now that we are both older'.[15]

It was not without some trepidation that she expected to find Douglas a different man in ways less obvious than the loss of his hair. Upon seeing Douglas after the expedition, Eric Webb described him as not only physically reduced but as 'chastened', 'quieter, humble' and 'much closer to his

God'.[16] In having to endure alone, he had reached a place from which he would never fully return. Whether his experiences would affect their future happiness was something Paquita could not know until his return. 'I want a letter telling me how you felt all those three weeks & if you are really alright now',[17] she wrote. She tried to console him, to assuage any guilt he might have been feeling by arguing that, 'Mertz was not so wiry as you' and that, 'they both knew the risks they took'.[18]

Douglas's contemporary, Cherry-Garrard, assistant zoologist on Scott's last expedition, was haunted for the rest of his life by the idea that he could have saved Scott, his guilt resulting in bouts of madness. In November 1912, Cherry-Garrard had unearthed the buried tent housing the yellow, frostbitten bodies of Wilson, Bowers and Scott and upon reading Scott's diary, he realised that a week before their deaths, at which time Oates was still alive, he, Cherry, was only sixty-three miles away, at One Ton Depot. He could have reached them in a few days with his team of dogs. Yet Douglas was a very different personality. As Eleanor Jacka pointed out in her lectures about Douglas[19], nowhere in his diaries does he ever blame himself for the tragedies that happened. Hayes, as previously mentioned, attributed the death of Ninnis to the wrong footwear. In this way, Douglas was responsible. As leader he ought to have ensured that his companions were wearing appropriate shoes at all times. 'Two lives had been lost for the want of one pair of snowshoes', Hayes argued, 'These fatalities were preventable, as Scott's disaster was preventable by knowledge available at the time'.[20] Yet, even when all the necessary precautions are taken, tragedies still happen. In 2005 two Argentines lost their lives when their snowmobile plunged into a crevasse along a well-trodden route.

Hayes conceded, although Douglas, when confined to the tent for some days, 'gallantly laid down his chance of life' for Mertz, he ultimately survived because 'his time had not yet come'.[21] This was the view Paquita took, that he was not meant to die, that he had been 'miraculously spared to do great things'[22] and Douglas was equally philosophical about it. David Madigan claims that his father and the five other men in the Hut in 1913 were 'disgusted' by the 'off-hand way' Douglas spoke about Ninnis and Mertz.[23] It is difficult to imagine that Douglas would have been off-hand about two men he had clearly greatly admired and cared for. Rather I think it very probable that he spoke of the deaths of Ninnis and Mertz in a matter-of-fact way. This was Davis's impression and it inspired in him admiration for Douglas. When he arrived at Commonwealth Bay in December 1913 to retrieve the party of seven, Davis described how Douglas related to him the details of 'his terrible journey' 'in a detached, matter-of-fact voice that enhanced, rather than detracted from, the tragic and stirring quality of his narrative'.[24]

Mertz and Ninnis were gone and there was nothing more Douglas could do for them and in his position as leader it would have been unprofessional and inappropriate to have burdened the men with his own grief, and he was not alone in not disclosing his private feelings. Even Mertz, who was recognised as a more emotional, demonstrative personality, revealed almost nothing in his diaries of his obvious grief over the death of Ninnis, except to say that he had lost his best friend on the expedition. He could have been writing about an elderly man dying of natural causes. Did he cry? He did not say so. Of his physical struggles, he wrote almost nothing. He pulled the sledge and broke and pitched camp until he could go no further, writing in his diary for the last time seven days before his death barely hinting at his obvious depression and failing health. There was no time to analyse and to nurse their feelings. Similarly, Douglas suffered in silence and found his own quiet way of dealing with the trauma he undoubtedly felt.

As it was, he would have to live with the memory of the horrendous deaths of Mertz and Ninnis for the rest of his life, which was part of his ongoing survival. The Far-Eastern Sledging Journey inadvertently became the focus of the expedition. In 1913, it already was, and Douglas would relive the details of it night after night in lectures he gave through Europe, America, Australia and New Zealand following his return from the Antarctic in 1914. Ironically, retelling the details of the journey helped considerably to pay off the expedition debt. This was punishment enough.

26

Coming Out of the Cold

At the first opportunity of good weather in Adélie Land the memorial cross for Ninnis and Mertz was raised on Azimuth Hill. If he helped in erecting it, there is no mention of doing so in Douglas's diaries. As the weather improved and the darkness receded, biological work resumed. Hodgeman made several bag traps for dredging in which he caught marine worms and crustaceans and they caught rock cod with hand lines and large purple and brown jellyfish, the latter of which they preserved. Some of the men accompanied Douglas in searching for geological specimens, which he identified as Pre-Cambrian in age and similar to the rocks of the Barrier Ranges in South Australia. They were collected in piles to be deposited at the Hut on sledges pulled by the dogs.

The penguins had returned to the bay to breed on 12 October the previous year and the men were all on the lookout for their arrival but the first were not sighted until 17 October by Madigan and Douglas, the same day that the pack-ice went out to sea. By 1 November the penguins were mating and on 9 November Bickerton found the first lot of eggs. Sea leopards and penguins were shot and their oil extracted from the blubber, skua gulls and Antarctic petrels were also killed and the parasitic worms found inside them, pickled by McLean. Bottles were sent out to sea to trace the direction of the ocean currents.[*] Wireless communication ceased from 20 November with the advent of continuous daylight and they all began to pack in anticipation of rescue at last.

Jeffryes, who had not improved, was under the impression he was going sledging and mimicked the men in whatever they did. In fact, it was Douglas who was going sledging with Madigan and Hodgeman and a team of dogs. They left the Hut on 24 November to recover some instruments Madigan's and Bage's parties had left behind the year before at a place they had named Mount Murchison, after Melbournian Roderick Murchison, who had donated £1000 to the expedition, spending a night in Aladdin's Cave along the way. Paquita was aware that Douglas was intending to make this journey, approximately fifty miles from the Hut, as she had been informed by the returned expeditioners in Melbourne. 'Leave those instruments—they'll be covered and something might happen as you search',[1] she wrote. These were not the words of a paranoid woman. As long as he was in Antarctica, Douglas was never free from danger. Before leaving he wrote to say that he had drawn up 'a fresh will'[2] that would be sent to her in the event of him perishing on the journey. From Paquita's point of view, he was putting himself in danger again, to her mind, unnecessarily. Perhaps she was afraid that his life would not be spared a second time; that they would be robbed of the happiness that was almost theirs. It seems she also feared that another sledging adventure would take him further away from her and rekindle his love for Antarctica. 'I can't do without you very much longer', she confessed '…Oh Douglas, don't, don't let Antarctica freeze you.'[3]

In truth, Douglas found the journey difficult. The dogs seemed unusually tired, the sledge repeatedly capsized, the cyclometer and the crossbar broke, the weather was awful. Deep snow had covered the valley where the instruments had been cached and Madigan and Hodgeman returned to Douglas at camp empty-handed on 29 November. So much snow had fallen in a year that less than a foot of a ten-foot flag pole that had been

---

[*] In 1912 Wild and his men also sent messages in bottles. In 1927, a man named George Bressington claimed to have found a bottle washed up on Tuggerah Beach, New South Wales, engraved by the members of the Western Base.

This photograph of Paquita holding a husky called Admiral
D'Urville appeared in *Life* magazine, 1 May 1914

planted on the summit of Mount Murchison was visible. Douglas studied
the clouds and noted the geological features as they travelled but his
diaries suggest he was weary of sledging. It was perhaps too soon after the
Far-Eastern Sledging Journey in that he was probably not as fit as he had
imagined and possibly the dogs and the rituals of polar travel reminded
him of all that he had endured the previous summer. His entry on
11 December seemed to sum up his feelings, 'Nothing visible—no hope
of travelling, direction nothing, the very ground invisible. Walking on,
one slips and falls, stubs the toes and stumbles on sastrugi'.[4]

After spending seven days confined to the tent in thick weather, they
made their way back to the Hut expecting the *Aurora* any day. With
most of the former officers and crew and some of the expeditioners, who
had returned to Australia in 1913, including Correll (mechanic and

assistant physicist) and Hurley (official photographer), Davis had set sail once again for Antarctica, from Hobart, on 11 November. He went via Macquarie Island to collect the party from there. Having received a wireless message informing them of the *Aurora's* departure, Douglas and his party celebrated with a special dinner, in all probability, fish. They had caught numerous fish, on one occasion, as many as fifty, and had begun to enjoy a varied menu, which also included scrambled penguin eggs.

Paquita would not see Douglas until February as a six-week oceanographical cruise to the Shackleton Ice Shelf and newly named Queen Mary Land, discovered and explored by Wild's party the previous year, via the Mackellar Islets and the Mertz Glacier Tongue, had been planned. 'In many a lesser man the anxiety to return home as quickly as possible would have been overmastering', wrote Davis of Douglas, adding, 'with utter selflessness, he took the view that a great many people had subscribed money to send the ship to the Antarctic for the third time and he was determined that it should not all be spent for the sole purpose of his own and his companions' rescue'.[5] However, privately Douglas longed to be home. He confided to Paquita: 'on account of the untoward delay, I shall not enjoy {it}, as I should otherwise…There are too many chances of accident to give a relish where my Soul is pining for you above all'.[6]

On Sunday, 9 November, two days before the *Aurora* left Australia, Paquita wrote what she claimed would be her last letter to Douglas before his return, '…I do hope this will be the last letter I'll need to write you for a very long time. This separation has been quite long enough.'[7] This, together with the letters she had written him since April went onto the ship with Davis. Yet, she was to write again two days later, inspired after seeing the *Aurora* set sail from Melbourne, bound for Antarctica. Encouraged by the 'splendid weather' she felt it was 'a good omen that the sun shone so brightly'. By then she had become frustrated by the inadequacy of letters. 'I'm not happy with the mail I've sent you already', adding, 'The letters are not warm enough but it is hard to write. When you come back to me I think I can show you that my love is warmer & stronger in spite of any lack of warmth I may have shown in letters'.[8]

Just before midnight on 12 December, as the three men, Hodgeman, Madigan and Douglas, descended the glacier above the Hut, Douglas looked through his field glasses and sighted, 'a faint black bar on the seaward horizon'[9], which he surmised could be nothing but the smoke of the *Aurora*. The last time he had seen her like that she had been steaming away from him. Now, at last, she was coming to rescue him. After summoning the four left at the Hut, all seven men huddled on the hills to watch the *Aurora* come into view and busied themselves making a bonfire. Returning to the Hut to rest after their tiring journey, they were roused by Davis who burst into the Hut, 'breezy, buoyant, brave and true'.[10] This was Douglas's version of events. Davis recalled the moment quite differently, of going to shore in the whaleboat with Hurley, Hunter, Hamilton and Blake with no one speaking a word when, 'the unaccustomed silence of that normally wind swept, noisy place was suddenly broken by a shout, "Turn out, you chaps! The BOAT is here!" It was Mawson's voice and, as we came ashore, he was there to greet us'.[11]

On the *Aurora* they enjoyed a special breakfast which included fresh vegetables and later, in brilliant sunshine, they sat out on deck and read the letters and papers Davis had brought with him. There were letters from some of the AAE members who had returned to Australia earlier in the year, among them one for Douglas from Eric Webb, written from New Zealand in October 1913. In his opening lines, he wrote: 'Quite how to greet you I do not know but I trust that it may and always will be in that spirit of comradeship which you so fully extended to me and which, I might add, I was so slow to appreciate'. With reference to a 'note' he had left for him in the Hut, in February when Douglas was still out on the plateau, feared dead, he hoped that he had received it and added:

What I felt at the time I wrote, and altho'{sic} our own recent experiences may have influenced our outlook, I think for my part I shd {sic} say much the same now. Without superfluity of word I wd {sic} like you to know that we admire the pluck, determination and endurance, the mental endurance as much if not more than the physical ability, which bro't {sic} you in as a man in thousands. Personally, from comparison with my own little experience, I feel convinced that your feat must rank with anything that has ever been accomplished in polar regions. There can be few more impossible places on this planet than Adelie Land and the adjacent country in 1912–13. Of Ninnis and Mertz I cannot write. What their loss meant to you few if any of us will ever fully understand.[12]

Douglas's survival was already regarded as unparalleled in the history of polar exploration but that one of his men, who knew him well and had experienced the conditions at Adélie Land first-hand, should endorse this opinion, less than a year after the event, is of particular significance. It is also significant that Webb's opinion did not alter with time. At the age of eighty-seven, as the last surviving member of the Main Base Party, he wrote a tribute to Douglas at the end of Lennard Bickel's book, *This Accursed Land*. It was then sixty-three years after the expedition. He might have been forgiven for embellishing but, interestingly, what he wrote does not differ much from the letter quoted above, written nine months after his return from the AAE.[13]

At some stage over the ensuing days, Douglas found his 1912 letters to Paquita on the ship, still in their box. They had sailed unnoticed to Australia and then back to Antarctica. 'You should have had that letter', he wrote, 'and, besides the wires referred to, many assurances to our being "all well"…Perhaps they did not tell you—Eitel and Davis are both very remiss'.[14] It was another reminder of the anxiety he had caused her, further evident in the recent correspondence from her, which he answered immediately, explaining that, communication troubles aside, he could never have given her his 'heart's feelings by wireless'.[15] He assured her that he understood she had changed, that he had expected it, that he was not frozen in heart and, in reference to her fear that he would go to Antarctica again, he wrote, 'No dearest, nothing like this will happen again'.[16] He read her letters quickly for news the first time but he felt quite differently when he read them for the second time. 'I don't know why', he wrote, 'but I shivered & all the blood seemed to go to my heart in one great whirling eddy. Your love made me shiver'.[17]

On Christmas Eve 1913, the men boarded up the Hut and blocked up the chimney. Much was left behind for future explorers, including a cache of plum puddings.* Huge waves crashed over the ship as they left Commonwealth Bay and the launch was lost. Christmas day was miser-

---

* After sampling the puddings on Mid-Winter's Day, 1912, all the men agreed that they tasted odd. Someone thought to inspect a piece under a microscope and discovered it was riddled with mites and their excreta. As nothing is thrown away in Antarctica, they buried the puddings near the hut. They were found and appreciated by a French expedition in 1950. The leader, Paul Émile-Victor, sent a wireless message of thanks to Douglas in Australia.

able with thick, falling snow. On several occasions Douglas mentioned in his diary that he was thankful the *Aurora* had strong engines, stronger than the *Gauss's*, but the voyage, though productive, was hard-going with the usual challenges of avoiding collision with an iceberg and conserving coal. 'This work is very trying on Capt Davis as he has to be on the alert so much', noted Douglas. 'I wish he would take more rest when he may. Of late he has talked a great deal in his sleep, and repeatedly starts up half asleep, addressing the officer of the watch who he imagines is calling him'. The physical repercussions of the sledging journey had begun to creep up on Douglas again, making this doubly harder to cope with, as he admitted in his diary: 'The anxiety is considerable and, especially when Capt Davis in present condition, I too am precluded from sleeping properly.'[18]

His head was already turned to home and to Paquita. 'I wonder where we shall meet first', Douglas had pondered. 'If it is on the ship I shall have to retire to the Captain's cabin and wait for your ladyship for I am sure I would be much too shy to receive you adequately under the public gaze...It is just possible we may make Adelaide'.[19] Paquita had claimed that she would be waiting for him, wherever he landed, assuring him that she was no longer the 'too-often tearful person'[20] he once knew, her tendency to be over-emotional being the reason why she had been prevented from seeing him off twenty-seven months before. Early on the morning of 26 February, she arrived in Adelaide by ship, sailing into Outer Harbour from Melbourne with her mother. Once on shore she read in the local paper that the *Aurora* was approaching Adelaide. Years later she could not recall how she knew to expect him on this particular day.

In the afternoon the *Aurora's* black hull emerged over the horizon and then a wisp of a sail as it sailed closer to Semaphore. It was hot and beads of sweat formed on Douglas's brow as *Aurora* steamed closer, the Australian blue ensign flying from the gaff. It had been 111° F in the shade only a week before. Aside from the heat, they were inundated with colour as they passed the stunted green of mangrove swamps. Three launches were put out from the jetty, one containing the press, and soon reporters and friends were scrambling over the bulwarks among the dogs, which began to fight. Douglas did not answer many questions as he boarded the Customs launch with a suitcase in his hand. Sporting white flannel trousers and a grey Norfolk jacket, he looked more like a returned holiday-maker than an Antarctic explorer. He walked briskly along the jetty with reporters in hot pursuit before leaping into a taxi. He was bound for the South Australian Hotel on North Terrace where he had asked Paquita to wait for him. She had caught a train there, but how she and Douglas had come to this arrangement was also something that she could not remember.

Paquita believed she would know more about how she really felt and about how Douglas felt once they finally reunited. 'I'm longing for your return to put me at rest'[21], she had written in one of her last letters, fearing that her feelings for Douglas, whose image had lived in her thoughts for so long, might dissolve on meeting him in person. They did not. In her recollection of this day, he entered their hotel room and she just had time to think, 'Yes, of course, that's what he is like!'[22] She recognised the smile that had captured her heart when she had first seen him from a distance at the University of Adelaide. 'Throughout the years that passed', she was to recall in *Mawson of the Antarctic*, 'whenever he returned from his many absences, that grin greeted me and took me back to the fateful moment: the misty day, the men in their sports clothes, the wet grass and the tall slim figure smiling at his friend'.[23]

a King Penguin

27

A Knight to Remember

I cannot see myself ever changing from a warm love, deep rooted,
and perpetual which will ever thrive in the radiance of your own
and, like a flood tide over all the little things which experience
teaches us are to be expected.

Douglas to Paquita, 24 June 1913

There was to be no peace or privacy for Paquita and Douglas for some time following the AAE. There was a public welcome for the expeditioners at the University of Adelaide on 2 March, just three days after their return, and another at the Town Hall the day after. This was the beginning of a long list of engagements that continued well into 1915. With the expedition debt to pay off, and the men's wages to pay, any dreams of settling down together were necessarily put on hold, even after they were married.

In a book by F W Norwood, I found a description of the welcome at the Town Hall. It was in a short story entitled, 'The Home-coming of the Explorers'. Norwood, who was a member of the audience at the Town Hall that afternoon in March 1914, provides an insight into what the public wanted, which was an opportunity to hero-worship, something Douglas didn't allow them to do. He was apparently a disappointment as a speaker, mumbling and failing to give the gritty details of the sledging journey they had known about for a year. Some people even walked out. On reading it, I appreciated how difficult it must have been for Douglas, a man of action, an unassuming geologist, who was not good at self-promotion, to sell his tale of survival, which is what he had to do to make the expedition a financial success. He was under enormous pressure from the moment he got back to Australia, and marrying immediately undoubtedly added to his money concerns but neither he nor Paquita wanted to delay it any longer. They had waited long enough.

They married in Melbourne just over a month after his return, at Holy Trinity Church, Balaclava, on 31 March. The Antarctic, which would forever be a part of their lives, was the theme of the wedding reception, held in the garden of the Delprat's Toorak home in a marquee, the entrance of which was made to look like the bow of a ship. The ushers were all former members of the AAE. Paquita's younger brother, Willy, was groomsman, and Davis was best man. There was an iceberg and tiny sledge dogs and Antarctic petrels on top of the wedding cake, which was surrounded by models of the *Aurora*. More models of the *Aurora* were placed on each table, and a sugar-coated penguin stood beside every plate for the guests to take home.

On the morning of the wedding, once again Davis came to the rescue. When he went to Douglas's hotel room, he found him dressed inappropriately in dark blue lounge suit trousers and persuaded him to go to the Delprats to get a more suitable pair. Paquita's dressmaker was horrified when Douglas arrived to collect his trousers and peeped round the door at Paquita. She shook her head and exclaimed that it was most unlucky for the groom to glimpse the bride before the ceremony. The black opal and diamond necklace Paquita was wearing, a gift from Douglas, she considered another ill-omen, as well as the fact that the bridesmaids, a school friend of Paquita's and her violinist sister, Carmen, were in green. Later it transpired that there were thirteen at the wedding table, Professor David being a late and unexpected addition to the party. Yet, the day was a happy one and the Mawsons defied superstition as they embarked on a marriage that would last for forty-four years.

The next day they boarded the *Orama* bound for Marseilles. The voyage was their honeymoon but it was a working honeymoon from the outset and they rarely had a moment alone together. Davis and McLean sailed with them. Davis was going to England to see his mother and sister, and to find work, and McLean, to help write and edit *The Home of the Blizzard*, which he and Douglas worked on daily throughout the voyage. They sailed via Egypt and Italy, Douglas giving lectures in Cairo and Naples.

In Marseilles he gave an address at the Royal Geographical Society, followed by a meeting with scientists in Paris before they all went to England. Shackleton and his wife, Emily, and Frank Wild welcomed them at Victoria Station. In the event that both Poles had been reached, Shackleton had set his sights on becoming the first to cross the continent from east to west and Frank Wild was to be his second-in command. That night Shackleton took Davis to dinner and tried, unsuccessfully, to persuade him to go south with him as captain of his ship, *Endurance*. Hurley had already agreed to go as photographer. The timing could not have been worse for Douglas. Not only did the commercially savvy Shackleton with his latest expedition plans, divert interest from the story and results of the AAE, but he also took Hurley away. Douglas needed Hurley to help select and arrange the photographs for *The Home of the Blizzard*, as well as prepare the film of the expedition, which Douglas eventually edited himself.

In London, they took an apartment in Buckingham Gate. The mornings were reserved for work on *The Home of the Blizzard* and every afternoon and evening, they rushed from one engagement to the next. Young and socially inexperienced, Paquita sometimes made mistakes. She overdressed when she went to Henley with Scott's sister, Monsie Scott, she underdressed for a party at the Ritz. She was reprimanded for introducing herself as 'Mrs Mawson' and not 'Lady Mawson' on the day that Douglas was knighted. On another occasion, it took the quick-thinking Davis to prevent her from standing for her own toast. Douglas was mostly too engrossed in his work to advise her on what to wear or do. Davis, who went to most of the functions with them, comforted and supported Paquita with his 'Irish flattery' and she later wrote that she could never have got through her honeymoon without him.

Among the people she and Douglas met during this busy time, was Kathleen Scott, who Paquita never warmed to. Kathleen had a reputation for enjoying male company and for not liking women. She was attrac-

From left: Jessica (Oma), Douglas and Pat, Jerbii 1930.
Douglas is seated in one of the leather chairs, now belonging to
the author's parents. (*Gareth Thomas Collection*)

tive and confident, she had thirteen years of experience as the wife of a
prominent explorer, she was on her home turf, she was recently widowed,
and friends with Douglas, the lion of London. All of these things made
her potentially dangerous to Paquita, then a young wife, not yet entirely
sure of herself.

Oma told me that, when her parents were back in England during
the war, Kathleen invited Douglas to dinner, adding, with reference to
Paquita, then heavily pregnant with Oma, 'Your wife won't want to come
in her condition'. Douglas apparently accepted the invitation, leaving
a hurt Paquita at home. Douglas obviously valued his friendship with
Kathleen Scott and they remained in touch until the end of Kathleen's
life. It seems Paquita did not suspect an affair but she never changed her

mind about Kathleen. Oma remembered that when, years after her father's death, a toilet paper called 'Lady Scott' came out, it amused Paquita who exclaimed, 'I must buy some', as if by way of exacting her revenge.

In May 1914, Douglas and Paquita met Ninnis's mother in London, (Douglas having written earlier in the year explaining the accident and giving assurance that Ninnis's death was instant). 'She was very sweet to us and I saw her many times' recalled Paquita. 'When we came back to England during the First World War Mrs Ninnis confided in me that she was now resigned to her son's death in the Antarctic: his regiment had been early cut to pieces in France. Somehow death in an icy crevasse seemed more fitting to his youth than slaughter in the mud of Flanders…'.[1]

In June Douglas was knighted by King George V at St James's Palace and in July he and Paquita went to The Netherlands briefly, to meet her Dutch relatives, and then to Basle in Switzerland, where they spent a day with the Mertz family, who were still completely grief-stricken. Oma told me that, while they did not say it in so many words, Douglas sensed that they blamed him for their son's death.

There had been quite a lot of correspondence between Douglas and the family prior to the visit. One letter from Mertz's father, Emile, written from Switzerland, two months before, in May 1914, indicates that he did not fully understand, or accept, Douglas's explanations, in earlier letters, for his son's death. It was not clear to him why no food depots were established on the sledging journey and he had asked Douglas to send him Mertz's small sledging diary so that he could evaluate his death himself. He longed for 'every last syllable'[2] his son had uttered and the letter is long and repetitive, as if he never wanted to finish it. Mertz had died for the cause of science, which must have been difficult to accept since he wasn't even a scientist. Added to this, Douglas, the leader, had lived, and now he was before them, 'Sir Douglas Mawson', newly married, outwardly bearing no physical scars, and furthermore, busy paying off the expedition debts by retelling the story of Mertz's death.

In describing the day, Paquita wrote: 'It was a grief to us to witness their sorrow. We sat for many hours answering their questions hoping in some way to make some response or to touch on an aspect that might lead their thoughts away from the actual tragic happening'.[3] However, there were no dying messages to relate. As Douglas had explained in a letter previous to his visit, on the last day of his life, Mertz 'was taken with a succession of fits, between which he remained delirious and was not able to communicate anything to me.'[4]

In August 1914, Douglas and Paquita returned to Australia, via Geneva, and Toulon. Douglas resumed work at the University of Adelaide, lecturing for a term and giving public lectures on the expedition. Paquita was, by this time, pregnant with her first child, my great-aunt, Pat (Patricia). In October, at the beginning of the university holidays, she and Douglas sailed back to England, to fulfill more engagements there, Douglas giving four lectures in New Zealand along the way. In January 1915, he went on to America to start an exhausting lecture tour. Travelling from city to city by train, he slept many nights on the trains, arriving at each new destination at 7 am in the morning. He sent a letter to Paquita from every place he visited, sometimes with illustrations of the countryside through which he was passing.

Meanwhile, Paquita went back to Australia via Cape Town and, six weeks later, in April 1915, Pat was born at home in Melbourne while Douglas was still in America. In the same month the film of the AAE was screened in England and afterwards, less successfully, in America. *The Home of the Blizzard* had, by then, been out since January. Published in two volumes with colour plates, only just over two thousand copies of the set had sold in America, Britain and Australia by the end of the war, out of a print run of 3500. A substantial number of copies had been given away, to the expedition members, major sponsors and other people and organisations.

Yet, the poor sales of *The Home of the Blizzard*, was less an indication of failure than of unfortunate timing. It was released when the world was at war, when Shackleton was in the Antarctic again, and in the wake of Scott's tragic death, which had been followed by a book and a film offering a more sensational story. The scope and value of the AAE's achievements was not appreciated at the time. It was not until some years later, in 1928, that the polar historian, Hayes, declared it, 'the greatest and most consummate expedition that ever sailed for Antarctica', and that no other expedition equalled it 'in the wealth and importance of the data collected and in results generally'.[5]

Paquita and Douglas with baby Pat (*Gareth Thomas Collection*)

On his return to Australia a few weeks after Pat's birth, Douglas and Paquita took a flat in Ruthven Mansions in Pulteney Street in Adelaide for six months while Douglas prepared the AAE scientific results for publication so that he would be free to do some work towards the war. He wanted to contribute his scientific knowledge to the war effort, and once again the University of Adelaide granted him leave. In early 1916, Douglas left Paquita again and went to England. During the voyage, he received a telegram on the ship advising him that he had been elected to the Shackleton Relief Committee.

Shackleton, with all his grand plans to traverse Antarctica, had failed to even reach the continent, and had only got as far as the Weddell Sea where his ship, *Endurance*, was crushed in the ice. After abandoning the sinking ship, his party had made their way to the nearest land, remote Elephant Island. Realising it was deserted and that there was no chance of rescue, Shackleton had then sailed in a whaleboat with five others, seven hundred miles across the tempestuous South Atlantic Ocean to South Georgia, where he knew there was a whaling station. He left the remaining men, among them Frank Hurley and Frank Wild, to endure months of harsh weather under upturned boats living on a diet of elephant seals, which were fortunately in abundance, and penguins. However, none of this was known at the time. Shackleton had been missing for two years and plans were being made for a voyage to the Weddell Sea to search for him.

Although he had assured Paquita, in a letter from the Antarctic in 1913, in reference to future expeditions to the Antarctic that 'nothing like this will ever happen again',[6] Douglas was tempted to volunteer to join the relief expedition to rescue Shackleton and his men. Fortunately for Paquita, it didn't come to this. Shackleton made it to South Georgia and the party he had left on Elephant Island was rescued with the help of the Chilean Government on 5 September 1916.*

With Shackleton safe, Douglas turned his attention to getting a wartime job and, in June 1916, he was appointed to the staff of the Explosives Supply Department of the Ministry of Munitions. He was sent to Liverpool in July as Liaison Officer with the Russian Government, supervising the loading and storage of high explosives being sent to Russia, a position that allowed him to draw on his chemical, geological and engineering knowledge. However, within days he was missing Paquita. In a letter to her, which revealed he was stressed and overtired, he admitted that his stomach was 'a little out of order' and that his hair was 'coming out again'.[7] Longing for her company, he wrote, 'You dear girl—I do so wish you were here now—this wretched dull snobby Liverpool would be a different place'.[8]

At this point Paquita made the difficult decision to join him and leave Pat as she and Douglas both felt it unwise to take a baby into a war zone. Paquita delivered Pat to her mother, Henrietta, in San Francisco

---

* A support party, minus three men, who had lost their lives, was later rescued from the other side of the continent, at McMurdo Sound, by Davis in the *Aurora*, which Douglas had sold to Shackleton for £3200 in recognition of his help raising money for the AAE.

on the way. Henrietta had taken Willy to America, to study medicine. It secretly pleased Paquita that for once the tables were turned and it was Douglas who was worrying about her safety as she crossed war-torn seas to England. He sent her a letter advising her to take a berth 'high up' so that she would be closer to the deck if the ship was torpedoed, stressing the importance of getting on deck and into a lifeboat as quickly as possible. However, the ship sailed without incident and Douglas met her at Liverpool, in full uniform, accompanied by two military officials. Longing for a stable home life, having lived out of a suitcase for so long, he had bought her a tea set as a welcoming present.

In Liverpool, in the mornings, Paquita made hospital dressings, which were then sterilised and sent to military hospitals. This was the first of many voluntary jobs she took. Later, in the Second World War, she worked almost full-time managing the Red Cross Civilian Relief Department in Adelaide, where clothes were sorted and mended and sent to air raid victims in England.* In Liverpool, in the afternoons she worked for Douglas, as his secretary, typing to his dictation every afternoon. He never excluded her from his work, always keeping her informed of everything he was doing and, unusually for the times, he involved her in the details of their financial affairs, and was open to her advice, encouraging a working partnership, despite her lack of experience in managing money, and her extravagant ways.

When Douglas was relocated to London, he and Paquita moved to a cottage at Egham-on-Thames, west of London, where they spent the summer of 1917. Although Douglas worked long days, made longer by the train trip to London each day, this was one of the rare times they were able to have some quiet moments together. For the first time the Antarctic wasn't the centre of their lives and they could enjoy relative anonymity, picnicking along the river under the flowering horse chestnuts.

In September they moved to London, to a house in Kensington, where Jessica (Oma) was born on 28 October, and where many members of the AAE stayed with them while on leave, including Davis, who was made godfather to Oma. Paquita cooked for them. Although she became a

---

* Paquita also started the Dutch Club in Adelaide during World War II, to help Dutch refugees from the former East Indies find accommodation and assimilate into Adelaide society. She was appointed OBE in 1951 in recognition of her services to the war.

Sir Douglas Mawson knighted, June 1914 (*Gareth Thomas Collection*)

very good cook, especially at desserts, mastering rice cream and crème caramel to accommodate Douglas's sweet tooth, her early attempts were not entirely successful. Oma told me that one night when they were entertaining in London in 1917, Douglas had to 'whip the gravy off the table' because it was so thick it wouldn't pour. At this time, he had more experience at cooking and apparently taught her how to cook a roast, a dish she was not familiar with, having grown up in a Dutch household.

After the War, in 1919, Paquita and Douglas returned to Australia on the troop ship, the *Euripides*, with Oma who was then two years old and they reunited with Pat, who had since been taken back to Melbourne from San Fransisco by Henrietta. By then Pat was four years old, Paquita and particularly Douglas, having missed most of her early years of growing up. One of Oma's oldest friends once said to me that it was always very obvious to her that Oma was her parents' favourite. Certainly Paquita and Douglas expected a lot more from Pat, which is not unusual as she was their first-born child, but that they had barely known her as a baby might also explain their high expectations of her.

The following year, 1920, their house, Jerbii,* named after Oma's imaginary afternoon tea friends, Mr and Mrs Jerbii, was built in King Street, Brighton, Adelaide, loosely based on the designs Douglas had drawn up in the Antarctic in 1913. A few blocks back from the sea, it was built on land given them by Paquita's father as a wedding gift. Unfortunately the house, surrounded by fruit trees, many of which GDD planted in the early 1900s, and a flourishing garden and grass tennis court, no longer exists. Paquita sold it a few years after Douglas died, as she could not bear to go on living there without him, and it was demolished and replaced by six flats. Now there is only a plaque on a park bench on the esplanade at the end of King Street, which tells you that the Mawsons once lived there.

Jerbii was their refuge in a marriage marked by comings and goings and they both had a flair for homemaking, something they have passed down to most members of the family. They shared a taste for fine things, for pewter and glass, Persian rugs, linen and Queen Anne and William

---

* The spelling of Jerbii was also Oma's invention. It is pronounced J'bye with the accent on the second syllable.

Paquita and Douglas, Adelaide circa 1915
(*Gareth Thomas Collection*)

and Mary furniture. In 1926, in their only other trip abroad together, they bought a lot of furniture, including two leather chairs that now belong to my parents, complete with the original cushions. Every time I sit down on them, I think of Oma telling me her memory of the day they arrived and of how her father was so happy as he removed the nails of the wooden boxes they were delivered in.

Oma had happy memories of her childhood at Jerbii. She remembered Douglas as an attentive and devoted father and she was very much in awe of him. He taught her and Pat how to swim. They practised diving off his shoulders. He insisted that they closed their eyes and threw things into the water for them to retrieve. He taught them how to shoot and they were not spared heavy jobs just because they were girls. Their chores included chopping wood for their three fireplaces and lining the tennis court. On Sunday nights Douglas made pancakes with them. He taught them how to toss them by practising with two books. One represented the frying pan and the other, the pancake. Later, when they had progressed to real pancakes, one was tossed so high that it left a stain on the kitchen ceiling that was still there when the demolishers took the house down.

Douglas was very family-minded and liked doing things with the family, although this almost always revolved around work of some kind. Perhaps to make up, in part, for his frequent absences from home, he wrote to Oma and Pat individually whenever he was away. His letters were always thoughtful and educational. From England he once sent Oma a leaf from the elm tree in Kensington Gardens, under which he had parked her when a baby in a pram.

He encouraged them in their studies. They collected rocks and butter-flies and sea creatures in jars and waited for him to come home from work to help identify them. Both Pat and Oma graduated from the University of Adelaide with science degrees, and they sometimes accompanied Douglas on geology excursions to the north of South Australia, although neither studied geology beyond first year. Oma majored in bacteriology and Pat went on to become a lecturer in zoology at the University of Adelaide and a world authority on parasitic nematodes.

Although neither Pat nor Oma had aspirations to become polar explorers (both were still in their teens when the first woman set foot on the Antarctic continent in 1935), they took after Douglas in many ways. They resembled him physically, and also inherited many of his qualities—his enquiring mind, his strong work ethic, his pragmatism, his frugality and his stoicism. I often wondered if Oma's habit of reusing teabags (incidentally only for herself, never for visitors), had come from Douglas. This was something he had needed to do on both the BAE and the AAE, and had perhaps continued to practise at home.

A family of two children was very small for the times and people have often wondered why Paquita and Douglas didn't have more. According to Oma, her mother had a terrible time during both births. Douglas was in the house when Oma was born at home in London and Paquita's screams of pain distressed him so much that he never wanted to make her go through it again. When my brother, Angus, was born a year before Paquita died, the third of my mother's five children, Paquita remarked that she thought my mother was marvellous and brave, admitting that she had wanted more children but that she could not have faced another painful labour. However, it was probably just as well that Paquita stopped at two, given that Douglas was so often away.

In 1929 the inevitable happened and he went to the Antarctic again. The British Australian New Zealand Antarctic Research Expedition

1929–1931 (BANZARE), which he led at the still relatively young age of forty-six, when Oma and Pat were in their early teens, was almost entirely conducted at sea. With the focus on marine science, the expedition entailed two oceanographic cruises over the summer months of 1929–1930 and 1930–31. It did not involve any long land journeys, man-hauling sledges, sparing Paquita much of the anxiety she had endured during the AAE, with regard to Douglas's safety and wellbeing. In recognition of the emotional strain this had put her under, she was given a copy of all the wireless messages that came through on the BANZARE, even though Douglas was only away for two three-month periods.

The first voyage began in Cape Town and Paquita was not present but, when Douglas returned to Australia in March the following year, she was there with Pat and Oma to welcome him home, something she had not done in 1914. They boarded *Discovery* where she lay at anchor and sailed with her to the wharf at Port Adelaide. Paquita recalled that, 'waves and cheers followed us as we drove to the town with Douglas'[9] and that it was her children's first experience of their father's fame in his hometown.

The second cruise left from Hobart and Paquita became more involved in the preparations than she had on the AAE. In 1911 she had remained in Adelaide for the month that Douglas spent in Hobart but, in 1930 she travelled with him to Tasmania where she worked on the ship, leading up to its departure, stacking books and sorting clothing. She and her mother made small parcels for each member of the scientific staff to open on Christmas Day and a large cake for the crew. At school, Pat and Oma and other members of their class made parcels for the men. Inspired by the expedition, Oma also made a print of a ship and penguins for her godfather, Davis, with his name etched above it, which is appropriately stuck inside the inside cover of Oma's copy (now mine) of his autobiography, *High Latitude*.

While Douglas was away, Paquita was left in charge of overseeing the running of their farm, Harewood, in the Adelaide Hills. It was one of three properties they owned in the hills, where they bred sheep and pigs and grew trees, and later had a working dairy.* Paquita, in jodhpurs,

---

* One of Douglas's many interests was timber. In the 1920s he joined with other local people in the Adelaide Hills and started a mill, initially using redgums, which were everywhere, and later pines, from forests they planted, which they sold to the government for railway sleepers and to BHP to make mine shafts.

Mawson family group, Adelaide 1988. **From left:** William McEwin (author's younger twin brother), Jessica McEwin (Oma) (nee Mawson), Emma McEwin (author), Pat (Patricia) Thomas (nee Mawson), Susie McEwin (next to author) (author's mother), Ally Lynch standing next to Pat (nee McEwin) (author's aunt), Alun Thomas (Pat's son), Pamela Thomas (Gareth's wife), James McEwin (author's younger twin brother), Gareth Thomas (Pat's eldest son and author's cousin), Angus McEwin (author's brother), Andrew McEwin (author's father) (The author's sister, Dimity, is not in the picture.) (*Gareth Thomas Collection*)

would drive from Adelaide in their Moon, and later their Essex, with the running boards piled high with plants and bags of manure. The farm was a considerable responsibility. There were two bushfires at Harewood while Douglas was in the Antarctic, which claimed trees and miles of fencing, and trouble with prospectors, who had a licence from the Department of Mines to prospect for gold but dug big holes which they often didn't fill in, and frightened the sheep. There were other things Paquita had to cope with alone, while Douglas was away, intermittently from 1929 to 1933. He was in the Antarctic when Pat was learning to drive, and in England when Oma was recovering from a shooting accident, serious enough to take her out of school for six months. Paquita had to learn to manage without him and she did.

When he died at Jerbii on 14 October 1958, at the age of seventy-six, Douglas was an old man. It is not so old now but it was old then. He far outlived his polar contemporaries, Scott, Shackleton and Amundsen, none of whom reached old age. Scott had been dead for fifty years. Shackleton had died of a heart attack at forty-five on his third expedition to Antarctica in 1922; Amundsen had been pronounced missing at sea in 1928 when in search of a lost ship in the Arctic. Even the *Aurora* was gone, posted missing with all hands off the east coast of Australia on her way to Chile with a cargo of coal in 1917, a few months after Oma was born. And Paquita lived for another sixteen years, six of which she spent writing Douglas's life, *Mawson of the Antarctic*, about the same number of years it has taken me to write their story.

They lie together behind St Jude's Church, Brighton. My great-aunt Pat died in 1999 and Oma in 2004. Yet, the Mawsons live on, immortalised in the legacy and in the family they have left behind. I wonder what I have inherited from them. It is exactly one hundred years this month that Douglas was sailing to New Zealand to meet the *Nimrod* to begin his first voyage to the Antarctic. When I think about the hardships that awaited him, I feel sure that I have not inherited his amazing resistance to the cold, nor his extraordinary powers of endurance.

I often wish I had been old enough to appreciate Paquita, to have known her, because it is my memories of her that inspired my interest in their lives and, also the stories that Oma told me. My favourite is one I gather Paquita and Douglas liked to repeat together. It went something like this. Douglas was with some guests in the living room at Jerbii and he began to explain the extraordinary mating call of the elephant seal. While imitating the sound the male made, he explained that the females would immediately appear, at which point Paquita called out, from somewhere else in the house, 'Douglas, did you want me?' 'It always brought peals of mirth', as Oma used to say.

Bull elephant seal roaring

Appendix

Abbreviations

BAE   British Antarctic Expedition 1907–09
AAE   Australasian Antarctic Expedition 1911–14
BANZARE British Australian and New Zealand Antarctic
             Research Expedition 1929–31

Metric Conversions

1 mile (1760 yards)	= 1.609 kilometres
1 foot (12 inches)	= 30.48 centimetres
1 pound (16 ounces)	= .4536 kilograms
1 ton (2240 pounds)	= 1.016 tonnes
32° F	= 0° C

Timeline of Arctic and Antarctic expeditions mentioned

ARCTIC

1845–1847
Sir John Franklin, in *Erebus* and *Terror*, leads an expedition in search of the Northwest Passage. All expedition members vanish.

1847–1849
Dr John Rae leads a Franklin search expedition to America's Arctic Coast.

1848–49
James Clark Ross leads an expedition to find Franklin in *Investigator* and *Enterprise*.

1850–1851
Dr John Rae leads a Franklin search expedition to Victoria Island.

1875–1876
George Nares in the *Challenger*, leads British Naval Expedition in search of the North Pole.

1879–1882
George Washington De Long, in the *Jeanette* leads US Naval Expedition, in search of the North Pole.

1881–1884
Adolphus Greely leads an American scientific expedition in the *Proteus* to Ellesmere Island in the Canadian Arctic and achieves a Farthest North. Only six of the twenty-four expedition members return alive.

1893–1895
Fridtjof Nansen (Norwegian) leads an expedition in the *Fram*, deliberately allowing his ship to drift across the Arctic Ocean and establishes a new Farthest North.

1903–1906
Roald Amundsen successfully navigates the Northwest Passage.

1907–1908
Frederick Cook claims to be first to reach the North Pole.

1908–1909
Robert Peary claims to be first to reach the North Pole on his fifth attempt and the public favours him over Cook although today many are skeptical that Peary ever reached the Pole.

1913–1918
Vilhjalmur Stefansson leads an expedition in the *Karluk* and discovers Meighen, Borden, Brock and Louheed Islands in the Canadian Arctic.

ANTARCTIC

1772–1775
Captain James Cook circumnavigates Antarctica and discovers the South Sandwich Islands and the Southern Ocean.

1810
Frederick Hasselborough discovers Campbell and Macquarie Islands, Southern Ocean.

1819–1820
Edward Bransfield, is second to sight the Antarctic continent and discovers the Antarctic Peninsula.

1819–1821
Fabian von Bellingshausen is second to circumnavigate Antarctica and first to sight the continent; discovers Peter I Island and Alexander Island.

1821–1821
James Weddell discovers Aurora Islands and South Shetland Islands.

1822–1824
James Weddell discovers the Weddell Sea

1837–1840
Jules Dumont D'Urville discovers Joinville Island and Adélie Land.

1838–1839
Charles Wilkes discovers Wilkes Land, Antarctica.

1839–1843
James Clark Ross discovers Victoria Land, Ross Island and the Ross Ice Shelf.

1872–1874
George Nares leads an oceanographic voyage to the Southern Ocean.

1897–1899
The Belgian Antarctic Expedition, led by Adrien de Gerlache, becomes the first party to winter in the Antarctic.

1901–1903
Erich von Drygaslski leads a German Antarctic expedition and discovers Wilhelm II Land.

1901–1904
Robert Scott leads the National Antarctic Expedition and is the first to attempt to reach the South Geographical Pole and discovers Edward VII Land.

1902–1904
William Speirs Bruce discovers Coats Land.

1903–1905
Jean–Baptiste Charcot leads an expedition to the Antarctic Peninsula.

1904–09
Ernest Henry Shackleton leads the British Antarctic Expedition in *Nimrod* and attains a Farthest South, coming within 97 miles of the South Geographical Pole. Professor Edgeworth David leads the first ascent of Mt Erebus with Douglas Mawson and Alistair Forbes Mackay, and is first to reach the South Magnetic Pole, again with Douglas Mawson and Alistair Forbes Mackay.

1910–1912
Roald Amundsen is the first to reach the South Pole, 14 December 1911.

1910–1912
Robert Falcon Scott is second to reach the South Pole, 17 January 1912. He dies on the return journey.

1911–1912
Lieutenant Nobu Shirase leads a Japanese Antarctic expedition to the Ross Ice Shelf and Edward VII Land.

1911–1912
Wilhelm Filchner leads a German expedition and discovers the Luitpold Coast.

1911–1914

Douglas Mawson leads the first Australian Antarctic Expedition, the youngest Antarctic expedition under the youngest leader. Discovers George V Land and Queen Mary Land.

1914–1916

Ernest Henry Shackleton leads the Imperial Trans-Antarctic Expedition in an attempt to become the first to cross the Antarctic continent from east to west but his ship, *Endurance*, becomes trapped and crushed in the Weddell Sea.

1921–1922

Ernest Henry Shackleton leads an expedition to circumnavigate the Antarctic continent by sea. But off South Georgia Shackleton has a heart attack and dies. The expedition continues under the command of Frank Wild.

1929–1931

Douglas Mawson leads two oceanographic cruises and discovers MacRobertson Land, Princess Land and Banzare Coast.

Members of the AAE (1911–1914)

MAIN BASE PARTY

Name	Age	Occupation
Douglas Mawson	30	Commander
Cecil Madigan*	23	Meteorologist/Dog handler
Lieutenant Belgrave Ninnis	23	Dog handler
Dr Xavier Mertz	28	Dog handler
Frank Hurley	24	Photographer
Frank Stillwell	23	Geologist
Archie McLean*	26	Chief Medical Officer/ Bacteriologist/Specimen Collector and Editor of *The Adélie Blizzard*
Frank Bickerton*	22	Motor Mechanic/ Wireless Mechanic/Operator
Eric Webb	22	Magnetician

Name	Age	Occupation
Charles Laseron	25	Taxidermist
Leslie Whetter	29	Surgeon
John Close	40	Assistant Collector
John Hunter	23	Biologist
Percy Correll	19	Mechanic/Assistant Physicist
Walter Hannam	26	Wireless Operator
Herbert Murphy	32	Manager of Expedition Stores
Alfred Hodgeman*	26	Cartographer/Sketch Artist/ Assistant Meteorologist
Robert Bage*	23	Astronomer/Chief Storeman
Sidney Jeffryes*	27	Wireless Operator

* Stayed for a second year throughout 1913 with Mawson at the Hut

MACQUARIE ISLAND

George Ainsworth	28	Leader
Charles Sandell	25	Wireless Operator/Mechanic
Arthur Sawyer	26	Wireless Operator
Harold Hamilton	26	Biologist
Leslie Blake	21	Cartographer/Geologist

THE WESTERN BASE, QUEEN MARY LAND

Frank Wild	38	Leader
Morton Moyes	25	Meteorologist
Andrew Watson	24	Geologist
Alec Kennedy	22	Magnetician
George Dovers	21	Cartographer
Charles Harrisson	43	Biologist
Evan Jones	24	Medical Officer
Archibald Hoadley	24	Geologist

Endnotes

Chapter 1: An Explorer in the House

1   Ranulph Fiennes, *Captain Scott*, Hodder & Stoughton 2003, p. 387.

2   Archibald Grenfell Price, *The Winning of Australian Antarctica: Mawson's B.A.N.Z.A.R.E. Voyages*, Angus & Robertson, Sydney, 1962, p. vii.

3   Newspaper article, circa 1969, publication not given, Jessica's (Oma's) scrapbook, property of the author.

Chapter 2: Adventure Bound

1   Paquita Mawson, *Mawson of the Antarctic*, Longmans, London, 1964, p. 15.

2   Ibid, p.22.

3   Ibid, p.23.

4   Fred Jacka & Eleanor Jacka, eds, *Mawson's Antarctic Diaries*, Allen & Unwin, Sydney, 1988, p. xixi.

Chapter 4: How Douglas Ended up in Antarctica

1   Paquita Mawson, *Mawson of the Antarctic*, Longmans, London, 1964, p. 25.

2   Ernest Henry Shackleton, 'The Race for the South Pole', *The London Magazine*, pp. 173-180, Paquita's scrapbook, year not given.

Chapter 5: Paquita

1   Douglas Mawson to Guillaume Daniel Delprat, 7 December 1910, Mawson Collection, South Australian Museum.

2   Guillaume Daniel Delprat to Douglas Mawson, 8 December 1910, Mawson Collection.

3   Paquita Mawson, *A Vision of Steel*, F W Cheshire, Melbourne, 1958, p. viii.

4   Guillaume Daniel Delprat to Douglas Mawson, 8 December 1910, Mawson Collection.

5   Ibid.

6   Paquita Mawson, *Mawson of the Antarctic*, Longmans, London, 1964, p. 50.

7   Lief Mills, *Frank Wild*, Caedmon of Whitby, North Yorkshire, 1999, p. xix.

Chapter 6: The Making of the AAE

1   Douglas Mawson, *The Home of the Blizzard*, Wakefield Press, 1996, p. xvii.

2   Paquita's scrapbook, Gareth Thomas Collection, newspaper article, publication and date not given.

3   *Daily Telegraph*, (Sydney), January, 1913, Paquita's scrapbook, year not given.

4   Douglas Mawson, *The Home of the Blizzard*, p. 10.

5   Douglas Mawson to Paquita Delprat, 27 September 1911, Mawson/Delprat papers, PRG523/3, Mortlock Library, Adelaide.

6   Louise Crossley, ed, *Trial By Ice: The Antarctic Journals of John King Davis*, Bluntisham Books and Erskine Press, Huntingdon and Norfolk, 1997, p. 11.

7   John King Davis, *High Latitude*, Melbourne University Press, 1962, p. 60.

8   Charles Francis Laseron, *South With Mawson: Reminiscences of the Australasian Antarctic Expedition 1911–1914*, George G Harrap, 1947, p. 9.

9   Douglas Mawson, *The Home of the Blizzard*, p. 10.

Chapter 7: South Bound

1 Mary Edgeworth David, *Passages of Time: An Australian Woman Recalls an Eventful Life and a Remarkable Family*, University of Queensland Press, 1975, p. 65.

2 Douglas Mawson to Paquita Delprat 27 September 1911, Mawson/Delprat Papers, PRG/523 Series 4-6, Mortlock Library, Adelaide.

3 Nancy Robinson Flannery, ed, *This Everlasting Silence: The Love Letters of Paquita Delprat & Douglas Mawson 1911–1914*, Melbourne University Press, 2000, December 1 1911, p. 20.

4 Douglas Mawson, *The Home of the Blizzard*, Wakefield Press, 1996, p. 14.

5 Louise Crossley, ed, *Trial by Ice: the Antarctic Journals of John King Davis*, Bluntisham Books and Erskine Press, Huntingdon and Norfolk, 1997, 9 December 1911, p. 13.

6 Ibid, Christmas Day 1911 p. 15.

7 Ibid, 26 December 1911, pp. 15-16.

8 Xavier Mertz, Sledging Diary 28 July 1911-1 January 1913, MD752/1, 16 May, 1912, p. 42, Southcott Files, Mawson Collection, South Australian Museum.

9 Nancy Robinson Flannery, ed, *This Everlasting Silence*, 3 January 1912, p. 25.

10 Ibid.

11 Nancy Robinson Flannery, ed, *This Everlasting Silence*, 3 January 1912, p. 26.

12 Fred Jacka & Eleanor Jacka, eds, *Mawson's Antarctic Diaries*, Allen & Unwin, Sydney, 1988, 18 May 1912, p. 83.

13 Paquita's scrapbook, Gareth Thomas Collection, source not given.

14 Roald Amundsen, *The South Pole: An Account of the Norwegian Antarctic Expedition in the 'Fram' 1910–1912*, John Murray, London, 1913, vol 1, p. 121.

Chapter 8: Winter Pursuits

1 Fred Jacka & Eleanor Jacka, eds, *Mawson's Antarctic Diaries*, Allen & Unwin, Sydney, 1988, 25 January-15 February 1912, pp. 57-58.

2 Nancy Robinson Flannery, ed, *This Everlasting Silence: The Love Letters of Paquita Delprat & Douglas Mawson 1911–1914*, Melbourne

University Press, 2000, Paquita to Douglas, 28 February 1912, p. 31.

3   Ibid, p. 32.

4   *Register*, Adelaide, 9 December 1912, 'Wireless Intelligence from Antarctica: Party all well' by Conrad Eitel, Paquita's scrapbook, Gareth Thomas Collection.

5   Ibid.

6   Charles Francis Laseron, *South with Mawson:Reminiscences of the Australasian Antarctic Expedition 1911–1914*, George G Harrap, London, 1947, p. 91.

7   Nancy Robinson Flannery, ed, *This Everlasting Silence*, 10 May 1912, p. 36.

Chapter 9: Sledging into the Interior

1   Ernest Henry Shackleton, *The Heart of the Antarctic*, Popular Edition, William Heinemann 1910, p. 103.

2   John King Davis, *High Latitude*, Melbourne University Press 1962, p. 84.

3   Eleanor Jacka, 'Mawson's Antarctic Diaries: as it happened' (4 lectures), 20 September-11 October 2006, The University of the Third Age, 186b Pulteney Street, Adelaide.

4   Nancy Robinson Flannery, ed, *This Everlasting Silence: The Love Letters of Paquita Delprat & Douglas Mawson 1911–1914* , Melbourne University Press, 2000, 9 November 1912, pp. 47-48.

5   Ibid, 3 January 1911, p. 25.

6   Ibid, pp. 39-42.

7   Ibid.

8   Fred Jacka & Eleanor Jacka, eds, *Mawson's Antarctic Diaries*, Allen & Unwin, Sydney 1988, p. 150.

9   Douglas Mawson, 'Out of the Jaws of Death', Strand Magazine, 48, pp. 199-211, p. 209.

10 John Gordon Hayes, *Antarctica: A Treatise on the Southern Continent*, The Richards Press, London, 1928, p. 293.

11 Douglas Mawson, *The Home of the Blizzard*, Wakefield Press, 1996, p. 161.

12 Mike Stroud, *Survival of the Fittest: Understanding Peak Physical Performance*, Yellow Jersey Press, London, 2004, p. 71.

13 Douglas Mawson, *The Home of the Blizzard*, p. 235.

14 Snow blindness results when unprotected eyes are exposed to sunlight reflected from snow. It is not necessarily a permanent condition.

Chapter 10: The Race Back

1   Charles Francis Laseron, *South with Mawson: Reminiscences of the Australasian Antarctic Expedition*, George G Harrap, London, 1947, p. 55.

2   John King Davis, Private Journal (14 August 1911-15 March 1913), 17 August 1911, Davis Papers, 3232/5, La Trobe Library, Melbourne.

3   Douglas Mawson, *The Home of the Blizzard*, Wakefield Press, 1996, p. 165.

4   Xavier Mertz, Sledging Diary 28 July 1911-1 January 1913 MD752/1, 22 December 1912, p. 80, Southcott Files, Mawson Collection, South Australian Museum.

5   Fred Jacka & Eleanor Jacka, eds, *Mawson's Antarctic Diaries*, Allen & Unwin, Sydney, 1988, 16 December 1912, p. 151.

6   Douglas Mawson, *The Home of the Blizzard*, p. 116.

7   Ibid, p. 172.

8   Ibid, p. 180.

9   Fred Jacka & Eleanor Jacka, eds, *Mawson's Antarctic Diaries*, pp. 39-40.

10 Douglas Mawson, *The Home of the Blizzard*, p. 179.

11 Roald Amundsen, *The South Pole: An Account of the Norwegian Antarctic Expedition in the Fram 1910–1912*, John Murray, London, 1913, p. 63.

12 Fridtjof Nansen, *Farthest North*, 2 Volumes, Macmillan and Co Ltd, London, 1897, Volume 2, p. 89.

13 Douglas Mawson, *The Home of the Blizzard*, p. 174.

14 Fred Jacka & Eleanor Jacka, eds, *Mawson's Antarctic Diaries*, pp. 151-155.

Chapter 11: The Loss of Mertz

1   Fred Jacka & Eleanor Jacka, eds, *Mawson's Antarctic Diaries*, Allen & Unwin, Sydney, 1988, 31 December 1912, p. 156.

2   Douglas Mawson, *The Home of the Blizzard*, Wakefield Press, 1996, p. 167.

3   Ibid, p. 181.

4   Lennard Bickel, *This Accursed Land*, Macmillan, Melbourne, 1977, p. 42.

5   Douglas Mawson to Emile Mertz, 16 May 1914, 175AAE, Southcott Files, Mawson Collection, South Australian Museum.

6   Xavier Mertz, Sledging Diary 28 July 1911-1 January 1913 MD752/1, Southcott Files, Mawson Collection, South Australian Museum.

7   Ibid, 15 & 16 February 1912, p. 25.

8   John Cleland and Ronald Vernon Southcott, 'Hypervitaminosis A in the Antarctic on the Australasian Antarctic Expedition of 1911–14: A Possible Explanation for the Illness of Mertz and Mawson', Medical Journal of Australia, Part 1 for 1969, pp. 1337-42.

9   Fred Jacka & Eleanor Jacka, *Mawson's Antarctic Diaries*, 31 December 1912.

10 Ibid, 22 November 1908, p. 24.

11 Charles Francis Laseron, *South with Mawson: Reminiscences of the Australasian Antarctic Expedition 1911–1914*, George G Harrap, London, 1947, pp. 216-217.

12 Douglas Mawson, *The Home of the Blizzard*, p. 181.

13 Fred Jacka & Eleanor Jacka, eds, *Mawson's Antarctic Diaries*, 6 January 1912, p. 157.

14 Xavier Mertz, Sledging Diary, 14 December 1912, p. 80.

15 Douglas Mawson, *The Home of the Blizzard*, pp. 6-7.

16 Fred Jacka & Eleanor Jacka, eds, *Mawson's Antarctic Diaries*, 3 May 1912, p. 78.

17 John King Davis, *High Latitude*, Melbourne University Press, 1962, p. 101.

18 Douglas Mawson, *The Home of the Blizzard*, p. 182.

19 Fred Jacka & Eleanor Jacka, eds, *Mawson's Antarctic Diaries*, 6 January 1913, p. 157.

20 Ranulph Fiennes, *Captain Scott*, Hodder & Stoughton, London, 2003, p. 366.

21 Douglas Mawson, *The Home of the Blizzard*, p. 184.

22 Xavier Mertz, Sledging Diary, 26 May 1912, p. 45.

23 Douglas Mawson (in Sydney) to Madame Mertz, 17 March 1914, 175AAE, Southcott Files, Mawson Collection.

24 Paquita's scrapbook, Gareth Thomas Collection, newspaper article, date and publication not given.

25 Fred Jacka & Eleanor Jacka, eds, *Mawson's Antarctic Diaries*, 8 January 1913, p. 158.

26 Ibid, 11 January 1913, p. 159.

Chapter 12: Surviving Alone

1 Pierre Berton, *The Arctic Grail: The Quest for the North West Passage and the North Pole*, Viking, New York 1988, p. 285.

2 Korn, Daniel, Radice, Mark, Hawes, Charlie, *Cannibal: The History of the People Eaters*, Channel 4 Books 2001, pp. 116-17.

3 David Parer and Elizabeth Parer-Cook, *Douglas Mawson: The Survivor*, Alella Books, Victoria, 1983, p. 145.

4 *New York Globe*, January 13 1915.

5 *Toronto Daily Star*, 22 January 1915.

6 Mike Stroud, *Survival of the Fittest: Understanding Peak Physical Performance*, Yellow Jersey Press, London, 2004, p. 73.

Chapter 13: Defying Death

1 *Traditional Hymns*, Ebury Press, London, 1996, p. 189.

2 Fred Jacka & Eleanor Jacka, eds, *Mawson's Antarctic* Diaries, Allen & Unwin, Sydney, 1988, 11 January 1913 p. 159.

3 Jessica McEwin's (Oma's) scrapbook, property of the author, newspaper article, publication and date not given.

4 Fred Jacka & Eleanor Jacka, eds, *Mawson's Antarctic* Diaries, p. xxix.

5 Marcus Aurelius, *Mediations*, Penguin Books, London 2004, Book 10.33, pp. 133-4.

6 Ibid, Book 6.29, p. 66.

7 Ibid, Book 5.18, p. 52.

8 Ibid, Book 7.33, p. 81.

9 Fred Jacka & Eleanor Jacka, eds, *Mawson's Antarctic Diaries*, 11 June 1912, p. 90.

10 Ibid, 20 July 1912, p. 101.

11 Ibid, 25 September 1912, p. 114.

12 Ibid, 3 October 1912, p. 116.

13 Lennard Bickel, *This Accursed Land*, Macmillan, Melbourne, 1977, p. 205.

14 Fred Jacka & Eleanor Jacka, eds, *Mawson's Antarctic Diaries*, 17 May 1912, p. 83.

15 Nancy Robinson Flannery, ed, *This Everlasting Silence: The Love Letters of Paquita Delprat & Douglas Mawson 1911–1914*, Melbourne University Press, 2000, 22 July 1913, p.95.

Chapter 14: A Will to Live

1 Nancy Robinson Flannery, ed, *This Everlasting Silence: The Love Letters of Paquita Delprat & Douglas Mawson 1911–1914*, Melbourne University Press, 2000, 3 January 1912, p. 27.

2 Douglas Mawson to Professor Edgeworth David, undated letter, 67DM, Mawson Collection, South Australian Museum.

3 Fred Jacka & Eleanor Jacka, eds, *Mawson's Antarctic Diaries*, Allen & Unwin, Sydney, 1988, 6 June 1913 p.192.

4 Paquita Mawson to Robin Lorimer of the publishing house, Oliver & Boyd, who Paquita approached with her manuscript of *Mawson of the Antarctic*, undated letter, PRG/523/6-7, Mortlock Library, Adelaide.

5 Nancy Robinson Flannery, ed, *This Everlasting Silence*, 9 November 1912, p. 47.

6 Lady Kennet (Kathleen Scott), *Self-Portrait of an Artist*, John Murray, London, 1949, 21 February 1913 p. 122.

7 Fred Jacka & Eleanor Jacka, eds, *Mawson's Antarctic* Diaries, 9 January 1913, pp. 158-59.

8 Ranulph Fiennes, *Captain Scott*, Hodder & Stoughton, London, 2003, p. 363.

Chapter 15: Love and Responsibility

1 Fred Jacka & Eleanor Jacka, eds, *Mawson's Antarctic Diaries,* Allen & Unwin, Sydney, 1988, p. xxviii.

2 Ernest Henry Shackleton, *The Heart of the Antarctic*, Popular Edition, William Heinemann, 1910, p. 307.

3 Ibid, pp. 260-261.

4 Fred Jacka & Eleanor Jacka, eds, *Mawson's Antarctic* Diaries, 23 October 1908, p. 13.

5 Ernest Henry Shackleton, *The Heart of the Antarctic*, p. 279.

6 Ibid, p. 278.

7   Fred Jacka & Eleanor Jacka, eds, *Mawson's Antarctic* Diaries, 22 November 1908, p. 24.

8   Ibid, 5 January 1913, p. 157.

9   Ernest Henry Shackleton, *The Heart of the Antarctic*, p. 269.

10 Ibid, p. 269.

11 Fred Jacka & Eleanor Jacka, eds, *Mawson's Antarctic Diaries*, 23 November 1908, p. 24.

12 John King Davis, *High Latitude*, Melbourne University Press, 1962, p. 107.

13 Fred Jacka & Eleanor Jacka, eds, *Mawson's Antarctic* Diaries, 8 January 1913, p. 158.

14 Lady Kennet (Kathleen Scott), *Portrait of an Artist*, John Murray, London, 1949, 21 February 1913, p. 122.

15 Robert Falcon Scott, *The Diaries of Captain Robert Scott: A Record of the Second Antarctic Expedition 1910–1912*, Volume VI, Sledging Diaries November 1911-March 1912 (B.M. ADD. MSS. 51033, 51034, 51035), University Microfilms Ltd, London, 1968.

16 Nancy Robinson Flannery, ed, *This Everlasting Silence: The Love Letters of Paquita Delprat & Douglas Mawson 1911–1914*, Melbourne University Press, 2000, 15 April 1913, p. 55.

17 Ibid, 26 December 1913, p. 122.

18 Mike Stroud, *Survival of the* Fittest *Understanding Peak Physical Performance*, Yellow Jersey Press, London, 2004, p. 87.

Chapter 16: A Miraculous Return

1   Lennard Bickel, *This Accursed Land*, Macmillan, Melbourne, 1977, p. 203.

2   Douglas Mawson (in Sydney) to Madame Mertz, 17 March 1914, 175AAE, Southcott Files, Mawson Collection, South Australian Museum..

3   Fred Jacka & Eleanor Jacka, eds, *Mawson's Antarctic Diaries*, Allen & Unwin, Sydney, 1988, 9 April 1913, p. 71.

4   Charles Francis Laseron, *South with Mawson, Reminiscences of the Australasian Antarctic Expedition 1911–1914*, George G Harrap, London, 1947, p. 50.

5   Ibid, p. 98.

6 Scott Huler, *Defining the Wind: The Beaufort Scale and How a Nineteenth-Century Admiral Turned Science into Poetry*, Crown Publishers, New York, 2004, p. 78.

7 Lennard Bickel, *This Accursed Land*, p. 203.

8 John King Davis, *High Latitude*, Melbourne University Press, 1962, p. 195.

9 Ibid, p. 198.

10 Nancy Robinson Flannery, ed, *This Everlasting Silence: the Love Letters of Paquita Delprat & Douglas Mawson 1911–1914*, Melbourne University Press, 2000, 9 November 1912, p.47.

11 Ibid, p. 81.

12 Douglas Mawson, *The Home of the Blizzard*, Wakefield Press, 1996, p. 77.

13 John King Davis, *High Latitude*, p. 195.

14 Fred Jacka & Eleanor Jacka, eds, *Mawson's Antarctic Diaries*, 13 October 1913, p. 122.

15 Ibid, 14 May 1912, p. 81.

16 Douglas Mawson, *The Home of the Blizzard*, p. 82.

17 Charles Francis Laseron, *South with Mawson*, p. 81.

18 Fred Jacka & Eleanor Jacka, eds, *Mawson's Antarctic Diaries*, 22 March 1912, p. 66.

19 Ibid, 18 June 1912, p. 92.

20 Apsley Cherry-Garrard, *The Worst Journey in the World*, 2 Volumes, Penguin Books 1922, Volume 1, p. 270.

21 Ibid, p. 1.

22 Douglas Mawson, *The Home of the Blizzard*, p. 72.

Chapter 17: Providence

1 Fred Jacka & Eleanor Jacka, eds, *Mawson's Antarctic* Diaries, Allen & Unwin, Sydney, 1988, 17 January 1913, p. 161.

2 Douglas Mawson to Kathleen Scott, undated letter, 177AE, Mawson Collection, South Australian Museum.

3 Philip Ayres, *Mawson: A Life*, Melbourne University Press, 1999, p. 80.

4 Mike Stroud, *Survival of the Fittest: Understanding Peak Physical Performance*, Yellow Jersey Press, London 2004, p. 86.

5   M. H. Abrams, General Editor, *The Norton Anthology of English Literature: Fifth Edition,* Volume 2, Norton & Company Inc., London 1986, p. 2193.

6   Nancy Robinson Flannery, ed, *This Everlasting Silence: The Love Letters of Paquita Delprat & Douglas Mawson 1911–1914,* Melbourne University Press, 2000, 3 January 1912, p. 25.

7   Lennard Bickel, *This Accursed Land,* Macmillan, Melbourne, 1977, p. 204.

8   Fred Jacka & Eleanor Jacka, eds, *Mawson's Antarctic* Diaries, 8 February 1913, p. 172.

9   *Toronto Daily Star,* 22 January 1915.

10 Nancy Robinson Flannery, ed, *This Everlasting Silence,* 13 April 1913, p. 58.

11 Douglas Mawson, *The Home of the Blizzard,* Wakefield Press, 1996, p. 191.

12 Ibid, p. 198.

13 Ibid.

14 Charles Francis Laseron, *South with Mawson: Reminiscences of the Australasian Antarctic Expedition 1911–1914,* George G Harrap, London, 1947, p. 220.

15 Fred Jacka & Eleanor Jacka, *Mawson's Antarctic Diaries,* Allen & Unwin, Sydney, 1988, 11 August 1912, p. 106.

16 Douglas Mawson, *The Home of the Blizzard,* pp. 200-201

17 Fred Jacka & Eleanor Jacka, eds, *Mawson's Antarctic Diaries,* 7 February 1913, p. 171.

18 Louise Crossley, ed, *Trial by Ice: The Antarctic Journals of John King Davis,* Bluntisham Books and Erskine Press, Huntingdon and Norfolk, 1997, 20 January 1913, p. 53.

19 Ibid, 18 January 1913, p. 52.

20 Ibid, 31 January 1913, p. 59.

21 Ibid, 20 January 1913, p. 53.

22 Ibid, 22 January 1913, pp. 54-55.

23 Ernest Henry Shackleton, *The Heart of the Antarctic,* Popular Edition, William Heinemann, 1910, p. 329.

Chapter 18: A Shadow of Himself

1 Nancy Robinson Flannery, ed, *This Everlasting Silence: The Love Letters of Paquita Delprat & Douglas Mawson 1911–1914*, Melbourne University Press, 2000, 14 October 1913, pp. 39-42.
2 Ibid, 10 May 1912, p.37.
3 Ibid, 28 February 1912, p. 32.
4 Ibid, p. 32.
5 Ibid, 10 May 1912, p. 37.
6 John King Davis, *High Latitude*, Melbourne University Press, 1962, p. 106.
7 Fred Jacka & Eleanor Jacka, eds, *Mawson's Antarctic Diaries*, Allen & Unwin, Sydney, 1988, 8 February 1913, p. 173.
8 Ibid, 12 February 1913, p. 174.
9 Douglas Mawson, *The Home of the Blizzard*, Wakefield Press, 1996, p. 316.
10 Fred Jacka & Eleanor Jacka, eds, *Mawson's Antarctic Diaries*, 2 February 1913, p. 244.
11 Paquita Mawson, *Mawson of the Antarctic*, Longmans, London, 1964, p. 107.
12 Related to the author by Jessica McEwin (Oma).
13 Mike Stroud, *Survival of the Fittest: Understanding Peak Physical Performance*, Yellow Jersey Press, London, 2004, p. pp. 66-87.
14 Lennard Bickel, *This Accursed Land*, Macmillan, Melbourne, 1977, pp. 204-205.
15 Fred Jacka & Eleanor Jacka, eds, *Mawson's Antarctic Diaries*, 8 February 1913, p. 171.
16 Ibid, 8 February 1913, p. 172.
17 Douglas Mawson, *The Home of the Blizzard*, p. 202.
18 Telegram, 8 February 1913, 28AAE, Mawson Collection, South Australian Museum.

Chapter 19: The Aborted Rescue

1 Louise Crossley, ed, *Trial by Ice: The Antarctic Journals of John King Davis*, Bluntisham Books and Erskine Press, Huntingdon and Norfolk, 1997, 8 February 1913, p. 61.
2 Ibid, 9 February, p. 61.
3 Ibid, 9 February 1913, p. 61.

4   Ibid.

5   David Madigan, *Vixeres Fortes:A Family Archive*, 2000, p. 287.

6   John King Davis, *High Latitude*, Melbourne University Press, 1962, p. 218.

7   Xavier Mertz, Sledging Diary 28 July 1911-1 January 1913, 8 August 1911, p. 4, MD752/1, Southcott Files, Mawson Collection, South Australian Museum.

8   Fred Jacka & Eleanor Jacka, eds, *Mawson's Antarctic Diaries*, Allen & Unwin, Sydney, 1988, 9 February 1913, p. 174.

9   John King Davis, *High Latitude*, p. 219.

10 Nancy Robinson Flannery, ed, *This Everlasting Silence: The Love Letters of Paquita Delprat & Douglas Mawson 1911–1914*, Melbourne University Press, 2000, 21 September 1913, p. 101.

11 Douglas Mawson, *The Home of the Blizzard*, Wakefield Press, 1996, p. 318.

12 Fred Jacka & Eleanor Jacka, eds, *Mawson's Antarctic Diaries*, 9 February 1913, p. 174.

13 Nancy Robinson Flannery, ed, *This Everlasting Silence*, 22 July 1913, p. 95.

Chapter 20: Telegram from Antarctica

1   Telegram, 7 March 1913, 28AAE, Mawson Collection, South Australian Museum.

2   Paquita Mawson, *Mawson of the Antarctic*, Longmans, London 1964, p. 102.

3   Fred Jacka & Eleanor Jacka, eds, *Mawson's Antarctic Diaries*, Allen & Unwin, Sydney, 1988, 22 February 1913, p. 183.

4   Paquita Mawson, *Mawson of the Antarctic*, Longmans, London, 1964, pp. 95-96.

5   Ibid.

6   Henrietta Delprat (in Holland) to Douglas Mawson, 18 October 1912, Inv DM 52, Mawson Collection, South Australian Museum.

7   Lica Delprat (in Vienna) to Douglas Mawson, 17 October 1912, Inv DM 53, Mawson Collection, South Australian Museum.

8   Douglas Mawson to Carmen Delprat 28 October 1913, MS7029, National Library of Australia, Canberra.

9   Nancy Robinson Flannery, ed, *This Everlasting Silence: The Love Letters of Paquita De,prat & Douglas Mawson 1911–1914*, Melbourne University Press 2000, 8 July 1913, p. 87.

10 Telegram, 1 April 1913, 28AAE, Mawson Collection, South Australian Museum.

11 Telegram, 3 April 1913, 28AAE, Mawson Collection.

12 Nancy Robinson Flannery, ed, *This Everlasting Silence*, 30 October 1913, p. 110.

13 Ibid, 1 June 1913, p. 65.

14 Paquita Mawson, *Mawson of the Antarctic*, p. 92.

15 *Register*, Adelaide, 27 February 1913.

16 Nancy Robinson Flannery, ed, *This Everlasting Silence*, 5 May 1913, p. 63.

17 Ibid, 15 April 1913, pp. 56-57.

18 Telegram, 1 April 1913, 28AAE, Mawson Collection.

19 Nancy Robinson Flannery, ed, *This Everlasting Silence*, 21 April 1913, p. 58.

20 Paquita Mawson, *Mawson of the Antarctic*, p. 91.

21 Nancy Robinson Flannery, ed, *This Everlasting Silence*, 15 April 1913, p. 55.

22 Ibid, 19 January 1912, p. 29.

23 Ibid, 21 April 1913, p. 58.

24 Ibid, 9 November 1912, p. 47.

25 Ibid, 15 April 1913, p.56.

Chapter 21: Lost Letters of Love

1   Louise Crossley, ed, *Trial by Ice: The Antarctic Diaries of John King Davis*, Bluntisham Books and Erskine Press, Huntingdon and Norfolk, 1997, 24 January 1913, p. 55.

2   Nancy Robinson Flannery, ed, *This Everlasting Silence: The Love Letters of Paquita Delprat & Douglas Mawson 1911–1914*, Melbourne University Press, 2000, 22 June, 1913, pp. 80-81.

3   Ibid, 5 May 1913, p. 62.

4   Ibid, 15 July 1913, p. 91.

5   Ibid, 14 October 1912, p. 42.

6   Ibid, 22 June 1913, p. 81.

7   Ibid, 15 December 1913, p. 24.

8 Ibid, 10 June 1913, p. 71.

9 Ibid.

Chapter 22: Descent into Darkness

1 Douglas Mawson, *The Home of the Blizzard*, Wakefield Press, 1996, p. 315.

2 Ibid.

3 David Cecil Madigan, *Vixere Fortes: A Family Archive*, 2000, p. 288.

4 Douglas Mawson, *The Home of the Blizzard*, Wakefield Press, 1996, p. 315.

5 Ibid, p. 316.

6 Fred Jacka & Eleanor Jacka, eds, *Mawson's Antarctic Diaries*, Allen & Unwin, Sydney, 1988, 17 July 1913, p. 198.

7 Nancy Robinson Flannery, ed, *This Everlasting Silence: The Love Letters of Paquita Delprat & Douglas Mawson 1911–1914*, Melbourne University Press, 2000, 21 April 1913, p. 60.

8 Fred Jacka & Eleanor Jacka, eds, *Mawson's Antarctic Diaries*, 22 June 1913, p. 194.

9 Xavier Mertz, Sledging Diary 28 July 1911-1 January 1913, 6 October 1912, p. 68, Southcott Files, Mawson Collection, South Australian Museum.

10 Fred Jacka & Eleanor Jacka, eds, *Mawson's Antarctic Diaries*, p. 117.

11 Fridtjof Nansen, *Farthest North*, 2 Volumes, Macmillian and Co Ltd, London, 1897, Vol 1, p. 246.

12 Katherine Lambert, *Hell with a Capital H: An Epic Story of Antarctic Survival*, Pimlico, London 2002, p. 141.

13 Apsley Cherry-Garrard, *The Worst Journey in the World*, 2 Volumes, Penguin Books, 1922, Volume 1, p. 220.

14 Fred Jacka & Eleanor Jacka, eds, *Mawson's Antarctic Diaries*, 23 March 1913, p. 185.

15 Ibid, 25 May 1913, p. 191.

16 Nancy Robinson Flannery, ed, *This Everlasting Silence*, 17 June 1913, p. 74.

17 Ibid.

18 Fred Jacka & Eleanor Jacka, eds, *Mawson's Antarctic Diaries*, 26 May 1913, p. 192.

19 David Cecil Madigan, *Vixere Fortes*, p. 288.

20 Douglas Mawson, *The Home of the Blizzard*, p. 318.

21 Fred Jacka & Eleanor Jacka, eds, *Mawson's Antarctic Diaries*, 26 May 1913, p. 192.

22 Ibid.

23 Ibid, p. 182.

24 Ibid, 8 June 1913, p. 193.

Chapter 23: Madness and Misunderstanding

1 Douglas Mawson, *The Home of the Blizzard*, Wakefield Press, 1996, p. 318.

2 Fred Jacka & Eleanor Jacka, eds, *Mawson's Antarctic Diaries*, Allen & Unwin, Sydney, 1988, 7 July 1913, p. 196.

3 Ibid, 7 July 1913, p. 198.

4 Fred Jacka & Eleanor Jacka, eds, *Mawson's Antarctic Diaries*, 3 January 1909, p. 36; 3 February 1909, p. 46.

5 John King Davis, *High Latitude*, Melbourne University Press, 1962, p. 230.

6 Fred Jacka & Eleanor Jacka, eds, *Mawson's Antarctic Diaries*, 11 August 1913, p. 201.

7 Ibid, 17 July 1913, p. 198.

8 Ibid, 30 July 1913, p. 199.

9 Nancy Robinson Flannery, ed, *This Everlasting Silence: The Love Letters of Paquita Delprat & Douglas Mawson 1911–1914*, Melbourne University Press, 2000, 10 June 1913, p. 71.

10 Ibid, 30 October 1913, p. 109.

11 Ibid, 22 June 1913, p. 81.

12 Paquita Mawson, *Mawson of the Antarctic*, Longmans, London, 1964, p. 93.

13 Nancy Robinson Flannery, ed, *This Everlasting Silence*, 1 October 1913, pp. 105-106.

14 Ibid, 21 April 1913, p. 58.

15 Ibid, 1 October 1913, p. 106.

Chapter 24: Anxiety about the Future

1 Lady Kennet (Kathleen Scott), *Self-Portrait of an Artist*, John Murray, London, 1949, p. 121.

2   Nancy Robinson Flannery, ed, *This Everlasting Silence: The Love Letters of Paquita Delprat & Douglas Mawson 1911–1914*, Melbourne University Press, 2000, 1 October 1913, p. 106.

3   Ibid, 17 August 1913, p. 97.

4   Ibid, 26 December 1913, p. 123.

5   Ibid, 15 September 1913, p. 102.

6   Ibid, 21 September 1913, p. 102.

7   Ibid.

8   Ibid.

9   Ibid, 11 November 1913, p. 115.

10 Ibid, 17 August 1913, p. 96.

11 Emma Wotton De Long, *Explorer's Wife*, Dodd & Mead & Company, New York 1938, p. 36.

12 Ibid, p. 70.

13 Ibid, p. 85.

14 Ibid, p. 1

15 Lady Kennet (Kathleen Scott), *Portrait of an Artist*, p. 102.

16 *The Accelerator*, December 1956.

17 Telegram, 30 September 1913, 28AAE, Mawson Collection, South Australian Museum.

18 *The Daily Telegraph*, Sydney, 13 January 1910.

Chapter 25: Thoughts of Reunion

1   Nancy Robinson Flannery, ed, *This Everlasting Silence: The Love Letters of Paquita Delprat & Douglas Mawson 1911–1914*, Melbourne University Press, 2000, 10 May 1912, p. 37.

2   Ibid, 26 December 1913, p. 127.

3   Ibid, 8 July 1913, p. 87.

4   Douglas Mawson, *The Home of the Blizzard*, Wakefield Press, 1996, p. 195.

5   Nancy Robinson Flannery, ed, *This Everlasting Silence*, 21 April 1913, p. 59.

6   Ibid, 1 October 1913, p. 107.

7   Ibid.

8   Ibid, 1 June 1913, p. 69.

9   Ibid, 17 August 1913, p. 97.

10 Paquita Mawson, *Mawson of the Antarctic*, Longmans, London, 1964, p. 111.

11 Nancy Robinson Flannery, ed, *This Everlasting Silence*, 17 August 1913, p. 97.

12 Ibid, 21 September 1913, p. 102.

13 Ibid.

14 Ibid, 9 November 1913, p. 111.

15 Ibid, 21 September 1913, p. 102.

16 Lennard Bickel, *This Accursed Land*, Macmillan, Melbourne, 1977, p. 204.

17 Nancy Robinson Flannery, ed, *This Everlasting Silence*, 21 April 1913, p. 60.

18 Ibid, p. 58.

19 Eleanor Jacka, 'Mawson's Antarctic Diaries: as it happened', 20 September-11 October 2006, The University of the Third Age, 186b Pulteney Street, Adelaide.

20 John Gordon Hayes, *Antarctica A Treatise on the Southern Continent*, The Richards Press, London, 1928, p. 293.

21 Ibid.

22 Nancy Robinson Flannery, ed, *This Everlasting Silence*, 21 April 1913, p. 58.

23 David Cecil Madigan, *Vixere Fortes: A Family Archive*, 2000, p. 290.

24 John King Davis, *High Latitude*, Melbourne University Press, 1962, p. 229.

Chapter 26: Coming Out of the Cold

1 Nancy Robinson Flannery, ed, *This Everlasting Silence: The Love Letters of Paquita Delprat & Douglas Mawson 1911–1914*, Melbourne University Press, 2000, 21 September 1913, p. 103.

2 Ibid, 20 November 1913, p. 117.

3 Ibid, 21 September 1913, p. 103.

4 Fred Jacka & Eleanor Jacka, eds, *Mawson's Antarctic Diaries*, Allen & Unwin, Sydney, 1988, 11 December 1913, p. 225.

5 John King Davis, *High Latitude*, Melbourne University Press, 1962, p. 230.

6 Nancy Robinson Flannery, ed, *This Everlasting Silence*, 20 November 1913, p. 111.

7   Ibid, 9 November 1913, p. 111.

8   Ibid, 11 November 1913, p. 115

9   Douglas Mawson, *The Home of the Blizzard*, Wakefield Press, 1996, p. 322.

10 Ibid.

11 John King Davis, *High Latitude*, p. 229.

12 Eric Webb to Douglas Mawson, 12 October 1913, 175AAE, Mawson Collection, South Australian Museum.

13 See *This Accursed Land* by Lennard Bickel, Macmillan, Melbourne, 1977, pp.201-06.

14 Nancy Robinson Flannery, ed, *This Everlasting Silence*, 26 December 1913, p. 124.

15 Ibid, p. 123.

16 Ibid.

17 Ibid, p. 127.

18 Fred Jacka & Eleanor Jacka, eds, *Mawson's Antarctic Diaries*, 2 February 1913, p. 244.

19 Nancy Robinson Flannery, ed, *This Everlasting Silence*, 22 July 1913, p. 94.

20 Ibid, p. 96.

21 Ibid, 9 November, 1913, p. 112.

22 Paquita Mawson, *Mawson of the Antarctic*, Longmans, London, 1964, p. 102.

23 Ibid, p. 47.

Chapter 27: A Knight to Remember

1   Paquita Mawson, *Mawson of the Antarctic*, Longmans, London, 1964, p. 107.

2   Emile Mertz to Douglas Mawson, 19 May 1914, Southcott Files, Mawson Collection, South Australian Museum.

3   Paquita Mawson, *Mawson of the Antarctic*, p. 117.

4   Douglas Mawson to Emile Mertz, 16 May, 1914, Southcott Files, Mawson Collection.

5   John Gordon Hayes, *Antarctica: A Treatise on the Southern Continent*, the Richards Press, 1928, p. 210.

6　Nancy Robinson Flannery, ed, *This Everlasting Silence: The Love Letters of Paquita Delprat & Douglas Mawson 1911–1914*, Melbourne University Press, 2000, 26 December 1913, p. 123.

7　Douglas Mawson to Paquita Mawson, PRG 523, July 25 1916, Mortlock Library, State Library of South Australia.

8　Ibid.

9　Paquita Mawson, *Mawson of the Antarctic*, p. 171.

Reference List

Books

Amundsen, Roald, *The South Pole: An Account of the Norwegian Antarctic Expedition in the 'Fram' 1910–1912*, 2 volumes, John Murray, London, 1913.

Antarctica: great stories from the frozen continent. Published by Reader's Digest Services Pty Limited, NSW, 1985.

Aurelius, Marcus. *Meditations*, Translated by Maxwell Staniforth. Penguin Books, 2004.

Ayres, Philip, *Mawson: A Life*. Melbourne University Press, Melbourne, 1999.

Berton, Pierre, *The Arctic Grail: The Quest for the North West Passage and the North Pole, 1818-1909*. Viking, New York, 1988.

Bickel, Lennard, *This Accursed Land*. Macmillan, Melbourne, 1977.

Branagan, David, *T W Edgeworth David: A Life*. Edited by Paul Cliff, National Library of Australia, 2005.

Caesar, Adrian, *The White: Last Days in the Antarctic Journeys of Scott and Mawson 1911–1913*, Pan Macmillan Australia, 1999.

Cherry-Garrard, Apsley, *The Worst Journey in the World*, 2 volumes, Penguin Books, 1922.

Conefrey, Mick, *A Teacup in a Storm: an Explorer's Guide to Life*, Harper Collins, London, 2005.

Cook, Frederick A, *Through the First Antarctic Night 1898–1899*, William Heinemann, London, 1900.

Crossley, Louise, ed. *Trial by Ice: The Antarctic Journals of John King Davis*, Bluntisham Books and Erskine Press, Huntingdon and Norfolk, 1997.

David, Mary Edgeworth, *Passages of Time: An Australian Woman Recalls an Eventful Life and a Remarkable Family*, University of Queensland Press, 1975.

Davis, John King, *High Latitude*, Melbourne University Press, Melbourne, 1962.

Davis, John King, *With the Aurora in the Antarctic 1911–1914*. Andrew Melrose, London, 1919.

De Long, Emma Wotton, *Explorer's Wife*, Dodd, Mead & Company, New York, 1938.

Fiennes, Ranulph, *Captain Scott*, Hodder & Stoughton, London, 2003.

Gurney, Alan, *The Race to the White Continent: Voyages to the Antarctic*, W W Norton & Company, Inc, 2000.

Gutteridge, Leonard F, *Icebound: The Jeanette Expedition's Quest for the North Pole*. Berkeley Books, New York, 1986.

Haddelsey, Stephen, *Born Adventurer: The Life of Frank Bickerton Antarctic Pioneer*, Sutton Publishing Limited, 2005.

Hayes, John Gordon, *Antarctica: A Treatise on the Southern Continent*, The Richards Press, London, 1928.

Hayes, John Gordon, *The Conquest of the South Pole: Antarctic Exploration 1906–1931*, Thornton Butterworth Limited, London, 1932.

Huler, Scott, *Defining the Wind: The Beaufort Scale, and How a Nineteenth Century Admiral Turned Science into Poetry*, Crown Publishers, New York, 2004.

Innes, Margaret, and Duff, Heather, *Mawson's Papers: A Guide*, The Mawson Institute for Antarctic Research, The University of Adelaide, Adelaide, 1990.

Jacka, Fred and Jacka, Eleanor, eds, *Mawson's Antarctic Diaries*, Allen & Unwin, Sydney, 1988.

Keneally, Thomas, *The Survivor*, Penguin Books Australia, 1970.

Kennet, Lady (Kathleen Scott), *Self-Portrait of an Artist*, John Murray, London, 1949.

Kirwan, L P, *A History of Polar Exploration*, Penguin Books, 1959.

Korn, Daniel, Radice, Mark, Hawes, Charlie, *Cannibal: The History of the People Eaters*, Channel 4 Books, 2001.

Lambert, Katherine, *Hell with a Capital H: An Epic Story of Antarctic Survival*, Pimlico, London, 2002.

Laseron, Charles Francis, *South with Mawson: Reminiscences of the Australasian Antarctic Expedition 1911–1914*, George G. Harrap, London, 1947.

McGregor, Alasdair, *Frank Hurley: A Photographer's Life*, Penguin Group, Australia, 2004.

Madigan, David Cecil, *Vixere Fortes: A Family Archive*, privately published, Tasmania, 2000.

Martin, Stephen, *A History of Antarctica*, State Library of New South Wales, 1996.

Mawson, Douglas, *The Home of the Blizzard*, 2 volumes, William Heinemann, London, 1915.

Mawson, Douglas, *The Home of the Blizzard*, Wakefield Press, 1996

Mawson, Paquita, *A Vision of Steel*, F W Cheshire, Melbourne, 1958.

Mawson, Paquita, *Mawson of the Antarctic*, Longmans, London, 1964.

Mill, Hugh Robert, *The Siege of the South Pole*, Alston Rivers, London, 1905.

Mills, Leif, *Frank Wild*, Caedmon of Whitby, North Yorkshire, 1999.

Mills, William James, *Exploring Polar Frontiers: A Historical Encyclopedia*, 2 volumes, ABC-CLIO, Inc, Santa Barbara, California, 2003.

Nansen, Fridtjof, *Farthest North*, 2 volumes, Macmillan and Co Ltd, London, 1897.

Nansen, Fridtjof, *The First Crossing of Greenland*, 2 volumes, Longmans, Green and Co, London, 1890.

Nasht, Simon, *The Last Explorer: Hubert Wilkins Australia's Unknown Hero*, Hodder Australia, 2005.

Niven, Jennifer, *The Ice Master: The Doomed 1913 Voyage of the KARLUK*, Pan Books, 2001.

Norwood, FW, *Sunshine and Wattlegold*, Lothian Book Publishing Company, Pty Ltd, Sydney, 1915.

Parer, David and Parer-Cook, Elizabeth, *Douglas Mawson: The Survivor*, Alella Books, Morwell Vic., 1983.

Pound, Reginald, *Scott of the Antarctic*, World Books, London, 1968.

Powell, Theodore, *The Long Rescue*, Double Day & Company, New York, 1960.

Price, Archibald Grenfell, *The Winning of Australian Antarctica*, Angus & Robertson, Sydney, 1962.

Riffenburgh, Beau, *Nimrod: Ernest Shackleton and the Extraordinary Story of the 1907–09 British Antarctic Expedition*, Bloomsbury Publishing Plc, London, 2004.

Robinson Flannery, Nancy, ed, *This Everlasting Silence: The Love Letters of Paquita Delprat & Douglas Mawson 1911–1914*, Melbourne University Press, Melbourne, 2000.

Rossiter, Heather, *Lady Spy, Gentleman Explorer: The Life of Herbert Dyce Murphy*, Random House Australia, Sydney, 2001.

Sale, Richard, *To the Ends of the Earth: The History of Polar Exploration*, Harper Collins, London, 2002.

Scott, Robert Falcon, *The Voyage of the 'Discovery'*, Macmillan, London, 1905.

Scott, Captain Robert, *The Diaries of Captain Robert Scott: A Record of the Second Antarctic Expedition 1910–1912*, Volume VI, Sledging Diaries November 1911-March 1912 (B.M. ADD. MSS. 51033, 51034, 51035), University Microfilms Ltd, London 1968.

Service, Robert William, *The Trail of '98: A Northland Romance*, Grosset & Dunlap, New York, 1910.

Shackleton, Ernest Henry, *The Heart of the Antarctic*, Popular Edition, William Heinemann, London, 1910.

Sprigg, Reg, *Geology is Fun*, privately published, Adelaide, 1989.

Stroud, Mike, *Survival of the Fittest: Understanding Health and Peak Physical Performance*, Yellow Jersey Press, London, 2004.

Suzyumov, E M, *A Life Given to the Antarctic: The Antarctic Explorer Sir Douglas Mawson*, Authorized translation by Tina Tupikina-Glaessner, Adelaide Libraries Board of South Australia, 1968.

Swan, Robert Arthur, *Australia in the Antarctic*, Melbourne University Press, Melbourne, 1961.

The Norton Anthology of English Literature: Fifth Edition, W W Norton & Company Ltd, London, 1986.

Thomson, David, *Scott's Men*, Penguin Books, London, 1977.

Watson, Moira, *The Spy Who Loved Children: The Enigma of Herbert Dyce Murphy 1879–1971*, Melbourne University Press, Melbourne, 1997.

Wheeler, Sara, *Cherry*, Jonathan Cape, 2001.

Young, Louisa, *A Great Task of Happiness: The Life of Kathleen Scott*, Macmillan, London, 1995.

Diaries, journals, newspapers, articles, letters

Register (Adelaide)

New York Globe

Toronto Daily Star

The London Magazine

'Gentle Scientist Found Famous Mine, Helped Blaze Way to Pole', *Daily Mirror*, Wednesday, 8 January, 1958.

Carrington-Smith, Denise, 'Mawson and Mertz: A Re-evaluation of their Ill-fated Mapping Journey during the 1911–1914 Australasian Antarctic Expedition', *Medical Journal of Australia*, 2005; 183 (11/12), pp. 638-641.

Cleland, J, Southcott, RV, 'Hypervitaminosis A in the Australasian Antarctic Expedition of 1911–1914: A Possible Explanation of the Illness of Mertz and Mawson', *Medical Journal of Australia*, 1969; 1, pp.1337-1342.

Jago, JB, Pharaoh, MD, and Wilson-Roberts, CL, 'Douglas Mawson's First Major Geological Expedition: The New Hebrides, 1903', Earth Sciences History, Volume 24, no. 1, 2005, pp. 93-111.

Mawson, Douglas, Obituary of Walter Howchin, Obituary Notices, Reprinted from the *Quarterly Journal of the Geological Society of London*, volume xciv, 1938, pp. cx1-cxxxv.

Mawson, Douglas, 'Out of the Jaws of Death', *Strand Magazine*, 48, 1914, pp.199-211 (Part 1), 311-23 (Part 2).

Obituary: Archibald Lang McLean, *The Medical Journal of Australia*, 3 June, 1922, pp.619-620.

Mertz, Xavier, Diary 1911–1913, translated into English by Gabriel Eisner from the typed German transcript, MD752/1, Southcott Files, Mawson Collection, South Australian Museum.

Pitman, Joy, ed, Diary of Alistair Forbes Mackay on the British Antarctic Expedition 31 November 1908 to 6 February 1909, Royal Scottish Museum, March 1982.

Rodhal, K, Moore, T, 'The Vitamin A Content and Toxicity of Bear and Seal Liver', *Biochemistry Journal*, 1943; 37, pp. 166-168.

Shearman, David JC, 'Vitamin A and Sir Douglas Mawson', *British Medical Journal*, 4 February, 1978, 1, pp. 283-285.

Southcott, RV, Chesterfield, NJ, and Lugg, DJ, 'The Vitamin A Content of the Livers of Huskies and Some Seals from Arctic and Subantarctic Regions', *Medical Journal of Australia*, Part 1 for 1971, pp. 311-13.

Mawson Collection, Australian Polar Collection, South Australian Museum (MC).

Mawson/Delprat Papers, Mortlock Library, State Library of South Australia, Adelaide, (MLA).

Mawson/Delprat papers held privately by Gareth and Alun Thomas.

Mitchell Library, Sydney.

National Library of Australia, Canberra.

Index

AAE (Australasian Antarctic Expedition),
30, 32; concept of, 34-37;
preparations for, 46, 59, 67-68, 77;
equipment, 42-43, 47; funding, 38-
40, 173, 196; perceptions of, 201-
202, 206

Adélie Blizzard, 103, 168, 177

Adélie Land, 37, 52, 56-59, 109, 126,
127, 131, 144, 152, 179, 193, 197;
map of, xiv; discovery of, 35; first
wireless sent, 154; Douglas's thoughts
on, 185

aeroplane/air tractor sledge, 46, 63

Ainsworth, George, 50, 52, 179, 221

Aladdin's Cave, 1, 59, 63, 137, 140, 141,
146, 194

Amundsen, Roald, 18, 36, 42, 45, 46,
55, 68, 80, 219, 221; returns from
South Pole, 62; success with dogs, 65;
kills dogs, 109, 168; donates dogs to
AAE, 180, 185; death, 216

artefacts, Antarctic, 1, 5, 6

Aurelius, Marcus, 101-102

Aurora, route on AAE, iv; used in rescue
of Greely, 9, 10; description of, 39;
bought for AAE, 40; on AAE, 42,
46-48, 50, 51-55, 57, 69, 81, 94, 138,
139-141, 146, 149-153, 154, 158,

160, 161, 168, 169, 189, 195-97,
199, 202; used to rescue Shackleton,
208; fate of, 216

BAE (British Antarctic Expedition);
Douglas Mawson joins, 24; 20, 21,
23, 25, 28, 32, 35-37, 40, 41, 64,
76, 78, 101, 110, 111, 115-116, 118,
119, 140, 144, 177

Bage, Robert, leads Southern Party, 63;
on Southern Journey, 136-137, 148,
167, 194, 223

Banks, Joseph, 182

BANZARE (British Australian
New Zealand Antarctic Research
Expedition), 3, 4, 6, 12, 41, 103-105,
152, 213-214, 218

Bickerton, Frank, 61, 139, 148, 166,
168, 174-175, 193; leads Western
Party, 63; makes memorial cross for
Ninnis and Mertz, 157; work on
wireless, 175, 178, 222

Blake, Leslie, 50, 197, 223

Bransfield, Edward, 15, 220

Bruce, William Speirs, 36, 47

cannibalism, 10, 22, 93-97, 186

Charcot, Jean-Baptiste, 38, 47, 221;

wives of, 185

Cherry-Garrard, Apsley, 129, 130, 131, 172; guilt regarding Scott, 191

Crean, Thomas, 130

Close, John, 75, 95, 126, 129, 222; Douglas's opinion of, 103

clothing, polar, 7, 42, 43, 59, 118, 126, 130, 131, 133

Commonwealth Bay, map of, xiv; Douglas names, 52

communications, *see* wireless

Cook, Frederick, 219; and North Pole, 44; his book, *Through the First Antarctic Night*, 171

Cook, James (Captain), 220; circumnavigates Antarctica, 16, 17, 41; as a husband, 186

Cook, Elizabeth, 186

Correll, Percy, 73, 110, 182, 189, 195-196, 223

crevasses, and AAE; 7, 54, 59, 64, 66, 67, 70-72, 76, 87, 105, 106, 112, 124, 132-134, 136, 139, 186, 191, 205; and BAE, 111, 115, 144-145, 191, 205

de Gerlache, Adrien, 38; first to winter in the Antarctic, 47, 171, 221

David, Professor Edgeworth, 202, 221; influence on Douglas, 21-24, 119; on BAE, 35, 36, 64, 78, 86, 99, 115, 116, 130, 141, 177, 182-183, 185, 202; character and appearance, 118, 119, 145; and AAE, 39, 44, 154, 202

Davis, John King (Captain); character and appearance, 40, 151-152; and AAE, 48, 112, 126, 127, 139, 141, 162-164, 173, 197-199; on Douglas, 192, 196; on Ninnis and Mertz, 89; and BAE, 40-41, 140, 145; as best man to Douglas, 202; in England with Paquita and Douglas, 202, 203, 209; godfather to Jessica (Oma), 209, 214

Delprat family

GDD (Guillaume Daniel), 26, 28, 56,

121, 146, 189, 211; background, 27; correspondence with Douglas, 30-32, 154-155

Henrietta, 32; description of, 27, 29; as a young wife in Spain, 31; help towards AAE, 59, 219; writes to Douglas, 156; in America, 208-209

Paquita, *see* Mawson

siblings (Lica, Mary, Leintie, Carmen, Theo, Willy) 28, 29, 30, 56, 189; correspondence with Douglas, 156, 202, 209

de Long, Emma and George, 183, 184, 219

Discovery, Scott's ship, 19, 66; on BANZARE, 105, 214

dogs, 1, 42, 46-48, 52, 64-67, 70-74, 76-82, 88, 124, 129, 136, 168, 191, 194, 195

Drygalski, Erich von, 34, 47, 221

D'Urville, Jules Dumont, 17, 220; sights and names Adélie Land, 35

Eitel, Conrad, 58, 149, 158-159, 173, 178, 198

Endurance, Shackleton's ship, 134, 203, 207, 222

entertainment, 59, 60, 61, 168-170

expeditioners, AAE, *see* list, 222, 223, and individual entries where appropriate

explorers, polar, *see* timeline 219-222, and individual entries where appropriate

Far-Eastern Sledging Journey, 5, 32, 64, 68, 69, 75, 85, 95, 109, 111, 118, 119, 120, 121, 138, 139, 147-159, 167, 188, 192, 195, (chapters 9-17)

Fiennes, Ranulph; on Douglas, 3; on Titus Oates, 91; on the death of Scott, 112; in the Antarctic, 68, 86-87, 115, 133, 146

Filchner, Wilhelm, 44, 48, 221

food/rations, for and on AAE, 39, 42,

43, 46, 53, 59, 62, 129, 149, 179,
196, 198; for sledging, 67-68, 71, 98,
104, 116-117, 126, 133, 136-137,
138, 177; and dogs as food source;
75-79, 83-86
Franklin, John, 17, 30, 79, 184-185,
219; is searched for, 94; wives of, 186
frostbite, 10, 62, 86; on Far-Eastern
Sledging Journey, 78, 86, 87, 90, 92,
133

Greely, Adolphus, 9, 10, 39, 78, 79, 94,
170, 219

Hamilton, Harold, 50, 197, 223
Hannam, Walter, 149, 223
Hasselborough, Frederick, 48, 220
Hayes, John Gordon, 18; views on death
of Ninnis, 72, 191; views on Douglas's
survival, 191; on achievements of
AAE, 206
Hodgeman, Alfred, 137, 148, 157, 168,
193, 194, 223
Hurley, Frank, iv, 56, 130, 137, 158,
166, 197, 222; leads Southern
Supporting Party, 63; with
Shackleton, 203, 208
huskies, see dogs
Hypervitaminosis A, 85-87

Jarvis, Tim, 7, 131
Jeffryes, Sidney, 149, 154, 168, 174,
175, 223; shows signs of mental
illness, 176, 177, 178, 194
Jerbii (the Mawsons' home), Douglas
designs and description of, 188, 211

Keneally, Thomas, 95

Laseron, Charles, 43, 59, 60, 75, 86,
102, 124, 222; on Mawson, 103, 117,
136, 124, 125, 168
Law, Philip, 96

Mackay, Alistair Forbes, 36; description

of, 115; on BAE, 64, 78, 86, 99, 115,
116, 118, 119, 130, 136, 140, 141,
145, 177, 182; Douglas's opinion of;
119; goes to the Arctic, 185, 221
Madigan, Cecil, 121 129, 137, 148,
154, 158, 174, 177, 196, 222; leads
Coastal Eastern Party, 64; sledging,
73-74, 126, 139, 194; as dog-handler,
168; Douglas's criticisms of, 174
Madigan, David (Cecil's son), 174; on
Davis, 151; on Bickerton, 166; on
Douglas, 191
Mawson, Douglas; childhood, 10-12;
education, 12, 21-22, 27; in New
Hebrides, 22; at Broken Hill, 23,
26-28; and University of Adelaide, 4,
5, 8, 22-24, 135, 201, 206-207; on
BAE, 24-25, 114-119; character, 61,
97-98, 99, 101, 103-106, 117-118,
119, 121, 138-139, 153, 158, 171,
215; is knighted, 211; marriage,
208; physical attributes, 22, 101;
philosophies on life, 101-102, 103,
111, 135; dedication to science, 109-
113, 135; leadership qualities, 12,
114-115, 119-120; cooking skills, 86,
117, 169, 211; physical hardships,
22, 124, 132-133, 146-148, 157,
167, 172, 178, 199, 208; inspired by
Paquita, 120, 121; as perceived by
others, 12, 22, 30, 51, 123, 147-149,
158, 159, 191-192, 197, 198, 201-
202; relationship with Kathleen Scott,
155-156, 204-205; burdened by
debt, 173-174, 201-202; expectations
and opinions of men, 53, 89, 102,
174, 177; plans for future, 188; war
work, 208; as a father, 212-213; on
BANZARE, 213-214; work in South
Australia, 23, 28; death, 216
Mawson, Paquita, (nee Delprat), 52, 53,
68, 95, 96, 109, 111, 138, 141, 148,
152, 154, 156, 152-164, 169, 177-
191, 194, 196, 198-213; in Europe,
56-57, 61, 69-70; author's impressions

of, 2, 27; *Mawson of the Antarctic*, 2, 3, 10-11, 22, 61, 155, 180, 189, 200, 216; on Douglas, 11, 22, 101, 105-106, 146; supports Douglas, 6, 7, 32, 39, 120-121, 135, 137, 143-144, 159, 189, 214; character and appearance, 27, 28; love letters, 8; meets Douglas, 26, courtship, 28-32, 45, 46; scrapbook, 50, 179; receives telegram on ship, 155; on Kathleen Scott, 203-205; death, 216

Macquarie Island, 37, 43, 47, 51, 52, 58, 196; description of and history, 48, 220; wildlife, 49-50

Mawson descendants and partners, *see* 215

Mawson, Margaret (Douglas's mother), 10; parental influence, 11-12, 104, 122; background, 12

Mawson, Jessica, *see* Oma

Mawson, Patricia, 8, 207, 208-209, 211-214, 216; birth, 206

Mawson, Robert (Douglas's father), 10, 121-122, 164

Mawson, William (Douglas's brother), 3, 10, 11, 12, 21, 164

McEwin, Peter, 30

McLean, Archie, 61, 73, 137, 148, 157, 169, 174, 194, 222; work on *The Home of the Blizzard*, 167, 202, 203; on *Adélie Blizzard*, 168

Mertz, Xavier, 7, 41, 59, 76, 96-100, 124, 205, 222; on Davis, 151-152, 158, 163, 166, 169, 191-193; background, 42; impressions of Antarctica, 52, 91; on Far-Eastern Sledging Journey, 66, 67, 71-80, 83-94; death, 91; Douglas's thoughts on, 89-90

meteorology *see* weather conditions

Murphy, Herbert Dyce, 53-54, 104, 163, 166, 167, 223

Nansen, Fridtjof, 42, 60, 219; on killing dogs, 80; in the Arctic, 106, 170

Nares, George, 41, 219, 221

Ninnis, Belgrave (Lieutenant), 7, 41, 67, 70-77, 86, 88, 112, 133, 158, 166, 169, 191-193, 205, 222; description of, 41, 75; death, 72; as perceived by others, 75, 89

North Magnetic Pole, 19

North Pole, 7, 42, 44, 55, 80, 106, 183, 185

Oates, Titus, 80, 91, 100, 191

Oma (Jessica Mawson), author's grandmother, v, 1, 2, 30, 95, 211; stories and memories of her father, Douglas, 80, 85, 101, 104, 105, 117, 135, 204; birth, 209; childhood, 211-217

Orme-Masson, David (Professor), 39

Pavlova, Anna; on *Aurora*; 6; dog named after her, 81

Peary, Josephine, 185

Peary, Robert, 42, 44, 45, 185, 220

Pharaoh, Mark, (curator of the Mawson Collection, South Australian Museum), 85, 96, 104

ponies, 18, 48, 64-66, 79, 116

Queen Mary Land, iv, 196, 221, 223

Rae, Dr John, 94, 219

Ross, James Clark, 17-19, 115, 219, 220

Sandell, Charles, 50, 179, 223

Sawyer, Arthur, 50, 179, 223

Scott, Kathleen, 111, 120, 133, 180, 181, 184, 203-204; hears of Scott's death, 155; letter from Douglas, 156; help towards AAE, 173

Scott, Robert Falcon, 3, 18-21, 35, 36, 109, 110, 112, 144, 155, 156, 170, 172, 174, 191, 216, 221; and Douglas, 36, 37, 41; makes first flight in Antarctica, 46; 48, 52; reaches South Pole, 55, 65; and dogs, 66, 80,

79; death, 95, 100, 112; Douglas's
thoughts on, 101
Shackleton, Emily, 181, 185, 203
Shackleton, Ernest Henry, 3, 11, 18-21;
BAE, 23-25, 35, 36, 37, 41, 51, 52,
69, 114, 221, 222; on dogs, 64; on
ponies, 66; on 1914–17 expedition,
109, 134, 206-208; as husband, 185;
death, 216
Shackleton Ice Shelf, 152, 196;
discovered, 54
Shirase, Nobu, 44, 45, 221
ships, see Aurora, Discovery, Endurance
snow blindness, 74, 78, 118
South Australian Museum, 5, 6
South Georgia, map of, xiv; 16, 35, 48,
130, 134, 208, 222
South Magnetic Pole, iv, 19, 24, 25, 36,
63, 64, 74, 77, 78, 86, 99, 114, 115,
116, 119, 136, 145, 177, 183, 221
South Pole, xiv, 3, 7, 19-21, 25, 35, 36,
40, 44, 45, 55, 62, 65, 66, 144, 189,
221
Stefansson, Vilhajalmar, 185, 220
Stillwell, Frank, 103, 222; leads Near-
Eastern Coastal Party, 63
Stroud, Mike, 86-87, 97, 115, 133, 146

weather: auroras, 61, 167, 175; blizzards,
on Far-Eastern Sledging Journey, 70,

93, 105, 137-139; in Adélie Land, 95,
105, 127; and Scott, 112, 155; snow,
in Adélie Land, 70, 158, 167, 194;
winds, in Antarctica, 47, 48, 158; in
Adélie Land, 57-59, 62, 69, 70, 93,
95, 124-131, 141, 149, 150, 151,
153, 167, 169, 175, 178
Webb, Eric, 222; on Douglas, 96, 104,
123, 126, 135, 147, 190-191; letter to
Douglas, 197-198
whaling, 130, 134, 208
Weddell, James, 17, 35, 53, 220
Whetter, Leslie, 60, 102, 126, 129, 222;
Douglas's opinion of, 102
Wilkes, Charles, 17, 19, 220
Wild, Frank, description of, 41; on
AAE, 52, 54, 59, 196, 223; with
Shackleton, 203, 208
wireless; on AAE, 37, 46, 50, 51, 57-59,
149, 157, 160, 174, 175, 178, 180,
182, 186, 194, 198, 214; first message
sent from Antarctica, 154
wildlife, polar: birds, 49, 51, 52, 71,
83, 194; penguins, 49, 52, 86, 129,
131, 193; sea creatures, 59, 193; sea
leopards, 52, 193; seals, 16, 48, 50,
52, 56, 131; killer whales, 79-80
women, see individual entries where
appropriate
Worsley, Frank, 130

ABOUT THE AUTHOR

Emma McEwin grew up on a dairy farm in South Australia, the eldest of five children.

After graduating from the University of Adelaide, she went to London where she lived for almost nine years before returning to write this, her first book.

Some other East Street titles:

All the Way Home – *Stories from an African Wildlife Sanctuary*
Bookey Peek
Autobiography, travel, wildlife
ISBN: 9781921037191

Between the Devil and the Deep Blue Sky – *Domesticity, danger and deadlines – confessions of a foreign correspondent in Iraq*
Gina Wilkinson
Autobiography, travel, journalism
ISBN: 9781921037160

Beyond Capricorn – *How Portuguese adventurers secretly discovered and mapped Australia and New Zealand 250 years before Captain Cook*
Peter Trickett
History, Australiana, Discovery, Exploration
ISBN: 9780975114599

Cool Hunting Green – *Recycled, repurposed and renewable objects that inspire a greener world*
David Evans
Design, popular culture, gift
ISBN: 9781921037276

Dandelion – *A 60s Memoir*
Catherine James
Memoir, popular culture
ISBN: 9781921037238

Don't Leave Home Without One – *A home leaver's survival guide*
Dennis Bills
Self-help, family wellbeing
ISBN: 9781921037115

Luca Antara – *Passages in Search of Australia*
Martin Edmond
Memoir, history, travel
ISBN: 9781921037085

Olive trees around my table — *Growing up Lebanese in the old South Africa*
Cecile Yazbek
Memoir
ISBN: 9781921037214

The Twelve Little Cakes — *A Memoir From Communist Prague*
Dominika Dery
Memoir
ISBN: 9781921037092

Through My Eyes — *The Autobiography of Lindy Chamberlain-Creighton*
Lindy Chamberlain-Creighton
Autobiography
ISBN: 9780975114537

Vintage Melbourne — *Beautiful buildings from the Melbourne city centre*
Susan Marsden and Peter Fischer
History, architecture
ISBN: 9781921037245 – hardback

What the Psychic Told the Pilgrim — *A Midlife Misadventure on the Camino de Santiago de Compostela*
Jane Christmas
Travel, memoir
ISBN: 9781921037207

With the Kama Sutra Under My Arm — *An Indian Journey*
Trisha Bernard
Travel, memoir
ISBN: 9781921037153

If you have any comments, suggestions and thoughts on any of our books we would welcome your comments on our website!

www.eaststreet.com.au